# For A Good Year

# For A Good Year

## Selected High Holy Day Sermons
## of Rabbi Larry Raphael

ORGANIZED AND EDITED BY
**Terrie Raphael**

YBK Publishers
New York

For A Good Year: Selected High Holy Day Sermons
of Rabbi Larry Raphael

YBK Publishers, Inc.
39 Crosby Street
New York, NY 10013

ISBN: 978-1-936411-66-5

Library of Congress Control Number: 2021934204

Manufactured in the United States of America
for distribution in North and South America
or in the United Kingdom or Australia
when distributed elsewhere.

For more information, visit
www.ybkpublishers.com

# Contents

# Preface

The book you hold in your hands is a work of love—Larry's love for the Judaism that formed the core of his beliefs, his identity, his work and his hopes; my love for my partner and best friend of more than fifty years; and the love of our three wonderful children for their father.

This collection was not Larry's idea, although the ideas are his. He approached life by looking forward and outward, occasionally inward and rarely backward. Yet the ideas, questions and values that he revisited over a lifetime light a path into the future. They can fill us with "wonder at our infinite capacity to learn and to grow . . . and to understand that our joy and our ability to be transformed can come from anyone, anytime, anywhere." (Lawrence Raphael, "My Spiritual Journey," *Paths of Faithfulness*, KTAV 1997)

The idea for this book began when I found neatly organized files of sermons in Larry's computer as my journey into the land of grief was accompanied by the banal process of bureaucratic paperwork that follows upon a death. I found 135 High Holy Day sermons, like gifts neatly wrapped and waiting for the right moment to open. And I knew these sermons! I had heard each one in real time, delivered to congregations in New York City, San Francisco and elsewhere. I knew these sermons because I had read many in the multiple drafts that Larry wrote as he honed his ideas to make the best use of time when people would be listening. I knew these sermons because I heard him rehearse aloud over and over to assure a compelling few moments from the *bimah*. And I knew how much thought, study and care he invested in each one.

From 1972 until 2003 when Larry became Senior Rabbi at Congregation Sherith Israel in San Francisco, the only sermons he regularly prepared were for Rosh Hashanah and Yom Kippur. In those years, in addition to serving as a dean and faculty member at the New York campus of Hebrew Union College–Jewish Institute of Religion, he was the rabbi of an unusual congregation that met just for the High Holy Days. (It was sponsored by the College and the New York Metropolitan Conference of the North American Federation of Temple Brotherhoods, an affiliate of the Union for Reform Judaism later known as Men of Reform Judaism.) He approached these annual sermons with serious commitment. This became his personal tradition for the High Holy Days and marked his work every summer from 2003 to 2015 for Sherith Israel and then in 2017 and 2018 for the Santa Ynez Valley Jewish Community, a small congregation he served in his retirement.

Preparing Rosh Hashanah and Yom Kippur sermons taught Larry not only about Judaism but also about himself. He learned that he preferred to study and share the wisdom of others more than the craft of writing. He learned that he liked to teach by asking questions and telling stories rather than giving answers. He learned that he could be vulnerable and personal instead of hiding behind a lectern dressed in a clerical robe. Is it odd that sermons are prepared in solitude but are intended to be shared face-to-face with a large audience? They are intensely personal and also purposefully public. Sermons for Larry were a journey of discovery, and he invited his congregants to join him on their own voyage of learning.

For me, reading these sermons with the insight of retrospection, I see anew how Larry grew into his life as a rabbi and into a teacher with an open mind and a generous heart. Some of the many sermons he prepared over the decades addressed events specific to a moment in time. The majority, some of which are collected here, speak to timeless concerns and prescient observations that illuminate a future beyond Larry's own lifetime. They are a gift from one life to many.

Finally, this book is dedicated to our children Matthew, Andrew and Rachel. Each embodies special qualities of the father they loved and admired deeply. They relied upon his calm and centeredness, his kindness and devotion to family. He helped them to learn and grow and honored their unique gifts. They brought him joy, laughter, wisdom and pride. Each encouraged me to gather and share their father's words.

My dearest Matthew, Andrew and Rachel: May you continue to draw strength and hope and understanding from these words for decades to come.

And may it be so for all of us.

*Terrie Raphael*

# Acknowledgements

A book like this is the product of many hands and hearts over a lifetime. Larry's teachers, students, colleagues, congregants and friends inspired him during his five decades as a rabbi. In his memory, I offer heartfelt appreciation for the many opportunities they gave him to learn and grow in understanding together.

The following people have my deep gratitude for their special contributions bringing this book to life:

**Norman Cohen** for a heartfelt tribute that commemorates both an abiding friendship and Larry's contributions to the New York campus of Hebrew Union College–Jewish Institute of Religion and beyond.

**Jessica Zimmerman Graf** for honoring and sustaining Larry's legacy at Congregation Sherith Israel.

**Barbara Paley** for a multidimensional friendship and showing us how to minimize regrets.

**Hara Person** for celebrating her deep connection with Larry by opening a door to publication and for sharing a special perspective as his student, colleague and friend.

**JoAnn Oswald** for nurturing those Larry loved most and sharing the friendship of sisterhood.

**Marc Raphael** for guiding creation of this book with the same wisdom and expertise that was a lifelong touchstone for his brother.

**Bernie Silverman** z"l and **Naomi Gale Silverman** z"l for their enduring support of Larry as the rabbi of the special Jewish community created by the free High Holy Day services in New York City that was Larry's annual congregation for decades and the first home for many of the sermons in this book.

**Rosalie Weider** and **Rabbi Gerald I. Weider** for a bond more than a half-century strong that began in Jerusalem, nurtured family for decades in Brooklyn and encompassed *simchas* and more in San Francisco.

**Gary Zola** for generous and thoughtful observations about his dear friend and for suggesting that Larry could continue to teach through his writings by welcoming his papers to the American Jewish Archives.

*Terrie Raphael*

# Introduction

## Marc Lee Raphael,
## Rabbi, PhD[*]

In Los Angeles, early in February of 1946, my parents filled the crib next to my bed with a baby brother whom I had eagerly anticipated for many months. Larry, as they called Lawrence William, would occupy the crib and then a bed (bunk and then twin) for the next nineteen years, until he left UCLA for the opening of the UC Santa Cruz campus in the fall of 1965 and I headed off to Jerusalem to study biblical history and archeology. We were brothers and very close friends, and the memories of our years side by side remain vivid.

Among the activities which occupied us both as we matured and influenced us throughout our lives was the Zionism and social justice activism of our rabbi, Albert Lewis. Whether writing to pen pals in Israel who were assigned to us in religious school in the 1950s, registering Negroes to vote in Watts and supporting freedom riders from our congregation in the early 1960s or learning about the plight of Soviet Jewry in that same decade, Rabbi Lewis' bold outreach motivated us continually. We both, then and later as rabbis, came to the rabbinate with well-established commitments to social action and a desire to live in Israel, at least for a few months. Rabbi Larry noted that "social justice was the core of [my] beliefs," an "obsession," and that nothing gave him "deeper satisfaction." He continually preached about the topic, calling it *tsedakah* or *tikkun olam* or Hebrew phrases from the prayer book. And his months living in Jerusalem and later

[*]Dr. Marc Lee Raphael is Professor Emeritus, Department of Religious Studies, William and Mary. He specializes in Jews and Judaism in the United States and has written many books about philanthropy, culture, politics and religion. His most recent book, *The Synagogue in America—A Short History* (New York University Press, 2011), has been his field of interest ever since he began doctoral studies, and it represents the culmination of many years of research in synagogue archives and attendance at worship services at more than 100 synagogues in every region of the country.

Safed became a subject of sermons and an important part of his professional life.

In those same Los Angeles years, from the mid-1950s through the mid-1960s, my brother and sister and I assembled for a family dinner every night at 6:00. Of course we had assigned seats, and usually the same main dish on a set day of the week (e.g., liver on Thursdays), and a pattern of conversation which was quite formulaic. When our mother asked what was new at school that day, I usually said "nothing much." I do not recall my sister's responses (she was not even a teen until the 1960s) but I do recall vividly how my brother would begin a monologue or story about his day. He loved people even more than subjects of study and would entertain the table with a tale from his day of adventures. As he would tell the worshippers in 1992, he would "draw [us] into what [he was] thinking about."

Decade after decade, as his sermons become "more personal, more individual, [with] more immediate concerns of the heart," his use of stories in his sermons also grew, and those who knew him will easily hear his voice as they read the tales he told. Sometimes they are from the tradition (e.g., by Rabbi Nachman of Bratzlav, the Baal Shem Tov, Martin Buber or a rabbinic colleague), stories about biblical heroes but not found in the Bible, other times from outside the Judaic tradition. He was a master at story-telling, something that of course a print sermon cannot capture.

From the mid-1950s until we left our bedroom for good, we played a baseball board game, APBA, endlessly. Our contests started with the entire 1955 and 1956 seasons and continued through the Dodgers versus Yankees of the early 1960s. We especially enjoyed competing with two classic teams, the 1927 and 1937 Yankees. I remember vividly, sixty years later, a game we played in 1960 with these two teams and my tenth grade brother asking me how I could plan to be a rabbi and read aloud prayers such as "We bless You God for giving the Torah to the people Israel." "For surely," he said to me, "as you have said many times, you do not believe God actually GAVE the Torah to the Israelites."

I cannot recall my exact words, but I am certain that I had ready an explanation I had used in a course I was taking at the Hebrew Union College while attending UCLA, and it involved phrases such as "figures of speech" and "language of poetry" or a word such as "metaphor." I had decided that both the Bible and the prayer book of our congregation were never to be taken literally. And for a few years after this discussion we explored this idea between innings of many a baseball game played on his bed or mine.

Recalling this conversation reminds me of Larry's interest, from the time he was in junior high, in theology, at least in our bedroom. Perhaps no theme occupies him more in these High Holy Day sermons, for even when he is not explicitly discussing God, he weaves his theological interest throughout his discussion of specific prayers, and even single words, from the liturgy he reads on these holy days. The fruits of our discussions when he was living at home continued when he was a rabbinic student as he struggled with a liturgy filled with a transcendent being and as he sought a "vocabulary to discuss our theological belief system." Unlike so many of his colleagues, "anxious . . . talking about their faith," Larry loved to discuss his "personal theology" throughout his career as a preacher. "We need God" was a constant refrain.

And of course it follows that Larry loved studying liturgy and preaching on it. Kol Nidre, kaddish, *teshuvah*, *al chet*, *tsedakah*, *teshuvah*, Book of Life, and so many other words and phrases from the liturgy, seemingly at least once each year, he carefully translated, historicized and made relevant in his sermons. Larry was especially sensitive to the multiple meanings of a liturgical word, translating *teshuvah* one year as "turning," another time as "change" and even the most common translation, repentance or atonement, at times. But he did so in order to examine the word, and of course the concept it embodied, thoroughly. If there had not been a professor of liturgy at the Hebrew Union College he would have loved to add liturgy to his teaching portfolio.

It is a great sadness that the words in this book cannot be heard any longer, as Larry was a writer of much elegance but a public speaker with extraordinary gifts.

# The Sermons

# The Sound of the Shofar

## Rosh Hashanah Morning—1974

We know that unlike other Jewish holidays—such as Passover, Shavuot or Succot—Rosh Hashanah is not tied directly to any seasonal event. Unlike Chanukah or Tisha B'Av, it is not in recognition of any historical occasion. Rather, its origin is in biblical times when it was known simply as "the Day of Memorial."

Rosh Hashanah falls on the new moon of the seventh month of Tishrei. We celebrate new moons each month in our liturgy, reciting special blessings and reading special psalms. This celebration of the new moon was adopted rather late in our recorded history as the official beginning of the festival cycle which follows. As such, we devote an entire evening and morning service to distinguish it from other days of the year. As a Day of Memorial, it is only secondarily a day of festivity. Its primary emphasis has been one of thoughtful reflection and a thorough review of the previous year.

Our tradition further has regarded this day as a Day of Remembrance. On the new year we remember the beginning of the world; historically, this day has been inseparable from the memory of the covenant between God and all people. This relationship is brought out in traditional lore by associating with this day a biblical story about God's promises. This is the story of Abraham and Isaac. As a result of Abraham's faith, God not only spares Isaac but also promises that his seed will be multiplied "as the stars of the heavens and as the sand which is on the shore of the seas."

It is not unusual that we read from the Torah on this day. While it is true that we skip to a special portion in honor of the day, one thing that makes this holiday unusual is the blowing of the shofar. The shofar service itself developed over many centuries into what we know it as today. The service includes blowing the shofar in three parts, with introductory, intermediary and concluding prayers. This morning I want to comment on mythical, historic and personal aspects of the shofar.

With the first blowing of the shofar, we are reminded of its strange and haunting qualities. The use of the instrument traces back in our mythical tradition to the horn of the ram which was sacrificed by Abraham instead of Isaac. One rabbinic source explains that just as the ram was caught in the thicket by its horns, so are we destined to be caught by dilemmas and entangled in troubles. It is our creative human potential that enables us to look beyond the daily blows and battering we all receive to future visions of our lives. Rarely should surviving be a goal in and of itself. We expect something greater from our lives and, perhaps in this way, do we seek to leave our individual stamp on existence. We create institutions to help us celebrate life. We seek from our own creations and those of others moments which remind us of the beauty and the pain of existence. From these moments we are at least temporarily able to disengage from the thicket of our mundane, everyday existence.

A second explanation for the use of the shofar is to remind us of our historic tradition. It is possible, according to Saadia Gaon, the ninth century sage, to associate the shofar with the giving of the Torah to Moses on Mount Sinai. We have heard of the use of the ram's horn by the troops of Joshua at the battle of Jericho. Our tradition also holds that it is the sound of the shofar which will announce the ingathering of the exiles and the coming of the Messianic Age. The sound of the shofar reminds us here today of the long tradition of our people—the past in its sadness and its glory and the potential for the future. We, who are the present link between what has been and what has yet to be, are reminded of our role as preservers of our tradition.

Even if we reject the literalness of such historical associations of the shofar, a symbolic meaning remains. The ram's horn has been a constant in the history of our people. The sound we hear is the same sound heard by the Jews who worshipped together when the Romans attacked and destroyed Jerusalem in 70 A.D. The shofar call is the same as that heard by the Jews who comprised the flourishing Jewish communities in the Spanish world which ended in their dispersion or conversion at the time of the Inquisition some five hundred years ago. We hear the notes now just as did the Jewish communities locked in each night behind ghetto walls and just like those who were liberated by the decrees of Napoleon and the advances of the Enlightenment. The shofar service we participate in each new year is similar to that conducted by our grandparents or even great grandparents in small towns or villages in Eastern Europe and Russia during decades of impoverishment and discrimination. Today, this shofar sound is a note of celebration in communities of Jews throughout the world. Of course, it probably is heard on the local news here in New York, but it also reverberates in synagogues of North and South America, Europe, Asia, Africa and throughout the State of Israel so that we share a common element of worship and purpose.

There is a third and more immediate level of meaning in the shofar service. Maimonides, the famous medieval philosopher, explains that the shofar sounds should awaken all who hear them from their lethargy. The shrill notes of the shofar might have had their origin in imitating the deafening noises of other peoples who at the time of their new year sought to frighten off evil spirits and demons. For us, these notes can serve as a prayer without words. The sounds may elicit a range of emotions that usually are not present at any other time. Coming as they do near the conclusion of the service, the repetition of the shofar blasts might serve to revive our energy and call attention to what we say and do here together today.

If the shofar reminds us of the celebration of life, provides us with a historic link to our past and awakens us to emotions otherwise left untouched, then its intrusion has served a useful purpose. The shofar sounds traditionally are heard during the entire month leading up to Rosh Hashanah. This morning they announce for us the beginning of the ten days of remembrance and repentance. These days should be ones in which we examine the meanings of the shofar sounds. These days are a fitting occasion to reexamine our own potential and capacity to create and celebrate. It is a time to remember where we stand in relationship to our tradition and the contemporary worldwide community. And, it is the time to awaken ourselves to our own shortcomings and what steps we can take to correct them.

# Prayer and Reform Ritual

## Yom Kippur Evening—1975

It has often been said that you are what you eat. This is the one holiday of the year when we concentrate on who we are by ignoring the food that makes us who we are the rest of the year. Those of us who decide to fast on the Day of Atonement do so for many different reasons. There also are as many habits and personal rituals concerning the food we just ate or will eat tomorrow when we break fast as there are people who do fast. Some of us will dip apples in honey to celebrate the hoped-for sweetness of the year ahead; some of us will partake of a special round challah symbolic of the fullness and fruitfulness we wish for the new year; some will break the fast gradually, and other will eat as quickly as possible.

And during the coming year, depending upon our own life experiences and personal styles, we will seek either the old and comfortable or the new and different. This kind of choice is made with other religious observances and in other aspects of our lives as well.

I have heard these same preferences—for the familiar on the one hand or the new on the other—made by people when they come to services or participate in a religious ritual. Take for example our services here. I know, because some of you have told me, that many people expect the kind of services that they remember from their own past. Whether the memories are good or bad, there remains something important that many people wish to recapture—some nostalgic episode that they are in search of. On a very realistic note I should say that that there is no common past which we all share and no exact set of prayers or melodies which could precisely recall what once was.

This sort of search for the known raises questions about the role of ritual and ceremonial forms themselves. It is possible to regard that which is comfortable and learned to the point of memorization as good. Those of you familiar with prayer in an Orthodox service are aware that the words and melodies are so well-known that they sometimes serve as backdrop for discussion or contemplation. It is possible that the prayers

6

in our Union Prayer Book may be to some a stiff and boring repetition of the same thing year after year. Alternatively, it is possible that persons not used to the words or melodies of the service find that change or innovation gets in the way, is too demanding of their attention, making it difficult to concentrate on quiet contemplation that to some is the essence of their prayers.

I think that all of you would agree that there are certain irreducibles that comprise the essence of the service itself. For example, earlier in the service we listened to the cantor chant Kol Nidre. It would not be Yom Kippur, it seems, if Kol Nidre were not chanted. This melody is intimately tied up with the entire theme of the holiday itself—forgiveness and atonement, seeking a clean slate before man and God to start the new year once again.

How disturbing it might be if we did not hear this prayer at the beginning of the service, how disconcerting for most if it was changed or put at another place in the service. This is the evening when we seem to want all things to be exactly as we remember in order to be comforted at a time when we are trying to examine so much. Is it not somewhat peculiar that so much meaning is attached to a prayer we know so little about? In our ritual, Kol Nidre asks for absolution from God for all future resolutions in the coming year which we may forget to abide by. What a strange way of beginning our service!

It seems that the origin of the prayer dates from a time of intense persecution when Jews were called upon to publicly deny their belief in Judaism in order to live. Therefore, once each year, these secret Jews expressed their grief at their apostasy and sought forgiveness for vows they had been forced to make or for vows made but forgotten.

The Kol Nidre prayer exposed Jews for centuries to the charge that the oath of a Jew was not to be believed. Explanations that such a prayer was only for vows between man and God did little to counter this argument. Most of us here do not know of an earlier time in Reform Judaism when the Kol Nidre was removed completely from the service because of these negative associations of what many considered to be an anachronistic prayer.

Thus, a Reform ceremony developed that included a Yom Kippur evening service without Kol Nidre. Such a radical departure from our tradition did not continue. By the time the prayerbook we are using was printed in 1945, Kol Nidre had found its way back into enough Reform services to be included. There remained enough resentment of Kol Nidre for the words of the prayer to still be left out. Clearly this prayer still serves such a basic need that it has become an integral part of our recognized Reform ritual. However, since few of us understand the history or context of the prayer and the dynamics of oath taking in a Jewish court and survival as Marranos is not immediate to our experience, Kol Nidre is significant on a different level.

Perhaps some of us seek an aspect of an experience a friend of mine recently related to me. He said, "You know I am not observant and never attend services, but this past Rosh Hashanah I went to synagogue." I asked him where he went, and he replied, "I went to the Orthodox shul on Tenth Street because I wanted to pray where everyone *davened*. The problem was that I did not understand anything that took place!" Apparently, he was searching for something that he could consider a legitimate experience but was frustrated in his attempt to participate in it. When we come together as a Jewish community on an occasion such as this, many of us seek something familiar wrapped up in a package that we can understand and participate in. Nonetheless, we want to feel that our service is an authentic one, and so we seek and are comforted by certain traditions, albeit Reform ones, that we accept as ritual.

It may seem contradictory to speak generally of "Reform ritual," but this seems to be something that is very real for many of us. The ritual of Reform Judaism is not a uniform body of material. It differs from place to place and, in fact, from person to person. Some of you may be very used to standing for the recitation of the *Sh'ma* and consider this to be a traditional practice. Indeed, this is not the case because in the traditional liturgy, the recitation of the *Sh'ma* has less importance than prayers of supplication found later in the service when the congregation stands. How unusual and disquieting it would be if I asked you to remain seated for the *Sh'ma* and then to stand for the prayers beginning with the *Avot* which recalls the God of Abraham, Isaac and Jacob. Of course, these procedural aspects of our liturgy have curious and sometimes even unknown origins. Some of them date back to the descriptions in the Talmud of the services held in the Temple before its destruction in 70 A.D.

The Temple was tremendous in size and contained courtyards, inner chambers and altars for sacrifice. Certain procedural arrangements had to be made to accommodate all the people who came, especially on the holidays. All of these orchestrations eventually found their way into writing and became part of our history. After the Temple was destroyed and sacrifice was no longer possible to expiate one's guilt or sin, prayer became the substitute. And, as prayerbooks developed, certain rituals and prayers became fixed. These continued for more than a thousand years—from the time of Saddia Gaon in the ninth century, who compiled the first prayerbook, to the nineteenth century when early reformers in Germany began to make some changes. By that time, the prayerbook had grown in volume because no one felt they had the authority to delete a prayer inserted by earlier generations. But the Reform movement, which began in Germany more than 150 years ago, concentrated on a significant revision of the liturgy of the synagogue.

The changes made by early Reform leaders encompassed the desire for sermons to be given in the vernacular, a considerable shortening of the prayer service itself and the addition of music, usually from the organ. Very quickly the reformers had "reformed" the service to their satisfaction, and a new fixed liturgical ritual was established. Of course, many communities developed their own liturgy. Shortly after the Reform movement spread to America, there were multiple prayerbooks competing for the attention of congregations and rabbis.

The content, order and length of the service has been challenged and changed over the centuries. Has the purpose of the service changed as well? Originally meant as a substitute for the Temple sacrifices and then abolished with the destruction of the Temple by the Romans, prayer services fill different functions for different people. Some of us seek the opportunity to formulate a personal supplication to God at a time of need. Some of us seek a like-minded community where we can celebrate personal or public occasions. Some of us seek the peaceful and familiar in order to have an opportunity for critical self-evaluation. Some of us seek a spiritual experience that can transcend the routine. And for all us, no one procedure, no one manner, no one aspect of what we say or do here will be totally satisfying.

Only if the old and comfortable can lead us to a critical examination of our own selves will the effort be successful. Only if the new and ever-changing can push us forward to a renewed sense of worth will the experience together, whether it be prayer or celebration, have meaning to each of us after we leave here tonight.

# On Three Things

## Rosh Hashanah Evening—1976

Who are we who are gathered here on Rosh Hashanah Eve in the year 5737? In a physical sense we form a congregation. To an observer looking in we might appear as a group, a unity. But who are we? Certainly, we share many things in common that a trained observer might detect: we are all New Yorkers (either native or transplanted), relatively young compared to the national average and upwardly mobile. In one sense our being together as a group is an accident. The idea behind this unique congregation is to serve a special kind of transient population: students, military personnel, newly arrived New Yorkers. In a word, people without roots here.

Each year when I consider what to speak about, I turn over and over in my mind the definition and parameters of this community. Some of us are friends of many years whose paths have fortunately crossed once again here in New York. Others of us have recently become friends and have met at times in between these holidays.

For myself, I am pleased to recognize familiar faces and renew old acquaintances. Some among you have been attending these services since their inception eight years ago. Others here tonight might not easily recall when they last attended a High Holy Day service. But the overwhelming majority of you here are strangers to me and to each other. In sum, this congregation is like that of our ancestors in the Sinai wilderness after the exodus from Egypt 4,000 years ago: a mixed multitude.

I am sure we are mixed in our ways of life in general and in our ways of practicing Judaism in particular. While we might feel comfortable with the description of ourselves as "liberal" Jews, I suspect little else would distinguish our common essence. Nonetheless, we come together at this time of year to mark our Jewish commonality and to share in that essence.

For centuries many people have tried to describe, identify and define the common essence of Judaism—what its beliefs are, what marks its uniqueness, upon what hook its philosophical coat can be hung. There is no end of difficulty with this task. The ground rules themselves are always in question. Are we a religious group? Most certainly, but not solely. Are we a people? In part, but not only. Do we have an ethnic identity? Of course, but in so many different ways. We share a common heritage, a common history, a common legacy, a common liturgical language and a common ethical literature.

Tonight I want to reflect briefly on one central aspect of that commonality which is both a reason for coming together and which transforms us from a heterogeneous and anonymous category of people into a group with a sense of unity based on shared understanding and values. What is this powerful element? I believe it is respect for and response to a particular ethical tradition or, perhaps, a perspective on a way to perceive and behave towards our fellow human beings.

Our ethical tradition is an ancient one. The first explanation of our origin is found in the Bible. Its application to specific situations and continued development is written in many volumes of rabbinic literature. One small part of that rabbinic literature, compiled during the second century, is the Oral Law—called the Mishnah. This material is crucial to our understanding of an important time in our history. The Temple had been destroyed in 70 A.D. The Pharisees and Sadducees were wrestling for control of Jewish life. Several Messianic movements (early Christianity among them) were threatening the stability of religious life at the time, and the Romans ruthlessly were forcing their rule upon the Jews.

Within that Oral Law there exists a chapter that is called *Pirke Avot*, Sayings of the Fathers. Unlike the other parts of the law code, *Pirke Avot* contains a collection of sayings, some by named teachers and other anonymous, without any strict adherence to a single point of view. This small volume has been more widely studied and more often quoted than perhaps any other part of rabbinic literature.

We find in *Pirke Avot* a very simple statement of the moral obligation which each person bears. Simeon the Just was one of the survivors of the Great Synagogue. He used to say, "Upon three things the world stands: upon Torah, upon Worship and upon Acts of Kindness"—*"Al shloshah dvarim haolam omeyd: al hatorah, al ha'avodah v'al gemilut hasadim."*

It is generally thought that this Simeon was a priest in the Temple of Jerusalem in the third century B.C.E. If so, his words are recorded almost 500 years after his lifetime and, as with much of our ancient literature, we do not know with any certainty what was the original intent of the author. Although Simeon's words are very simple, our contemporary interpretation suggests that Simeon believed each individual had a complex and far-reaching obligation.

The first of the three things upon which the world stands is Torah. In the literal sense, Torah is the term used to describe the Five Books of Moses: Genesis, Exodus, Leviticus, Numbers and Deuteronomy. It is used to name these books because the precise definition of Torah is "law": the 613 commandments which traditional Judaism defines as continually binding are contained in the Torah. Torah also is history. It offers a general interpretation of the creation of the world, a recorded history of the Jewish people from Abraham to the conclusion of the wanderings in the Sinai desert and the story of the giving of the tablets of law to Moses on Mount Sinai.

Torah also is revelation. It is God's word to mankind and, hence, every word is considered sacred. For us, Torah is best understood as study. Often referred to as a "people of the book," Jews have valued books and study as an integral part of our lives. With no land to call our own for many centuries, Jews were able to maintain their identity through the study of the written word. This study of our common ancient history of the Torah and the rest of the Bible, our common ethical and religious law complied in rabbinic literature and scores of medieval commentaries and codes lead to the advancement of knowledge and increased self-awareness.

The second concept according to Simeon the Just on which the world stands is *avodah* or worship. Unlike its definition as "work" in modern Hebrew, *avodah* as worship refers to a very specific concept in Jewish life—the Temple sacrifice. If in fact Simeon the Just was a priest in the third century B.C.E, then he meant that *avodah* was the worship of God that took place through animal sacrifice at the Temple in ancient Jerusalem. Originally constructed during the time of King Solomon, probably about 1,000 B.C.E., the Temple and its sacrifices were an integral part of Jewish life in ancient Israel for more than one thousand years.

Not only did Jewish life in general change with its destruction in the first century, but Jewish worship in particular underwent a revolution. The previous obligation of Jews to go up to the Temple in Jerusalem at the times of the pilgrimage festivals of Succot, Passover and Shavuout could no longer be maintained. Instead, what evolved slowly over many decades, perhaps even centuries, was the development of the synagogue. No doubt quite unlike our contemporary examples, the early synagogues provided a place of meeting for Jews where prayers were instituted to replace the animal sacrifices of the Temple period.

The substitution that came to be an integral part of Jewish life and history was a creative response to the trauma of the Temple's destruction. Prayers that we now consider to be basic to our worship service were individually introduced by rabbis and scholars over many centuries.

Thus, worship underwent a radical change from sacrifice in a single central shrine or Temple to words of prayer according to an ever-growing body of liturgy in synagogues wherever Jews were scattered. What this response meant was not only a decentralization of worship but an all-important consequence of this change, the democratization of prayer. No longer did the Temple priest control how, who, when and for how much sacrifices would be offered. Rather, worship became the property and responsibility of the individual communication by each person and uncontrolled by any others—something we take for granted today.

*Avodah,* worship, has changed its meaning from the time Simeon the Just spoke of it 2,200 years ago. Now we understand worship, or prayer, to be a contemplative act reflecting our innermost thoughts whether it is conducted when we are part of a congregation as we are today or alone in the stillness of our chosen surroundings. This, then, is the second component of our common heritage that we carry forward to the present day.

We have seen that our contemporary understanding of Torah and *avodah* as pillars that uphold the world have evolved beyond what our ancestor Simeon possibly intended. However, little has changed in the definition of the third pillar—*gemilut hasadim*—which are acts of lovingkindness. A definition and a possible explanation are offered in another part of the Mishnah. We are told that each one of us is expected to perform certain deeds. They include feeding the hungry, clothing the naked, visiting the sick, burying the dead, visiting the mourner, educating and providing shelter for the orphan.

The words of Moses Maimonides, an eleventh century Spanish Jew of Alexandria, explain in considerable detail the manner in which these acts of charity should be performed. Maimonides said that the lowest degree is to give but with reluctance or regret. The second is to give graciously but less than is fitting. The next degree is to give but only after the poor person asks. The fourth degree is to place the gift in the poor person's hand but before the person asks. The fifth is when the poor person knows from whom the gift is received but the giver does not know to whom it is given. The next higher degree is when the giver knows to whom the gift is given but the poor person does not know from whom it is received. The seventh degree of benevolence according to Maimonides is to give to the needy in such a manner that the giver does not know to whom the gift is given, and the recipient does not know from whom it came. The eighth and highest degree is when a person anticipates poverty and assists a poor person whether by a gift or a loan or by teaching that person a trade or helping to find employment, putting that person in such a position where it is no longer necessary to seek charity.

Maimonides emphasized both willingness to help others and the personal reward of doing so. This detailed list of steps of charity takes into consideration our greed, our selfishness and our duly recognized attempts for self-aggrandizement. Acts of kindness or charitable acts are difficult to perform, more difficult when they are performed anonymously and even more difficult when they involve giving more of one's self than money.

If little has changed in the definition of what constitutes acts of lovingkindness, certainly much has changed in how we try to accomplish them. Perhaps there was a time when these tasks could be attempted on an individual level and some may still be. But over the centuries there have evolved organizations and institutions which were formed specifically to care for these practical problems. One consequence has been that these urgent and intimate human needs often are dealt with so as to remove the sense of involvement and personal responsibility of the giver. But Maimonides sought anonymity in the relationship between giver and receiver because he respected the integrity and pride of the recipient.

Today we live in a society where only professionals deal with the various aspects of human needs. We have administrators and legislators determining how many food stamps the hungry should receive. We have organizations which repair old or out-of-style clothes to give to those who cannot afford to shop. We are not surprised to learn that usually only relatives and clergy, who consider it their professional duty, visit the sick and arrange for burial of the dead. In these areas, we have turned over responsibility to others and consider it the duty of public or private agencies to care for those less fortunate than ourselves.

It is easy to lose sight of our personal obligations. Individual responsibility is where acts of kindness occur. To put it in a different way, the essence of *gemilut hasadim* can best be understood as *mitzvah*. In the strictest sense, *mitzvah* is a commandment, one of the 613 duties in the Bible which every Jew is expected to fulfill. An act of lovingkindness is not a *mitzvah* in this sense. But *mitzvah* has another, broader meaning: it is a good deed, consideration shown for another person that is beyond the technical or prescribed. Acts of lovingkindness are *mitzvot* in this sense.

Simeon the Just called upon us to perform these special acts, to seek out occasions of need and to respond before misery takes too great a human toll. We each have an obligation not just to give but to give willingly, generously and, more than that, to take action.

I believe that the words of Simeon the Just have special meaning for us on this evening of the new year. As we come together for these brief hours, it is vital that we be able to take something home with us. Our fragile community will separate and go in different directions. Our Judaism and Jewishness should not be left behind here in this sanctuary. As we celebrate new beginnings, as we contemplate past actions, let us also recall a message that remain as vital today as it was centuries ago: *Al shloshah dvarim haolam omeyd: al hatorah, al ha'avodah v'al gemilut hasadim.* Upon these three things the world stands: upon Torah, upon Worship and upon Acts of Lovingkindness.

# Three Women

## Rosh Hashanah Morning—1976

I would like to share with you a new view on our traditional Biblical text.

There are two main ways of analyzing the story of Abraham and Isaac. The first is to investigate the theme of how Abraham responds to God's challenge to sacrifice Isaac in order to demonstrate his commitment of faith. This allows us to see Abraham as trusting in God, grieving for his much-loved son as a stern and determined parent. At the same time, the biblical passage portrays God as compassionate, having mercy for Isaac and not intending to allow Abraham to kill his son.

Another approach to the *Akeda* story is to take the perspective of the apparent victim: Isaac. This way allows us to consider the dilemma which the child faces when his parent presents him with a radical and terrifying demand—in effect, the son's trust in his father is facing the ultimate test. It is a struggle between the generations. When we follow Isaac through his years of maturation, we understand the event of the *Akeda* as a crystallization of self-awareness, of independence and aloneness like those each one of us may face at moments of deep crisis and challenge.

Over the past years on Rosh Hashanah mornings, I have explored both of these themes in some detail. But absent in these analyses is the perspective of the third member of the cast: Sarah—mother of the victim, Isaac, and wife of Abraham, the person being tested by God.

Just before the passage we read in Genesis this morning, the Bible tells us that God appears to Abraham and Sarah in order to tell them they will have a child. Sarah is naturally shocked and tends towards disbelief because she is already ninety and Abraham is one hundred. But in a year's time, Isaac is born, the same son whom Abraham takes away intending to offer as a human sacrifice to God.

We are told about Abraham's behavior regarding this commandment of God, but what is Sarah's reaction? No one has spoken to her to reveal that Isaac is to be sacrificed like God has spoken to Abraham.

Unlike Abraham, who fathers another child, Ishmael, Sarah is mother of only one child, Isaac. Nothing is said of Sarah's behavior or thoughts in the biblical story. For some revealing commentary on the elusive story in Genesis, it is necessary to turn to a non-biblical source. One Midrashic legend tells us that Abraham lied to Sarah rather than reveal the truth about the impending journey and sacrifice of Isaac. Abraham told her that it was not time for Isaac to study in the service of God under the tutelage of two priests. We are told that Sarah believed Abraham but nonetheless was quite saddened upon discovering Isaac's departure.

The legend continues that Satan visited Sarah after Abraham and Isaac had departed on their momentous journey. Satan revealed to Sarah that Abraham had deceived her, and the truth of the matter was that Isaac was to be sacrificed. Sarah was deeply troubled by this information and went in search of the two priests with whom Isaac was supposed to study. Of course, Sarah did not find them, and later she received another visit from Satan who told her that Isaac had not been sacrificed after all. When she heard this, she was overwhelmed with emotion and literally died from the shock of her joy.

This traditional source of Jewish folklore expressed several themes that are not reflected in the Bible. Sarah was shown to be naïve, highly impressionable and very emotional. She could not be told the truth about Abraham and Isaac's journey presumably because she did not have the same faith and strength that Abraham did. She is deprived of the insight and communication that Abraham is privileged to receive, deceived by her husband and led on by Satan. It is an incomplete portrait of the mother of the sacrificial victim and one that is anything but complimentary.

The crucial, yet often overlooked, role that Sarah plays has special relevance at the beginning of the new year: Sarah represents the creativity and fertility of life. While it is true that the Bible and specifically the Mosaic legislation and the Garden of Eden narrative places women in a subordinate position, it is also evident that woman is the custodian and perpetuator of life itself. This theme is most explicitly presented in the paradigmatic biblical story dealing with creation and woman's central role in it—the story of Adam and Eve.

Adam, alone on earth, asks God for a partner, and Eve is created. Eve is seduced by the serpent and misleads Adam into eating the forbidden fruit. Nonetheless, as the mother of Cain and Abel, she is the source of all later creation. The authors of the Bible portray Eve in a very uncomplimentary light. To begin with, she herself is not created out of the dust of the earth like Adam. Rather, she is fashioned from Adam's rib, clearly emphasizing her dependency on the man. This tale is related in Genesis (Chapter 2, 22-23):

> And the Lord God fashioned into a woman the rib that He had taken from the man, and He brought her to the man. Then the man said,
> "This one at last
> Is bone of my bones
> And flesh of my flesh.
> This one shall be called Woman,
> For from man was she taken."

God inflicts upon Eve a much harsher punishment than upon Adam. Adam's burden for eating the forbidden fruit is that his work in life will only be accomplished by hard labor that will bring sweat to his brow. Eve is more severely punished for her sins, which include both eating the fruit and offering it to Adam. The penalty is women's central role as mother in the creation of future generations is forevermore an act filled with the pain of childbirth. As it says in Genesis (Chapter 3:16):

> And to the woman God said,
> "I will make most severe
> Your pangs of childbearing;
> In pain shall you bear children."

The theme of creation is a recurrent one and has held the fascination of scholars, philosophers and mythmakers for centuries. In the vast Jewish literature outside of the Bible, there are various myths and legends which deal with the role of women in creation. Although sources often are contradictory, the legend of a woman named Lilith emerges as a creation myth which strongly contrasts with the familiar story of Eve. Indeed, it is the differences between Eve and Lilith which are central to the legends. Here we have access to the stereotypes by which earlier generations expressed their views of what are appropriate roles for Jewish women.

In the ancient and anonymous collection titled *The Alphabet of Ben Sira*, Lilith's origin is explained in the following way:

> After God created Adam, He said, "It is not good for Adam to be alone." He created a woman, also from the earth and called her Lilith. Adam and Lilith quarreled immediately. She said, "I will not lie below you." Adam said, "I will not lie below you but above you. For you are fit to be below me and I above you." Lilith responded, "We are both equal because we both come from the earth."

Lilith persisted in her position and, as a result, she was exiled from the Garden of Eden. Adam wanted her to return, but she refused. God decreed that her sin of disobedience to Adam is punished more severely than Eve's. Lilith ceases to be a creator because her children all will die in childbirth. Indeed, it is written that "hundreds of her children will die every day."

The conclusion is that Lilith is transformed from a woman into a demon. Indeed, her very name means "night demon," as compared to Eve's name which means "mother of life." It is this demonic image that forms a substantial part of the centuries of later mythology about Lilith. Myth blends with superstition, and Lilith, because of her attempts to defend her inherent equality with Adam, comes to be viewed as a threat to kill child-bearing women, to injure newborn babies and to excite men in their sleep. For centuries, Jews have worn amulets and recited prayers to protect themselves from the dangers that Lilith portends.

Sarah, Lilith and Eve can be seen as contrasting dimensions of the "female" in our traditional literature. Together they form a composite of the role of creating which can apply equally to men and women. They remind us of the risks and consequences of each act: both of self-assertion and passivity as well as each instance of creation.

Eve, who commits the sin of giving in to temptation, is punished with pain at the time of her crucial role of giver of life. Lilith, who refuses to subjugate herself to Adam and fights for a place equal to his, is punished with the death of all of her children and is blamed for causing the death of countless generations of pregnant women. Sarah, who does not believe she really can bear children when she is ninety years old, is eliminated from the drama which takes place involving God, her husband Abraham and her son Isaac.

Our new year holds open for each one of us the endless possibility of renewal and re-creation. In the biblical passage we read this morning, Abraham and Isaac began life together again after the challenge with which God confronted them.

Let us hope that in the days and months to come in the new year 5737, each one of us has the courage to seize the opportunities for renewal and growth, the determination to endure the risks of uncharted ventures, the confidence to create a life that moves beyond the limitations of stereotyped images and roles about ourselves, about others and about the world in which we live.

# Worship and Prayer

## Rosh Hashanah Morning—1977

Some of you are becoming like old friends to me. We meet together at this time each year, comfortable in the knowledge of what to expect from one another. You know you can depend on a seat you need not pay for, a place which hopefully you will feel familiar with, words and melodies which you might recognize and people who seem to have much in common with you.

I have expectations which appear similar to yours. I know I can count on people coming here at a pre-arranged time who will assemble quietly and wait patiently for our service to begin. I know that you will respond when requested to rise or sit when asked and listen silently, if not always attentively, to what I have to say.

Have you reflected on why and how all this socialized behavior takes place? For the past few months, I have wondered about this and other aspects of our public rituals. My thoughts have been greatly influenced by some experiences during this past year which were very different for me.

From November through April, I lived with my wife in the small Israeli town of Safed. Located high up in the northern hills of the Galilee, Safed is an isolated community of about 15,000 people. Most of the town is built on the sides of the hills, and one part contains the old city where a number of centuries-old synagogues are found. These synagogues are a chief attraction for tourists who come to town, but they also still are regularly used by some local Jews for worship.

A major division exists in these synagogues between those who are Ashkenazi and those who are Sephardi. This label applies to both the ritual and customs which are followed as well as to the countries of origin of the worshippers. Every Shabbat I went to a Sephardic synagogue. Most of the men came to Israel originally from North Africa, primarily Tunisia. (Unfortunately, women are not admitted to this particular one; in some others they are provided with a small balcony area.)

20

In this synagogue, named after the seventeenth century biblical commentator Alsheich, worship is arranged rather differently than it is here. For much of the prayer service, there is no designated leader, whether a rabbi or cantor. Various people read parts of the service; the rest of the congregation knows what he is reading, whether to join in or not, whether to stand or sit down, when to sing and when to take over and have someone else lead the reading. Everyone feels at home in this small synagogue. Young children wander about, adults talk casually with others, and everyone sits on benches along the walls so that everyone can see everyone else. At first glance, chaos seems to reign. But, on closer inspection, it is evident that everything is very organized and circumscribed. The organization is the result of centuries of ritualized behavior.

Of course, one of the big differences that distinguished this service from most of ours is one of scale. If only ten or fifteen of us pledged to worship together every Friday evening and Saturday morning as well as holidays, week in and week out, we would evolve a rather different sort of social behavior that what we do here.

How we behave when we come together is, then, greatly affected by our physical environment here: this building, these pews, this pulpit, our public manner, our clothes, our strangeness to each other, our public behavior in front of strangers, as well as the reasons why we are here.

It seems to me that there are perhaps three main reasons why we gather together at this time of year. Well aware of the fact that most of you attend services only a few times a year, I offer the following possibilities as major motivations.

Living as we do in a general non-Jewish environment—although New York City offers some relief for this—we seek opportunities to express our Jewishness in acceptable forms. Products of secular culture, influenced by all the forces of assimilation and acculturation to a much greater extent than we are aware, we know that attendance at such a place as this is not only approved of but often expected of us as well. How many of us have experienced non-Jewish friends being surprised at how lightly we sometimes take our Judaism? We come here to show other people that at the really important times we do remember who we are and where we come from. So one possible motivation for why many of us are here is that it is expected—or what will other people think of me if I don't go to High Holy Day services?

Very closely related to this but perhaps the opposite motivation lies in our way of life as American Jews. For most of us, we do not have very many opportunities to express our Jewishness. We don't belong to those parts of Judaism which deliberately set themselves off from other parts of society, like Hasidim and other strictly observant Jews. Most likely, very few of us observe kosher dietary laws, we do some sort of work or play that would be considered a violation of the traditional Jewish notion of the Sabbath, and we don't attend synagogue on a regular and fixed basis. We may express our Jewishness through such actions as rallies in defense of Israel or protests against the treatment of Jews in Russia, but our work and leisure are not being defined by our Jewishness. So we can assert this aspect of our identity by attending a worship service. We can renew our ties to the Jewish people; we can manage, if only for a few hours, to recall our history and draw closer to our mutual present by being part of this miniature and temporary Jewish community. Here one of the only things we have in common is the fact that we all are Jews. We can figuratively reach out and touch each other and become one with another because of the shared aspect of our identity. This is a positive motivation for gathering together on these holidays. We care enough about our identity as Jews to want to congregate, and where else in our society can that be so easily achieved except in places such as this?

A third possibility exists for why so many more of us come to services at this time of year than any other. Perhaps we are interested in that form of communication called prayer. Previously I have described psychological and sociological motivation for our attendance, but there is the possibility that a theological one exists as well.

The Hebrew word for prayer is *tefillah*. The word comes from the verb *palel* which has a number of meanings. Most central to our discussion is that the word can mean "hope" or "plead" or "entreat." A common definition given to *tefillah* is "requesting from God." This fits with a good deal of what we know about Jewish liturgy. Many of our prayers take the form of requests or supplications. Central to the Jewish notion of prayer is that we are making a request to some sort or form of divine being—which means that there is a listener.

We raise our voices in speech or song when we are here together, and sometimes we give thanks or tell stories. But most of the time, we make requests. If we stop to analyze this whole concept carefully, there are a number of steps. First, there should be someone or something listening. Second, we think that our words have some effect upon that listener. Third, there is something we would like to receive as a result.

What I have described so far is a description that can as adequately describe human interaction and our relationships with others just as easily. If so, what difference is there between requests of other people and our supplications to God? Do not most of us think that God is like that benevolent parent who exists as the boundless source of plenty? Most of us can conceptualize our relationship with God in terms that parallel human relationships.

We are consistent with a good deal of Jewish tradition in such a conceptualization. Our ancestors in the Sinai Desert knew God as a power that acted daily in their lives. God spoke to Moses, revealed laws to the multitude, and even went before them in a cloud above the Holy Ark. The prophets describe God in human and vivid terms. The Psalms are filled with anthropomorphic metaphor and allusion which relate us to a God of vengeance, God as a warrior king, God as a kindly father or God as a beautiful musician.

It is not until many centuries later that we come across a negative reaction to this language and these concepts. We have to wait until the medieval philosopher Maimonides to find a clearly articulated Jewish theology that rejects this human God. Maimonides, in his monumental philosophical work *Guide for the Perplexed* reasons that God has no attributes that can be understood in human terms. To think and perceive God this way reduces God to humanness. Maimonides postulates that God can only be understood by what God is not—by negative attributes. For example, God is not human, God is not mortal, God is not limited in time and space. To assert that God is eternal or immortal immediately begs the question of what it means to be eternal or immortal. Can we understand such terms in any way other than those which are bound by our own human examples? Can we truly comprehend what it means to be immortal in any way other than to say that it is the negation of mortality?

Maimonides leaves us in a quandary if we insist on claiming that there is a logical and rational system to comprehend God as a figure in human history who daily intercedes on behalf of those who believe. But there are many different notions of God and approaches to theology in Jewish tradition. I have briefly touched on two. Whatever approaches we have to the existence or definition of God, it should influence the intention and direction of prayer.

Let me explain a little further what I mean. Prayer can serve many different functions. One important function that it often performs is communication. It is possible to appreciate and comprehend moments of group prayer, such as when we are here together on occasions like this, as an opportunity to relate to those around us. To reach out and to be reached out to means we recognize for a few moments that we are not always so alone in our human existence as we fear we might be. The act of communal prayer can serve as a bond among us and as testimony or a statement of our faith in ourselves and each other. Each of us has built up walls against others, and we need to find moments when we can try to lower them just a bit. We speak and sing in unison, we stand and sit together, we respond to cues as one, and in all of this we can seek a thread that ties us together. This links us in the chain of centuries of tradition which began with our ancestor Abraham about whom we read this morning.

There is another way in which some of us perhaps are a little bit like Abraham. In the biblical passage we read today, we can understand that Abraham was, as the Danish philosopher Søren Kierkegaard described him, a "knight of faith." Abraham chose to suspend the rational and place his trust in the irrational or mystical. How was it possible for Abraham to believe that God truly wanted him to sacrifice his only son? How was it conceivable that he would ignore his rational faculties and follow such a course of action?

Is it conceivable that each of us has a little bit of the same behavior in us? Until quite recently, I would not have imagined that is it is possible for someone who tries to reason and act according to rational motives and values ever to knowingly suspend reason. Recently, I have begun to understand that it is possible for there to be elements of reason and pure emotion, rationality and mystical forces in each of us. As humans we have many different aspects of our being in competition within us.

If I choose to believe Maimonides, the great Jewish rationalist and his systematic theology, how can I read the prayers that we all utter which describe God in human form? Maimonides himself provides us with an answer. The great rationalist was able to suspend his reason and claim that he believed with perfect faith that God would speedily send peace and comfort, heal the sick, end oppression, bring the Messiah and intercede in the daily events of human history.

It seems to me that it is possible and perhaps even necessary to be able to understand that along with cool reason goes passionate hope that prayer is a communication, a metaphysical language of hope and desire as well as a pleading and entreaty.

Prayer for me can be a vehicle of communication with others and with the Other. It can serve as an assertion and an awareness of our own self in relation to generations that have come before us. In addition, it can answer a need that some of us feel that the world and all that is therein is not yet complete. We not only work towards that goal but hope and pray that it is in the process of becoming.

# Determination and Free Will

## Rosh Hashanah Evening—1978

Six years ago, I began serving as rabbi to this most unusual congregation. In 1973, many of you were in other places, involved in other projects and perhaps feeling very differently about yourself and your Jewish identity than you do this evening. Many things were different at that time in my life as well. Not only was I still a rabbinic student, but I had some different attitudes about how I should talk to a congregation like you on an occasion like this. My attitude and outlook have changed from being pretty sure I knew what I wanted to say—and why I wanted to say it—to something else. Like a student who ventures into new areas, experience from the pulpit has shown me how very much there is that I still do not know.

For example, what do I know about many of you individually or, for that matter, as a group? I now know how you sing; how quickly you stand up or sit down; how many of you like to come early or arrive late; what those of you sitting near the front wear and how many of you like to participate in the service. But it is difficult to even begin to enumerate how much I don't know about you and, more specifically, how much I don't know about you that might be of relevance on an occasion such as this. What do you know about Judaism, about ritual, Zionism, Bible, Jewish history, Hebrew language and literature, prayer and so on?

This makes my task as your rabbi on these holidays more difficult. Not only do I not know who amongst you is seeking comfort, consolation, relaxation, answers to spiritual or philosophical questions, but I also don't know where you are coming from as Jews. Perhaps some of you are thinking, "Why is this guy giving us such a lengthy rationalization about why he had trouble writing a sermon." If so, you are not too far off the mark because for me, sermons are a means to communicate about something the person up here feels is important enough to, in a sense, force upon people like you sitting out there. For this communication to be effective, it not only must be concise, thoughtful and well-delivered, but it also should speak to common concerns of us all.

In the past, I have spoken about Israel and Zionism. Certainly, we all have a shared concern for Israel. I have spoken to this congregation about discrimination, education, the future of the Jewish community and other topics that are areas of interest shared in varying degrees by us all. Tonight I want to talk to you about a much more difficult subject to organize my thoughts about: belief in God.

Theology, I have often felt, is not a Jewish science. We Jews have pondered very little about the nature of God. Rather, we have concerned ourselves with what we as Jews should do as opposed to what we should believe. For many reasons, Jews in the contemporary world seem more concerned about theology and belief. Perhaps this is a reflection of a general lack of context for traditional Jewish observance. As we are less sure of what we do that is particularly Jewish, we sometimes find ourselves thinking about what we believe that is particularly Jewish.

To illuminate some aspects of theology, I would like to turn to the Bible for two examples. The examples I have chosen are not necessarily typical of what the Bible says about our human perception of God. In many places, the authors of the Bible cast God as all-powerful, all-knowing, ever-present as well as vengeful, mighty and destructive. Here are two stories that shed a slightly different light on our people's monotheistic perception many years ago.

In Genesis, the first of the Five Books of Moses, early on we encounter the patriarch Abraham. We will read about his interaction with his son Isaac tomorrow morning, but this evening I want to read to you a few verses from Chapter 18 of Genesis which comes a few chapters before the sacrifice of Isaac. The passage describes Abraham arguing with God about the possible destruction of the evil cities of Sodom and Gomorrah.

> The Lord said, "The outrage of Sodom and Gomorrah is so great, and their sin is so grave! I will go down to see whether they have acted altogether according to the outcry that has come to Me; if not, I will know." Abraham came forward and said, "Will You sweep away the innocent along with the guilty? What if there should be fifty innocent within the city; will You then wipe out the place and not forgive it for the sake of the innocent fifty who are in it? Far be it from You to do such a thing, to bring death upon the innocent as well as the guilty, so that innocent and guilty fare alike. Far be it from You! Shall not the Judge of the earth deal justly?" And the Lord answered, "If I find within the city of Sodom fifty innocent ones, I will forgive the whole place for their sake." Abraham spoke up, saying "Here I venture to speak to the Lord, I who am but dust and ashes: What if the fifty innocent should lack five: will You destroy the whole city for want of the five? And God answered, "I will not destroy if I find forty-five there."

Abraham goes on arguing and concludes by saying, "Let not the Lord be angry if I speak but this last time. What if ten should be found there? And God answered, "I will not destroy Sodom and Gomorrah for the sake of the ten."

Traditional Jewish commentators make much of the significance of the number ten which Abraham gets God to finally agree to. That, however, is not the point I wish to illustrate. Rather, I wish to comment on what the authors of this passage reveal as an important dimension of Jewish belief that strikes a responsive chord within me. Abraham says, "Shall not the Judge of all the earth deal justly?" Abraham wants to use the same criteria to judge God that he believes God uses to judge us. This approach, one that all of us may use at one time or another for getting the other person to try and live up to their own words, seems to be what Abraham pulls off in his conversation with God.

Here is an intensely personal and immediate experience in which God and Abraham seem as near equals. Not only does Abraham argue with God, but the premise of the argument is that a just God must do justly—and that compromise is possible. Here we have Abraham's encounter with God brought down to a personal and humanly understandable level.

In Chapter 21, Jacob, the grandson of Abraham, runs away from his brother Esau after stealing his birthright. Upon awakening from a sleep in which God had visited him, Jacob makes the following vow: "If God remains with me, if He protects me on this journey that I am making and gives me bread to eat and clothing to wear, and if I return safe to my father's house, then the Lord shall be my God."

Incredible as it may sound, Jacob also tries to strike a bargain with God. This time, however, it is not on behalf of the people of Sodom and Gomorrah or even to score a few points as a good bargainer. Rather, Jacob is striking a deal that God has to live up to if He wants Jacob's allegiance. If God comes through for Jacob, then Jacob will come through for God.

Some of you may find these stories a contrast with what you believe are the attitudes and viewpoints expressed in much of Jewish thought—and you would be correct. Judaism often expresses a belief in an abstract, unspecified and unmaterialized deity. But the Bible has dozens of examples of a concrete, specific and immediate Supreme Being. My opinion is that this is so because this is the best way that we can relate to God. It seems to me that our understanding of God cannot be only on an incorporeal and abstract level. God must also be comprehended in our human terms, even if doing so means limiting God's attributes to humanly understandable ones.

The further implications of my argument are as follows: Abraham's ability to strike a bargain with God and Jacob's promise of obedience if God delivers His part of the bargain has another side. There is a certain responsibility each of us has in this potential relationship with God. We are not free to place all the blame for the bad or credit for the good literally on the shoulders of God. Abraham and Jacob each enter into a dialogue and then a sort of contract with God. Responsibility goes both ways. It is my belief that God is limited in the extent of effect upon our condition and predicament by the actions and freedom with which we all are endowed.

There is a phrase in rabbinic literature that helps to amplify what I am trying to say. In the Sayings of the Fathers, it is stated that "All is determined, but free will is given." Apparently contradictory, as much of Jewish literature is, I suggest the following interpretation. One part of our tradition teaches that God creates and decides on the order and nature of things in this world. That power, however, has limits. The limits end where the responsibilities that we human beings have for our actions begins.

We have an infinite capacity for evil as well as good. Judaism always has recognized this and refers to *yetzer ha-rah* and *yetzer ha-tov*, the evil inclination and the good inclination within each of us. The course of human history and the future of our own lives is in large part determined not by what a supernatural deity ordains, but rather by what we can try and make it into. I believe God is limited by our human frailties and capacities. The bargains of Abraham and Jacob assert the basic humanness of our tradition. Judaism recognizes that we, too, have a hand in our future. It is up to each of us to try and shape it in the direction we would like it to go.

At the onset of the new year 5739, in a world filled with evidence of all of human frailties but open to the infinite possibilities each one of us can bring to it, let us not leave the determination of our own future to someone or something beyond ourselves. Rather, let us face our challenges by relying on our own strengths and abilities. The new year should bring an opportunity for each of us to enter into our personal dialogue, strike our own bargain and work out our compromise. May each one of us find the *yetzer ha-tov*—the good inclination—within us. May we recognize the limits that God and other people have over our lives. We have free will and must exercise it and assume responsibilities for our actions.

# Ethical Wills

## Rosh Hashanah Evening—1983

One summer weekend experience I had at the beach has stayed with me as I consider the meaning of Rosh Hashanah and the holiday season that we begin tonight. On the way back from the beach with some friends and my wife and four-year-old son, I found myself instructing my son about something my parents had taught me when I was his age. We were cleaning up from our day at the beach and making sure that the litter we had created was picked up. I said to my son that we should be very careful about cleaning up after ourselves and, in fact, we should try to leave the place that we were in a little bit cleaner than we found it. He turned to me and asked, "Why should we leave it cleaner?" I explained that if we each leave our place a little bit cleaner, it will help clean up everything around us.

What I want to reflect with you about is how we should see our job, our role, our obligation, our life, in this world as cleaning up after ourselves in such a way as to leave things better than we found them. That is, how can we as Jews work to improve the world in which we live?

In Jewish mystical tradition there is the notion of *tikkun olam*, the repair of the world. The specific reference or technical meaning of this term has to do with a particular way of seeing creation and chaos in the world and how we are obligated to repair the chaos around us. How can we go about being repairers of our world? It is a strange and peculiar world that we live in where a religion such as ours that teaches reverence for life as its highest principle is often derided. Where a religion such as ours that teaches that to destroy a single life is to destroy an entire world and that to sustain a single life is to sustain an entire world is often ignored. A world where a religion like ours that yearns above all things for the day when swords will be beaten into ploughshares and spears into pruning hooks is laughed at, sometimes by the descendants of those prophets as well as others. This is a world of great abundance and great privations—a world of great contrasts between rich and poor, north and south, black and white; a world where still some people are born into slavery of the body and others are born into the slavery of the mind; a world that is still greatly in need of repair; a world in which at the beginning of the year 5744, we offer up a prayer and a plea to God to remember us unto life, to inscribe us in the book of life, O God of Life.

The world we live in is just as much in need of repair as any in our long history. Rosh Hashanah is the day that our tradition tells us the world was created—so it also is the day to repair the mistakes of the world. That work at repairing the mistakes, collecting the dispersed sparks of creation, is human work. It is not God's work but the work of people like you and me.

There are many legends in our tradition that speak of our existence in an imperfect world. One such teaching that is repeated in the form of many different stories with the same theme is as follows:

> If you, God, seek justice, there will be no world, and if You seek to have a world, strict justice cannot be exercised. Do you think you can take hold of a rope at both ends? You desire the world to endure but You, God, desire true justice also. If You will not relent a little, the world will not endure.
>
> (Adapted from *Pesikta D'Rav Kahana* 19:1)

So we live in a world without true justice, a world as the rabbis of old said is one "of flesh and blood". What is our responsibility in this world and how can we carry it out?

There is a tradition of parents writing a special letter to their children—an ethical will—in which they tried to sum up what they had learned in life and to express what they wanted most for and from their children. They left these letters or wills because they believed the wisdom that they had acquired was as much a part of their bequest as material possessions, often noted in a separate document.

Ethical wills have been a part of Jewish life since biblical times. Jacob gathers his children around his bedside to tell them how they should live after he is gone. Moses makes a farewell address, chastising, prophesizing and instructing his people before he dies. David asks Solomon to complete the task he has begun but was unable to finish and warns Solomon to be wary of certain persons when he becomes king. The Apocrypha, the Talmud, medieval and modern Hebrew literature also contain examples of ethical wills.

It certainly is not easy to write an ethical will. For us to do so we must look inward for essential truths and must face up to the failures as well as the triumphs, to consider what things there are that really count. In this way, we learn a great deal about ourselves when writing such a will.

In our history, ethical wills were written by many people from many countries. They were written by scholars, and they were written by simple men and women. Some were prepared in rare times of freedom in our history and times of safety, and some in trenches and bunkers. They were written in many languages—in English, Hebrew, Yiddish, German. They were precious spiritual documents—windows into the world, perhaps of ethics, perhaps of ordinary life and aspirations of the people who wrote them. They tell us how Jews express their concern for and their desire to create a better world for themselves and others. How might we think of the future and the task before each one of us?

One example is that of Sholem Aleichim, pen name of the famous Yiddish writer, whose will he asked to be opened and published on the day of his death (*New York Times* May 17, 1916). An inspiring example of an ethical will, the document has ten sections with detailed instructions for how he wishes to be remembered. It reads in part (Section IV):

> At my grave and throughout a whole year, and then every year on the Jahrzeit, my remaining son, and my sons-in-law, if they are so minded, should say Kaddish after me. And if they do not wish to do this, or if they have no time for it, or if it be against their religious convictions, they can be absolved from this duty only if they all come together with my daughters and my grandchildren and with good friends, and read this my will, and also select one of my stories, one of the really joyous ones, and read it aloud in whatever language they understand best, and let my name be mentioned by them with laughter rather than not be mentioned at all.

We all know that we should write a will that concerns insurance, property and trusts. But what about the non-material items in our life, the other valuables that are perhaps beyond measure? How can we catalogue them, leave some message for others about what we hold most dear? How can we fulfill the obligation that is written in *Pirke Avot*, where Rabbi Tarfon is quoted as saying: "The work is not upon you to finish, nor are you free to desist from it."

To make our place a little cleaner than we found it, to try and make the world a little better for others to live in is the beginning of our ethical action. The effort of writing an ethical will can be a beginning, not an end, for us to try and capture what is special and unique within us that we can contribute and what we think is most important.

As these days of repentance and introspection begin, I would like to invite each of you here to pick up a pen and take responsibility upon yourself and consider writing an ethical will that best expresses how you wish to be remembered—how you hope to leave this world a little better than you found it. So that this will not be an empty exercise for each and every one of us, I invite any of you here who plan to be with us on Yom Kippur day to have an opportunity to read your ethical will to those of us who will be gathered together after the morning service and before the afternoon discussion. This will provide all of us an opportunity to share with one another those ethical values and standards that we wish to convey to others who live on after us.

I began this sermon tonight with recalling an incident that occurred at the beach some weeks ago. The experience at the beach has reminded me of the sands on the shore that we read about in our Torah portion that we will hear tomorrow morning. God promised Abraham, after Abraham refuses to sacrifice his son Isaac, that Abraham's seed will grow to be as great in number as the sands in the sea and the stars in the sky. All of us here tonight, descendants of Abraham, have a special responsibility and different ways of repairing the world, of trying to accomplish *tikkun olam*.

And I leave with you the thought tonight that each of us has a different path to reach that goal. As we conclude this evening's service on the symbolic day of the world's creation, let us remember that ours is a task to create a better world. But, as the rabbis of old have indicated, though the task is great and the time is short, even so we are not released from beginning it.

# Gates of Repentance

## Yom Kippur Evening—1984

There was a folk tradition passed on orally through the hillsides sur-
rounding Jerusalem in the years that followed the Temple's demise that
once there had been an enormous gate opening into the Temple court-
yard. It was said that when the gate opened and closed, the sound could
be heard as far away as Jericho some miles away. Observers today might
well wonder about the veracity of this tale. Even in the quiet of early
morning or late evening, it would have required quite a gate to echo so
far through the hills. Yet the image of a gate opening and closing at the
Temple has remained with us. Through gates we enter; through gates
we leave. Our liturgy is termed "gates"—portals to prayer, repentance,
forgiveness and understanding. The Bible speaks of the gates of heaven.

All of these images come together during our Yom Kippur services. We have seen the gates open and, tomorrow at the concluding
service called Neilah (which literally means "locking"), the gates will
be closed. The prayer book titled *Gates of Repentance* that we have
been using since Rosh Hashanah began will be put back on shelves
and locked as we leave for home tomorrow evening, just as the massive
gates of the Temple used to be shut against the backdrop of the desert
sun sinking behind Jerusalem. And the gates to heaven? Those gates,
the ones that open to God's presence, are never locked to us says our
tradition.

Struggling with these images in my own mind, I thought of a story
that I read some years ago. At the end of Kafka's *The Trial* (1925), he
tells the story of a man who comes from the countryside, reaches the
Law which is surrounded by a wall and finds a door. He waits—for
days and eventually years—for the doorkeeper to give him permission
to enter. With the last of his strength as he is dying, the man asks the
doorkeeper why no one else has asked to be admitted through this door
and is told that the door is meant only for him.

Kafka was a master storyteller and, in my opinion a writer of considerable religious sensibilities. His quest has no easy solution; his con-

cerns have no easy resolutions; his questions are difficult to answer. In my struggle with this parable, I wondered: For every gate there must be a wall or some comparable barrier, or else why would a gate be necessary? Kafka's wall surrounds the Law, a concept very much part of Jewish tradition. How can we be more successful in getting permission to enter the gates than Kafka's man?

Let me try to respond to the image of gates and walls by explaining something about Yom Kippur. Unlike all the other Jewish holidays, Yom Kippur and Rosh Hashanah have no outstanding association with major events in Jewish history. But rabbinic tradition insisted that a central biblical episode did occur on Yom Kippur. On this day Moses finally brought the second set of tablets of the Ten Commandments to the Jewish people.

The original tablets of the Ten Commandments were fashioned by the Divine, untouched by human flaws. But when the people of Israel sinned and created a Golden Calf, God despaired and wanted to get rid of them. Moses was so distressed that he smashed the tablets. It was almost as if the tablets were too pure to be left in human hands. Then came forty days of working through the heartbreak. Reconciliation and catharsis were followed by forty days of Moses's labor fashioning new tablets. This set—product of hard-won repentance, built on realism, forgiveness and acceptance of the limitations of others—could dwell among the Israelites and guide them for centuries to come.

The walls that surround us are ones of our own making. They are walls that we set up between us and others—and walls that we set up to try to hide our imperfections. In our individual fantasy of perfection, we think that no flaws or breaks can be permitted or discovered. Many of us fear that once there is a break, not even atonement can restore our original wholeness. This is a superhuman—and therefore inhuman—conception of tradition. Yom Kippur teaches us that humans inevitably fail, miss the mark or sin. The book of Ecclesiastes (7:20) teaches us that "There is no righteous person on the earth who does only good and never sins."

The first wall that we must open is the wall to our own hearts which close us off to our human failings—the wall which we build up to keep us from admitting that it is all right to have failed, to have sinned.

And who is the gatekeeper? For us, the gatekeeper is our own heart. When we turn and open our hearts, admitting that we were wrong or that we have failed, then we can come out stronger. When we have internalized the drive for perfection, we find it difficult to admit imperfections. So then how can we obtain forgiveness? The medieval scholar

Maimonides asserted that the indispensable first step in repentance is to admit the flaw or sin. The confirmed sinner is afraid to turn back. He or she may dread that with one moment of letting go and admitting failure an entire life will fall apart.

Entering the gates for us begins with a desire to truly see ourselves, the good and the bad parts. Admission of failings is what follows. This admission should carry with it the realization that out of the brokenness—like the brokenness of the tablets of the Ten Commandments—we become stronger than when we claimed to be whole.

How can we convince the gatekeeper to let us in before the gates are locked? Or before our strength fails us, and we cannot manage to get in? Do we have the strength to go through the gates?

The gates of righteousness are always open. True, but perhaps there are only certain times we feel fit enough to be able to enter them. We help prepare ourselves by admitting our weaknesses and by opening our sealed hearts.

During these few hours of Yom Kippur, we are in the time expressly set aside for our prayers to rise. And it is tonight and tomorrow when are fates are said to be sealed in the Book of Life.

Sealed: there is such finality is that word. "On Rosh Hashanah" we read, "it is written and on Yom Kippur it is sealed who shall live and who shall die." Is our fate really sealed on Yom Kippur? Is it really known for certain who shall live and who shall die? Most of us will accept that this image is a little narrow-minded and too literal, just as we react to the literal image of the Temple's booming gate. But on a symbolic level, both images have something to say to us. The closing of the door was heard psychologically, not just in Jericho but wherever Jews gathered to come to terms with their lives before God. They now faced the fact that the annual opportunity to renew their lives was nearing an end.

As for living and dying, some of us indeed will have determined our fate by Yom Kippur's conclusion. If we have not opened ourselves to the possibility of change, if we have not seriously atoned, if we have not turned in repentance to God and to those we love, then we have determined that next year sadly will be similar to the one just ending. Even if we still are physically alive twelve months from now, something in us will have died. And we will have sealed ourselves in spiritless coffins already at Yom Kippur this year.

For each of us to be admitted through the gates, we must prepare ourselves. We may have different gates, different barriers to overcome, different gatekeepers to get passed. If we wish to have greater success than the man in Kafka's parable, we must learn how to admit our own failings so that out of our brokenness we can become stronger.

The Temple has been destroyed, the gates no longer can be heard in Jericho or elsewhere. The gatekeepers exist only in our imagination. Nothing stands in our way of entering except our own courage.

AMEN.

# Reform Judaism and Who is a Jew?

## Rosh Hashanah Evening—1985

This evening we come together to celebrate something special in our lives and in the lives of the Jewish people. A short time ago, the Jewish year 5746 began. As the new year begins it is only natural to reflect on how the old one has been. We have our private thoughts and summing up for the past twelve months—individually and communally. Part of that is reflected in the liturgy that we read this evening and will read tomorrow morning as well. But a bigger part of that summing up lies within our hearts and minds as we reflect on life, death, loss, gain, victories and defeats during the past year.

We as the Jewish people are not only a stubborn lot—this we know from as good a source as our Bible—but we are a people that has had a very hard time getting along with one another. Our differences appear to be minor to the world of non-Jews who look at us from the outside. To those of us on the inside, they loom large. We are here this evening with worship services conducted, sponsored, arranged and developed by the Reform movement. That does not seem to be very important most of the time. This can, however, loom as a very large issue for many in the broader Jewish community elsewhere in the United States and in other countries, especially Israel.

To traditional Jews, there are some important developments that recently have underscored the differences between them and us. One such difference is the issue of determining who is a Jew. It is not only the definition that is important but how we non-traditional Jews arrive at our definition.

Jumping back in time to almost two centuries ago in Europe when reformers started speaking to the German Jewish community, it would be difficult for us to appreciate how revolutionary liberal Jewish thinkers were at that time. They proclaimed that Judaism always had changed with the times and still needed to do so. We today can hardly imagine what it might be like to conceive of the world in relatively static terms.

37

In fashion or government, things seem to hold still only momentarily before proceeding with further transformation. We take for granted Darwin, Marx and Einstein—their views of reality as constantly in motion. None of them had written when the liberals early in the nineteenth century proclaimed their notion of religion as substantially a human creation, one that therefore continually adapted itself to new knowledge and circumstances.

Almost everything I have to say here this evening, and for that matter at any other time, rests on the liberal conception of Judaism as a dynamic process of human spiritual discovery. For me, Reform Judaism is selling autonomy and doubt. We moderns are part of a world that forces us to stand between the two worlds: one where we know all the answers and the other where we doubt everything.

Reform or liberal religion teaches me that I am not sure what happened at Sinai. Did God in fact reveal to Moses all 613 commandments or just ten? Did 600,000 Jews witness the event or only Moses? I question exactly what happened. I have thoughts and doubts about the revelations that took place then and about their veracity. For me, and for those of you who share my doubts, our task of determining where in the human process of spiritual discovery we stand is extremely difficult. Are there absolutes that we can hold with certainty? For me, being human is recognizing that I am not certain about very much, but I do possess reason and the ability to examine what is.

For me, truth is and always has been something dynamic, a process of finding more adequate understanding of the universe and where we fit into it. With that in mind, I want to approach the controversial issue of patrilineal descent.

In March of 1983, the Central Conference of American Rabbis passed a resolution stating that "the child of one Jewish parent is under presumption of Jewish descent." The resolution goes on to state that timely participation in the rituals and education of Judaism are necessary for that individual to be considered a Jew by the Reform Jewish community. The most controversial part of the resolution means that the child of a Jewish father and a non-Jewish mother is under the presumption of Jewish descent. That is different from the centuries-old concept of the child of a Jewish mother is Jewish regardless of the faith of the father and that the child of a non-Jewish mother is not Jewish regardless of the faith of the father.

The traditional Jewish community has had a good time attacking Reform Judaism as divisive and creating a new sect of Jews over this issue. But, as is the case in many other matters, there is more here than meets the eye. In 1983 the Reform rabbinate affirmed a principle that had been part of the movement's agenda for a generation. In the 1940s, the *Rabbis' Manual*, that handbook for Reform rabbis, stated a similar position in its advice to rabbis. The Orthodox Jewish community is concerned that this violation of Jewish law will lead to the inability of the Jewish community to agree on who is a Jew.

This is not the time or place, nor am I the right person, to be discussing the development of Jewish law. I can offer the following observation that Orthodox law is not always objective. One has only to remember the Israeli rabbinate's refusal to deal with the problem of Brother Daniel (a man born of two Jewish parents who converted to Christianity and applied for Israeli citizenship under the Law of Return). Or the better-known situation of David Ben Gurion's daughter-in-law whose conversion to Judaism was not recognized because her conversion had been performed by a Reform rabbi. She gave birth to a boy on Shabbat and, on the following Shabbat, the *brit* was scheduled according to Jewish law. The Israeli rabbinate forbade the ceremony because they did not recognize the Jewishness of the child. We live in a world where Khrushchev's grandchild is Jewish because his son married a Jewish woman, but Ben Gurion's is not.

Now that my digression is completed, I wish to return to the point that even though we have ample biblical evidence of patrilineal descent, the rabbinic law makes clear that the child follows the religion of the mother. We know that the manner in which Jewish law evolved during the rabbinic period was entirely the product of men. The roles assigned to women were created by men and that the exegeses cited to justify these roles were developed by men, and so on. Rabbinic Judaism and its legal character reflect their original cultural environment, one that took for granted that the world ought to be as men have shaped it. If as it is to be hoped that that environment is now passing into obsolescence, it is not obvious how we ought to treat its artifacts. Obviously, I suggest by this line of reasoning that matrilineal descent is such an artifact.

One other such artifact that Reform Judaism struck out at some years ago is the necessity of a Jewish woman needing a Jewish divorce before she could remarry. In traditional Judaism, if this was not accomplished, then the resulting children are considered *mamzerim*, legally bastards, and unable to marry anyone other than other *mamzerim*. In many ways this is more of a threat to the hegemony of the Jewish community because someone who is not a Jew according to Jewish law always can convert, but once a *mamzer* always a *mamzer*. Again, this requirement of a Jewish divorce in order for a woman to remarry and bear legal children has significant consequences for the traditional Jewish community.

So how does Reform Judaism come to think and talk and act concerning these matters of personal status within the Jewish community? Our frame of reference is recognizing that we understand Judaism as dynamic and evolutionary. Religion has not stood still and, more importantly, our understanding of our spiritual and religious experience is a changing one. This means that there exists for each and every Jew a degree of autonomy.

For earlier generations of Jews, the definition of a "good Jew" was self-evident: a good Jew was one who follows Torah. A minority of American Jews live essentially among their fellow believers and uphold traditional Judaism. For them, the old standards for the good Jew remain in effect. Unlike them, most Jews lost their theological certainty and communal insularity when they modernized. Some of us base our lives on the possibility of changing Jewish tradition even as we partially continue it. Despite our debates and experimentation, we have no consensus as to how one can be fully modern and authentically Jewish. Ideologically, we Reform Jews range from those who identify Judaism with purely universal ethics and culture to those particularists who insist that everything truly human is found in the Torah. Hardly an intellectual or social movement surfaces in American culture which does not speedily generate a Jewish counterpart. Amid this cacophony of opinion and practice people ask, "Who is a good Jew?"

Our Jewish problem is not unique. Western civilization itself can no longer specify clear standards for "good" human behavior. As soon as we have made some tolerable adjustment to the latest insight into human nature and social relations a new cultural theory emerges, and we must again adapt. As it is, we can no longer specify who is a good person and, thus, modern Jews are doubly troubled by the related issue—who is a good Jew?

Now to the end, and, in a way, to where we began. Jews also face the critical problem of communal authority. Who among us today has the right to tell other Jews what they ought to do? Some generations back, we would have looked to the rabbis and sages to define our obligations. But as Jews accepted the need to change Jewish practice in ways their leaders thought were improper—for example, the use of the vernacular in prayer, mixed seating, attendance at a university—the old authority of the rabbinate effectively ended for them. In fact, today we face a dilemma that has no easy answer. And that is: by what right, by what authority, are we as moderns to act? For indeed, modernity has made individualism central to contemporary Jewish life.

I offer one final thought. It may be possible to claim that a good Jew is someone who lives connected with the notion of the Covenant that exists between God and the Jewish people, whose existence takes shape from a relationship with God as part of the Jewish people, who carries out in traditional and modern ways the ethical and religious duties of a personal, familial and communal sort, who is dedicated to the survival of the Jewish people and the enhancement of its way of life, who is devoted to the continuation of the State of Israel and the betterment of humankind generally and is determinedly hopeful that a messianic fulfillment awaits us.

As 5746 begins, we can hope and pray that this year will see increased understanding and cooperation between Jews and non-Jews and among Jews and Jews—enabling different Jews to try to understand one another, to talk to one another, to learn to respect the differences in the plurality of the Jewish people. When that day comes, we will be better able to understand what the biblical prophet meant when he said, "Who shall go up to the mountain of God, who shall ascend God's holy place . . . they who have clean hands, pure hearts, who never speak with malice, and who never swear deceitfully. They shall receive blessing from God."

May all of us here this evening, as well as Jews everywhere, remember what the purpose of this season of renewal is about: that is, to make peace with ourselves, peace with one another and peace with God. May each of us find our own way of accomplishing these tasks in the days and weeks ahead.

AMEN.

# Justice and Mercy

## Yom Kippur Evening—1986

It has been ten days since we last gathered together. Since Rosh Hashanah, we have lived days of repentance and reflection. Our tradition tells us that the Book of Life is opened and written in at the beginning of the new year, and at Yom Kippur it is sealed. We are taught that the sort of life we will have during the coming year will have been determined by the time this day concludes.

There exists another powerful tradition that has been part of Yom Kippur for many centuries. I am speaking of Kol Nidre, the declaration that was sung at the beginning of our service this evening. For many of us, this eerie chant is the most powerful Jewish experience of our year. We may remain far from the synagogue for the rest of the year, but for the evening of Yom Kippur we go somewhere that enables us to hear the chanting of this prayer. Some leave shortly thereafter, and most of us who remain do not have a firm idea of where the prayer comes from and what it means. Nonetheless, it is powerfully seductive in its hold. I believe the reason this is so has a lot to do with other equally important aspects of our religious experience, so I would like to explore the Kol Nidre prayer with you.

What we find in our prayer books is the full Aramaic text that has been preserved for Ashkenazi Jews (that is, Jews whose heritage is traced back to German and Eastern European Jews.) Our text refers to the vows between people and God from this Yom Kippur to the next. (Some communities use a text that refers to vows from the previous Yom Kippur to the present one.) We ask God's pardon, forgiveness and atonement for the sin of failing to keep a solemn vow.

Most scholars would agree that the origins of the Kol Nidre prayer are unknown. The first declaration of the prayer is found in the beginning of the eighth century of the common era. Amidst some controversy, it may have found its way into the liturgy of some Jewish communities at that time.

Why the controversy? Perhaps it was because of the notion that a public prayer would have the effect of canceling the oaths of Jews. Even though it is clear from the formula and language that the prayer refers to oaths between people and God, much has been made of the notion that the word or oath of Jews is considered worthless. As early as the thirteenth century in France, there was an attack on Jews because of the prayer. To counteract these accusations, Jewish apologists have cited the severe limitations that the Jewish law code imposed on Kol Nidre.

In 1860, a Hebrew introduction to Kol Nidre was included in prayer books in Russia on the recommendation of a rabbinic commission. It explained that Kol Nidre was not meant to apply to oaths taken before courts of law. In Germany in 1844, an assembly of the Reform movement recommended that Kol Nidre be removed from the liturgy. Later Reformers offered substitute versions. In the edition of the High Holy Day prayer book published by the Reform movement just prior to the one we use today, the prayer appears in its Aramaic original—but there is no English translation. (Perhaps this suggests that if there was no translation, then no one would object to the prayer.)

Some of you may be familiar with the theory that this prayer found its most popular usage during the persecutions of the Jews in Spain. Forced to convert to Christianity, it was popularly held that this prayer would in effect apologize to God for the false oaths that they had made to the church during the year. While this may be true, there is a body of scholarship suggesting that the origins of Kol Nidre predate the Marranos of the Iberian Peninsula.

On another level, I wish to explore with you the emotional reaction that this prayer holds for us and to wonder aloud if it might not reveal some important aspects of our faith and our approach to our religious beliefs.

I believe that this tells us a lot about our approach to Judaism and our approach to God. On the eve of the most important holy day in our year, it is time to go beyond the easy and superficial approaches we might have for religion and grapple with the more difficult. This is the day when we each stand by ourselves before whatever deity or whatever supreme being we imagine as a force in the universe. This is the day that we have approached by asking forgiveness from one another before we seek forgiveness and judgment from God.

What sort of image and what sort of approach does this leave for us in imagining this God of ours? What attributes does this God of ours possess that make it so important for us to think about?

There is a rabbinic story that deals with God's role in creation in the Book of Genesis. God is referred to there as both Adonai and Elohim. How are we to understand these two names or aspects of God? Picture a king who wants to fill a precious vessel with water. If he pours ice water into the vessel, it will contract and crack. If he pours hot water into the vessel, it also will break. If the king pours a combination of the hot and the cold, the vessel will withstand the water. So, too, with God in creation: God used both justice and mercy together to create this world of ours. And let us hope it will survive. This is the same God who supposedly is to inscribe us in the Book of Life, for that God combines the justice and mercy of our tradition, bringing both of these to bear in the judging that takes place.

What of our faith? What of our belief? What serves for each of us as that ultimate answer or that ultimate question and perhaps that ultimate meaning in the universe? Each of us stands primarily before God on this Judgment Day. We learn from the biblical text we will read tomorrow that God gives us the choice of choosing life or death, blessing or curse, and in so doing we can help determine whether we shall live or die.

Should then we approach God as if the deity is an admonishing parent in the sky? A mamma or papa who tells us whether we have done right or wrong? We should struggle to find out for ourselves about God as God is rather than our projections that we have placed on God. Struggling with the notion of judgment and God must surely raise for many of us whether we in fact want a God who stands in judgment over us at all.

What shall we make of judgment? Does it offer us cruel justice or undemanding love? Might there be an alternative such as the one discovered by the king in his attempt to fill the precious vessel with water. Perhaps God can be seen and understood in terms of human relationships. Perhaps God can be understood at the One who loves us as we are—and as we are yet to be. Like in a loving human relationship, the other can help me become the one I ought to be and not a failure.

It would be easier to not tell you about the times that I failed so that I did not run the risk of judgment, rejection or the possible change in our relationship. What if, as a result of my failure, I only received rejection and not forgiveness? What if this time the relationship comes to an end?

The High Holy Days help us restore our proper relationship with God with whom we stand in personal and communal covenant. We say that God is One, the First and Foremost. This God is not mythic. God is not just a Sovereign over us, though we proclaim that God rules. This symbolizes that we stand in covenant with the ultimate significance in the universe.

If God is only a cruel superego, then Freud was right in calling it a neurosis. And then this relationship is not only at risk but should not exist. But Yom Kippur comes to remind us that this God, who knows and understands us, holds us in a special relationship, a covenantal one. God loves us and, if we make a lasting and honest effort to repent, then God will forgive us.

Judaism teaches that God will not let us go. God will love us and judge us, for the judgment is in the context of love. Each of us, as we have been told, needs to first seek forgiveness from one another before seeking forgiveness from God.

With a clean heart and a will to seek forgiveness, I urge all of us to spend the time of Yom Kippur renewing the relationship between ourselves and God.

AMEN

# The Miracle of Life

## Rosh Hashanah Evening—1987

We cannot know who first discovered water, but we can be sure it was not the fish. Why not the fish? Because water is all about them. They breathe it, taste it, swim in it. For them, water is too obvious to be noticed. Could it be that only when they are caught in the fisherman's net, trembling, gasping for air, that the revelation occurs to them?

Water is life, and air is life. Both water and air are our life. Tonight we celebrate life. *Hayom Harat Haolam*—today the world was created. Tonight, as we celebrate Rosh Hashanah, we celebrate the birthday of the world. Our Jewish tradition teaches that the world was created 5,748 years ago today. Judaism helps us understand that our creation was with purpose. Yet, like the fish in the sea, all too often we take for granted the air we breathe and many other things that surround us as well.

An ancient story relates how we can hunt for something precious far, far away, and, in the end, find it nearby. This tale, most likely a folktale of Medieval origin, is attributed to Rabbi Nachman of Bratslav. The story goes as follows:

> Once there was a poor woodcutter who lived with his family at the outskirts of the forest and sold firewood to the other poor people who lived there. One night, this man had a dream in which he travelled down a path until he came to a bridge. A soldier was stationed on the bridge and crossed over it, back and forth. Led by a strange certainty, the man went beneath the bridge and began to dig. Before long he struck something and, when he had uncovered it, he found a treasure chest. And when he opened the chest, he found a treasure inside. The treasure was so precious that he gasped when he saw it. Just then, the man awoke and realized he had been dreaming.
>
> During the day, as he worked cutting wood in the forest, the man daydreamed about that treasure. The thought crossed his mind that he could search for it. But he dismissed this thought as foolish. After all, it was only a dream. So he went about his work and forgot about it.
>
> That night, however, the man again dreamed about the bridge beneath

which he found a treasure. And this time the dream was even more vivid. In the morning he laughed at himself for taking the dream so seriously. For how would he ever know where to begin the search?

But when the dream recurred for a third night, the man realized that his destiny was calling to him and vowed to find that treasure no matter how difficult it might be. And so the man set out into the world to search for a bridge he had only seen in a dream.

But where does one find such a bridge? Once he reached the town, he tried to ask people about the bridge, but when he was unable to say which one it was or what river it crossed, they just shrugged their shoulders and walked on. He thought for a long time, and then he remembered the guard on the bridge had worn a special helmet. So the next time he asked someone he mentioned the helmet, and soon he learned that the guards of the king wore helmets like that in the capital of that country. Now the capital was a great distance away, but when this detail of his dream turned out to be real, the woodcutter decided he must go there at once. For he had become confident that his dream might be true after all.

After many months and many hardships, the woodcutter reached the capital at last and the very bridge he had seen in his dream. Not only that, but there was a guard pacing up and down upon it—the same guard he had glimpsed in his dream! He greeted the soldier and asked him if he might dig beneath the bridge. When the soldier heard this, he seemed startled and asked the man why he would want to do such a thing. With no other choice, the woodcutter told the guard about his dream. When he heard it, the man laughed heartily and said, "If you have come all this way just because of a dream, you are indeed foolish. Your dream is merely a common one. Why, I have just dreamed three nights in a row of a treasure beneath an old oak tree at the entrance of a forest." And the soldier went on to describe the tree and the place he had found the treasure.

And as he did, the man suddenly realized that the guard was describing the woodcutter's own home in a distant province of that land. It suddenly dawned on the woodcutter that the dream had led him to that bridge not to dig beneath it but to hear the dream of that guard. And as if to confirm this, the guard suddenly became stern and said, "As to your request to dig here, why that is out of the question. This bridge belongs to the king, and if I permitted the ground beneath it to be dug up, I would soon be deprived of my head. Go now, and if I see you here again, I will not hesitate to arrest you!"

So it was that the woodcutter traveled back to where he had come from, to his family and home. But no sooner had he kissed his wife and children than he hurried out to the giant oak tree at the entrance to the forest and dug beneath it. And, before he had dug very far, he struck something which turned out to be the very treasure he had seen in his dream, buried behind his own house.

The treasure we seek is not somewhere else. It is close to us, in our own neighborhood, all about us. What is this treasure that so many of us are so anxious to travel so far for, only to find right in our own backyards? What we take for granted so often is the greatest miracle of all, the miracle of life. On Rosh Hashanah, the birthday of the world, we can celebrate our birth and celebrate living. As we examine our lives on this day of soul searching, we need to ask the question that comes next: Why this life and how are we to live this precious treasure of an existence?

Those are the questions I would like to address myself to tonight. The first is why this life—that we should live in this world, at this time, in this way? What purpose does it serve, and what can we learn from our Judaism that tells us about the reason for this life? We can understand something about the "why" of life by talking about what being a good person is. By contemporary standards, one who refrains from evil would have been enough to be considered a good person. For Judaism, there is more. There is the commandment to "do good." Further, there is a complexity to issues of goodness and justice which gut feelings alone cannot unravel. Difficult moral questions go to the heart of the particular Jewish way of doing good. They indicate recognition of the imperfect ethical results we, because we are human, inevitably turn out. Yet, we are not freed from thinking these matters through and taking the most useful good and just action that we believe is warranted. Doing this affirms our allegiance to God's presence in our midst. This is where we can capture a sense of holiness, or, to use the Hebrew word, *kedushah*. One meaning of this is the sense of God's presence and our search for it when we are trying to do what is just and the good.

For us Jews, we can learn from our tradition that there are some subtle differences from the world of secular ethics in how we can accomplish this. First, the Jewish understanding of what is required of us in doing righteousness legitimates the "good" in the face of the "best." This helps us keep faith with our will to improve our world by allowing us to face the task realistically. As we try to improve the world, or as Judaism says, *tikkun olam* (repairing the world), we repair our own houses. We know full well that sooner or later something else will need to be fixed. We do not abandon our homes because of this. Instead, we try to keep up with the necessary work.

Second, the Jewish way in good and justice refuses to leave the behavioral agenda alone. First and foremost, it speaks with the force of *mitzvah*, a common calling for active obedience. Beyond that, it wants to know how ethical objectives will be reached. It seeks ways for every member of the community to participate in reaching those objectives. It does not merely preach or demonstrate. It organizes the ways and means, figures out the cost and creates the day-in, day-out mechanisms by which plain people like us can contribute to some great ethical project. It wants us to have the pleasure, the *nachas*, of knowing that we counted, that our penny contributions can become a great sum.

In a society that seems to concentrate on the big, only major violations of ethics are deemed significant. Only threats of world destruction or the theft of millions make the news. The same point of view promotes the idea that only totally self-sacrificing persons are capable of doing anything about it all. The Jewish way to social justice bids us to let our people and our society know that in a world created by God and inhabited by a humanity made in God's image, refraining from littering the street is an act of affirming God and the possibility of holiness in the world. Little is not insignificant if it is a little bit of good. Indeed, nothing in our world is insignificant when we recognize the presence of God the Creator in it. The bit of dirt beneath our feet has a right to decent treatment because it is created by God.

Finally, it is Jewish to note that our tradition recognizes that there is more than one ethical vision or more than one possible path of truth. There can be conflicting ethical positions; we can try to decide between them and then act. We can realize that those who have decided differently are still in the camp of the righteous. We can try to understand that by seizing the opportunity for pursuing justice, we can give meaning and purpose to our lives.

In this way, we can attempt to answer or respond to the "why" of living. Specifically on the occasion of this birthday of the world, I also would like to address the question of how we can live such a life so that we can find that precious treasure under our own tree. Our own biological presence and our own physical behavior dictate to us needs that we have and ways in which we need to act.

Next week on Yom Kippur we will recite the list of the ways in which we have sinned. We all say "for the sin which we have committed against You by malicious gossip." How can we better understand how to live by remembering to refrain from the sin of gossip? When we gossip, relate stories, tell tales, we usually end up hurting someone we did not mean to hurt. We probably do not think that it is particularly sinful. But in fact, our tale ends up creating something we did not plan to create. Our slander ends up having a life of its own, a world that was created for it. We never do know where that might end up. What we told someone, who told someone, who told you, just may end up truly hurting someone. Our tradition understands this is not only an offense to others we may have hurt, but this is a sin against God as well. It shows our disrespect for God's creation. We have offended God, and we have hurt our friend or perhaps someone we did not know. In the process, we certainly have demeaned ourselves by this kind of talk.

Our words can be used to destroy and to injure. Our words can destroy a world. We possess this amazing power to both create and to destroy merely by the words we choose. We create worlds when we speak, in a sense mirroring the brilliance of the creation when God spoke, and the world came into being. Have we not all heard someone teach us something we did not know. In so doing, it is almost as if a new world has been opened up to us. Sometimes it is even like a revelation when two people meet and begin a conversation that turns into a lifetime of conversations. A new world is created because these two people have found a way to speak, to connect, with one another. We help maintain the world when we say things we should say to our families. We maintain the world when we confront a painful issue with a loved one or friend who is in need or in great pain. We confront a problem by speaking and, in so doing, we reconstitute the world that once was hidden by our silence.

We have destroyed a world when we have remained silent and do not protest the inhumanity that is all around us. When we offer silence instead of anger, it resolves nothing. When silence replaces talking the anger through and dealing with the issue, then silence may destroy worlds that could be saved by talking.

Yet silence sometimes creates a healing world when we have the self-discipline to say nothing. We have the potential to destroy when we have told someone that we do not like the way they part their hair or that they should lose some weight just because we are uncomfortable. We hurt others when we offer words that we think will be helpful but, in fact, our suggestion meets our needs rather than theirs.

Silence can be very powerful. It can be the most supportive, helpful thing we can do in the worlds we have created. Silence is very hard. For God, silence is when God rested after God spoke, after God created the world.

Words create worlds, but they also destroy. At Rosh Hashanah, we commemorate the birth of the world that was created when God spoke and the world came into being. When we are seeking the "how" of our life, let us remember in what way we speak and in what way we are silent.

In seeing how we can find the treasure placed beneath our door and how we can utilize the treasure of our words to heal or to hurt, we can get a better sense of who we are in this world of ours.

There is another story that I want to share with you tonight, a much shorter story than the first. In this story, the angels band together to conspire against God's intent to form Adam and Eve in God's image. They are jealous that ordinary men and women should inherit such spiritual treasure. The angels plot to hide goodness and truth from the human beings. One angel proposes to hide God's mystery in the highest mountains. Another suggests concealing it beneath the deepest seas. But the shrewdest angel counsels, "Men and women will search for godliness in the remotest of places. Hide it within them. It is the last place they will search for the miracles of godliness."

The water is all around us. Let us hope that we can swim in it and, at the same time, notice it. Water and air we can easily take for granted and, frequently, life itself. What we can learn on the occasion of our birthday 5,748 is that we must continue to search for the why of our lives and how we can fulfill it.

# Our Jewish Calendar

## Rosh Hashanah Evening—1989

Imagine with me a time long ago when the Bible tells us Adam and Eve were the first people on earth. The long daylight hours are near an end, and the sun is about to set in the western sky. As the first night that Adam and Eve experienced is about to begin, they might have said, "It is because we have sinned that the world around us is dark. The universe will now become void and without form. This is the death to which we have been sentenced by Heaven."

Of course, we know that this part of their story concludes with the sun rising and light returning. When the dawn breaks in the east, Adam and Eve now understand that this is the usual course of the world.

To our ancestors in ancient times, the immediacy of the natural world around them had a tremendous impact on their lives. Other cultures and religions of the ancient Near East perceived one force that controlled the light and another that controlled the darkness. The Psalmist understands that God will protect us from the night, and the prophet Isaiah repeats what the Book of Genesis first tells us—that it is God who forms light and creates darkness.

It is our tradition of counting days to measure from the setting of the sun or, more exactly, by the twilight created when darkness is about to begin. Much of the rest of the world is accustomed to measuring the day with the rising of the sun, or in more recent times with the advent of measuring time mechanically, beginning with the hour of midnight. We Jews began our association with time in the mythic era even before Adam and Eve when God said, "Let there be light!!," and day was created.

We have remained different in how we calculate time even to the present day. How many of us know about and use Jewish Standard Time? That time that exists over and above the measured time of the clock, when we understand custom and tradition are more important than the accuracy of measure. What a concept that the clock that divides up the twenty-four hours of the day needs to have a special adjustment to allow for the customs and usages of different people.

So, we Jews measure our days and celebrate our holidays not by the clock but by a much more ancient unit of measure—the setting of the sun. Imagine Thanksgiving beginning on Wednesday night, January 1st celebrations starting at 7:00 p.m. on December 31st, Independence Day getting underway on the evening of July 3rd!

Our Rosh Hashanah celebration begins not in the morning but in the evening. We still are governed by the ebb and flow of nature—though we live in the most industrialized society that has yet to be created.

The inheritance of Adam and Eve helps us understand the "when" of our celebration. I want to look with you a little bit further as to the "why" of our marking this day. We Jews who come to synagogue on the High Holy Days are here for many reasons. The manner that we mark time has something to do with the why in addition to the when. We understand that the marking of time is more than a physical act. We understand that measuring another year needs more than a party; in fact, it requires some type of religious commemoration.

Rather than ignoring the spiritual and religious side of ourselves, tonight and again on Yom Kippur we turn to our spirit and let it outgrow the physical space that contains it the rest of the year. We come together tonight to see again the drama unfolding.

Any student of Judaism knows that the central essence of Jews is the calendar that we live with—a certain type of internal clock that ticks away during the year, measuring the months and seasons in addition to the minutes and hours. Each one of us, no matter what our level of religious observance is, responds in some way to that calendar— even, if you will, to ignore it.

This marking of time, the beginning of the month of Tishrei, is a different time than all the other Jewish days of the year. There are holidays throughout the year that are holidays for the Jewish people, national or militaristic in their origin and in their nature. We celebrate Sukkot in just two weeks to remind us of the time that our ancestors dwelled in temporary houses while living in the desert. We celebrate Chanukah in the beginning of the winter when we recall the Maccabees and the Jewish people in their struggle against the Greeks centuries ago.

We celebrate Purim at the end of the winter, when we Jews observe the role that Esther and Mordecai played in saving the Jewish people from Haman and the villainy of the Persians. We Jews celebrate perhaps our greatest historical experience at the beginning of spring, when we commemorate the exodus of the Israelites from Egypt and the oppression under Pharaoh.

Rosh Hashanah and Yom Kippur are different holidays.

These are holy days for individuals, not as a people, for you and me, here and now. The "Days of Awe" as we call these special days are moments in time that touch our individual experiences and are an attempt to relate each one of us to our cosmic origins. This, if you will, is a transcendence of the historical experience.

We have a unique quality of observance and task incumbent upon us at this time of year according to our tradition. We are given the opportunity during these days of reflection and observance to pause from the daily events of our lives and take an accounting of ourselves and then to decide if we are able to refashion our lives in some new way.

An ancient Jewish legend teaches us that when God wanted to create the world, the first step was to create a model. But this original model that God created fell apart because there was no *teshuvah*, no repentance. So this artificially created model of the world could not endure. What is *teshuvah*? It is the Hebrew term used to describe what we might understand to be repentance.

*Teshuvah*, however, can be better translated as "turning" or "return." This is the time to turn, the time to return.

This is the time of year dedicated to the review of the human self— understanding of ourselves at the time of the High Holy Days. The traditions that we are the inheritors of are many centuries old. It is possible that they speak to us today as poignantly as they spoke to our ancestors many centuries ago.

One of the messages is that there are transcendent forces peering through the cracks of the visual universe. There are the unexplainable, the unknowns that even the most learned among us have yet to understand—the mysteries of life, the mysteries of the universe. These are what we should think about and ponder during these days dedicated to reflection and the determination to act upon a renewed commitment we bring to our task.

In addition to the mysteries of the universe, we need to delve into the mysteries of our individual psyches. It is part of our life experience to learn that we humans inevitably fail, miss the mark or sin. The Book of Ecclesiastes teaches us, "There is no righteous person in the earth who does only good and never sins."(Eccl.7:20) How can we act upon this knowledge that not only are there things beyond our comprehension, but there are words and actions that we wish might not occur?

These ten days of repentance are the opportunity to make this turn, to understand and open our own hearts so that we are not closed off to our human failings. We need the strength to remove the wall which we build up to keep us from admitting that it is all right to have failed, to have missed, to have sinned. ·

The chief obstacle to this opening is us. When we find and use the time to turn and open our hearts, admitting that we are wrong or that we have failed, then we can come out stronger.

When we have internalized the drive for perfection, we find it difficult to admit our failings. So then how can we obtain forgiveness? The medieval scholar Maimonides asserted that the indispensable first step in repentance is to admit the flaw. We may dread that once letting go and admitting failure, then our entire life will fall apart.

But the task ahead of us can only be accomplished if we begin with the desire to truly see ourselves. We need to see the good and the bad parts which follow after the admission of our own failings. This admission should carry with it the realization that out of the brokenness we become stronger than when we claimed to be whole.

Like the mythical first man and woman on earth, we stand in awe and perhaps in fear of what we cannot comprehend and what we have not experienced. Today we need to light the darkness not only for our physical safety but for our spiritual safety as well. Adam and Eve, who were afraid that when the sun set it would never rise again, have their contemporary parallels. We need the light to shine upon our spirit to enable us to understand our own failings and our own limits. We shall neither curse the darkness nor bless the light because we need both of them to survive whole as Jews and as human beings.

The time we use to find the answers to the spiritual questions we seek is time that is precious to us all. Time passes, never to return again. Unlike the human spirit and the human experience, we can turn and try to experience again the act of love, the act of forgiveness, the act of seeking comfort and consolation as we begin a new year.

AMEN

# The Meaning of Yom Kippur

## Yom Kippur Morning—1989

We have heard in the special Torah portion read this morning how each one of us bears personal responsibility in the decision-making process. As some of you are aware, this biblical passage differs from the one read in traditional synagogues for the morning of Yom Kippur which is from Leviticus (Chapter 16) where Aaron and his priestly progeny receive their instructions for performing the cultic minutiae for Yom Kippur.

Almost one hundred years ago in the 1894 Union Prayer Book, it was decided to incorporate a passage from Deuteronomy instead of the one from Leviticus. Early reformers firmly believed in the importance of denying the traditional belief in the eventual restoration of the cult and also firmly wished to end distinctions of class based on presumed priestly birth. Verses from Deuteronomy 29 and 30 stressing the importance of personal responsibility were selected. Therefore, we read that we have been given the choice of blessing and curse, good and evil, life and death. All of these options are within our grasp—and we can see ourselves able to make the choice.

Today on Yom Kippur there is another step of investigation that may be helpful in understanding the importance of this holy day. There are, as some of you know, three letter roots for all Hebrew words. Such is the case for *kippur*—known by us as "atonement." It might be helpful to examine this word and the different meanings that are possible to create with the three letters that make up this word: *kuf, phay* and *raish.*

The simple vocalization of the three letters is *"kaphar"* which gives a noun that translates as "tar," "bitumen" or "pitch." The word is used in this way in a famous biblical passage in the Book of Genesis. God is giving Noah instructions on how to construct the ark which will carry him, his family and the animals to safety. God says, "Make yourself an ark of gopher wood; make it an ark with compartments and cover it inside and out with pitch." (Genesis 6:14)

Can one of the meanings of this special holy day be related to the covering of Noah's ark? Perhaps we can understand *kaphar* as a symbolic covering we use to hide those things about ourselves which we do not want ourselves or others to see. Are any of us totally perfect? Are we each without blemish in our hearts or in our souls that we feel we ought to cover up during the year? Today is the day when we can, individually through prayer, through reflection, uncover what we might want to keep hidden all during the year.

The legends about Noah also can provide us insight into another meaning of Yom Kippur. Noah, who was described as a righteous man, built the ark to save a remnant of human and animal life from the flooding that God was to bring upon the world because of human violence. Many rabbinic sources portray Noah as offering an opportunity to the rest of humanity to repent from their sins. For the people of Noah's generation, God kept open the gates of repentance until the very end.

By changing the vowels of these same three letters, we have the word *kopher*, which in both biblical and modern Hebrew can be translated as "ransom." In the Bible, we can ransom animals. In contemporary usage the word also is used to ransom people. What does it mean to ransom someone or something? Each one of us has something precious that we would be willing to pay any price to get back if it were taken from us.

I am not speaking of our loved ones who might be taken or any particularly expensive material acquisition that we might have purchased with money. Rather, I am speaking about what we are born with and develop over time as we grow up—that is, our personality. Is there not a part of us, a deep down basic part of each one of us that we would like to redeem or ransom back and start all over again.

Can we imagine what we would like to start over with if we could? As we develop from trying to stop hiding what is covered up inside us, trying to get back and re-do what has escaped us, perhaps we move a little closer to the deeper meaning of Yom Kippur.

The third use of the three letters—*kuf, phay, raish*—is one which has the most common associations with this holy day. We find the word *keepair* translated as "pardon," "atone" or "expiate", particularly in the Book of Leviticus. One well-known use of the word is found in Chapter 4. Here the priest of the community of Israel is given the responsibility of properly sacrificing a bull to expiate the guilt of the priest and the community. A large body of law exists which explains in great detail the exact steps of animal sacrifice necessary for the priest to seek pardon for the guilt of the community. The biblical text goes on to talk about the steps necessary for an individual to atone for his or her guilt after doing anything which violates God's commandments. A female goat or sheep is to be sacrificed by the priest, and the individual will be forgiven.

The Jewish people have lived for almost 2,000 years since the destruction of the Temple cult without being able to use animal sacrifice as the process of expiation for our sins. Nonetheless, our basic liturgy—when we pray and what we say—is shaped by and greatly influenced by these ancient rituals.

Prayer has become one of the main vehicles of atonement for Jews since the destruction of the Temple. On the Day of Atonement, we may seek to strip away that which we have covered up. We may try to ransom or redeem that which we have done which we could like to do over again. And, finally, we may pray as individuals before God for those deeds or misdeeds which we cannot redeem or ransom back and for those we no longer can cover up. The final solitary act of prayer which we come to synagogue for today is not to be accomplished by the priest of old who would sacrifice an animal, thereby carrying away our guilt or sins—but rather by us as individuals in our own way and through our own strength.

Perhaps the deeper meaning of the High Holy Days lies in our own contracts, understandings and prayers we offer to God. A Midrashic source gives further illustration of this. When interpreting the passage of Moses receiving the Torah on Mount Sinai, we learn:

> When we, the Jewish people, received the Torah on Sinai, we heard the voice of the shofar. The Bible teaches us that the voice of the shofar was exceedingly strong. Moses spoke, and God answered with a voice."
>
> The Midrash asks, "How was that voice of God heard by all of Israel?" And the answer is "*Kol echad l'phe cocho.*" Each person heard that voice according to his or her own power; according to his or her own spiritual capacity, they heard the voice of God.

We come full circle this morning. At the end of our Torah passage we, too, hear God's voice which instructs that the choices are in our own hands and hearts. The command is near to us; we can accomplish it. The challenge for us is to strip away any false coverings, re-do what has led us to misdeeds; try to find peace and insight according to our own spiritual capacity; and seek to understand ourselves, one step at a time.

AMEN

# Horizontal Time
# and Vertical Time

## Rosh Hashanah Evening—1990

Twelve months ago, we watched on television the trains bringing East Germans to the West by way of Czechoslovakia. I remember speaking about some of the memories and images conjured up by these events, which we thought were remarkable. It was hard to imagine where they would lead. Ten months ago we watched as the Berlin Wall was breached, and East-West relations reached a new plateau. In the intervening months, new realities, new relationships and new opportunities for emigration and freedom have occurred like few other times in recent years.

Modern Jewish history and Jewish life have been rushing to catch up with the almost daily changing events in Europe and the Soviet Union. While increased anti-Semitism has threatened some of the fabric of Jewish life, the challenges are leading to a possible transformation of political realities. And it has been almost two months since the armies of Iraq invaded Kuwait. Whatever side we take in this struggle over limited natural resources and the aggression of one sovereign nation against another, we might all agree that the Middle East as we have known it since World War II has been dramatically changed.

To paraphrase Charles Dickens, it has been the best of times and may lead us to the worst of times. Where will the upheavals, the opening of borders, the collapse of Communism and the massing of troops in the Persian Gulf lead? I believe you can find better informed geopolitical answers in the *New York Times*.

What I want to share with you on this holy day is a closer examination of time—the notion, the concept, the idea of time that we use as our reference point. Intervals enable us to comprehend what happened yesterday, last month and last year because they have a beginning and an end.

There are many ways to measure, describe and even talk about time. Stephen Hawking, the theoretical physicist, has provided some insights into the concept of time in his book *A Brief History of Time* (1988). I learned that the theory of relativity put an end to the idea of absolute time. Instead, each individual has his or her own personal measure of time that depends on where we are and how we are moving. This concept comes from the physicist's knowledge that space and time are intricately related. This is different from our own subjective perceptions of when time moves too quickly, such as when we are having a good time at a party, or when time moves too slowly, such as when we are listening to a rabbi's sermon.

Hawking probably did not mean to suggest that we Jews have a different way of measuring time than others. Not only do we speak about Jewish standard time, but we even measure the passing day from when the stars rise at the end of one daylight period to sunset the following evening. This Jewish manner of measuring time reminds me of a Midrashic story about Adam in the Garden of Eden. When Adam saw the sun first setting and the very first evening of darkness arrive, he was terrified that the world had come to an end. Only after the sun rose the next morning did he realize that daylight and the possibility of re-birth, discovery and the challenges of new beginnings had returned.

At this time of Rosh Hashanah, when our tradition teaches that we are celebrating not only a new year but also the birthday of the creation of the world, we might look further at the elusive nature of time. What are the different types of time, and how are they measured?

External time is beyond measure and beyond measurer: in the waves of the seas and on earth and what lies beneath; in the heavens beyond even the Hubble telescope. What is in that mystery? How long has it been: the sun, the moon and stars?

Another aspect of nature's time: it is the moaning of the wind, the tattered and shredded loneliness of a winter tree or our imaginings of the length of time that it takes for the ocean to wear smooth a rock on the seashore. It is sometimes the suffocating and clinging heat of summer. It is the final leaf of autumn when the color of the world is muted, soft with resignation. It is still nature's time but measurable for us and within the scope of our understanding. Thus, we impale time on the lance of a single year—and we thrust aside 5750, as we did to 1989, and give brief center stage to 5751. We can speak of a kind of horizontal time which pours from the eternity behind us, across the face of our present and into the eternity that is before us.

This is horizontal time. On the one hand, it is forever beyond calculation, with the measurelessness of the waves of the sea, of the bright and burning star. On the other hand, there is the other kind of horizontal time, a time which is divisible into days and seasons, into years and centuries, a time within our reach.

It is the measurable time of our life set against the immeasurable time of the universe that we are trying to comprehend on Rosh Hashanah. It is measurable time in which we say that 5750 has ended and 5751 is here. We need this measurable time or else we would be meaningless wanderers in a meaningless desert without beginning and without end. With all our intellectual efforts, we humans may be establishing a small corner of order in an increasingly disordered universe. The answers to "what" and "where" are pointless without answers to "when."

Indeed, there is more than horizontal time. There is a kind of vertical time as well. It is the time of God's presence moving downward and the time of our personal quest moving upward. The time that beats through the time of the fear of death and the time of the uncertainty of what lies beyond. The time of concern about our unworthiness, of our incapacity to face up to life. The time that looks with love from a lover's eyes, the love that moves hearts to warmth and can fill every corner of life with light. The time of affection, measurable like the time of the seasons and immeasurable like the time of the heavens and the stars.

The time in our hearts beats with different rhythms for each age: slow and solemnly paced for those of any age who know that their time is limited now. For others, time beats carelessly and high, the pendulum swinging in a wide and joyous arc. There is no need to reckon the individual minutes nor the quickly passing hours. There is spendthrift time when our calendar of life is thick with pages and the ticking of the clock is cheerful, the sound is music and the pendulum's arc traces a rainbow. This is expansive time when the world that we experience has no frontiers, when all of life is a song and a growing and a reaching.

There is thankful time: when the harvest of the years of love and hard work are bearing fruit. But the thankfulness is sometimes tinged with a bit of sadness. Parents' eyes see the clock move faster for themselves than for their children; when we adults wonder whether our attainments have reached their highest point; when time slips through grasping fingers that try desperately to stop or at least slow its flow.

There is wisdom's time: the time for listening to the heavens, for the beat of the Eternal's time descending to us. This is the time when the clock's face is not easy to read and when there are few who can read it truly. Wisdom's time: when we learn what to treasure and what to discard. If we are among the fortunate, what the minutes are for and how to use the hours; to know how much time we have and what time it is in our inner lives.

Some of us never do hear the ticking of wisdom's time. Some of us never learn more than spendthrift time, and, with thoughtless gesture, scatter the years. Some of us never learn thankful time and never appreciate the blessing of the years nor comprehend what the clock and the days are telling us.

If we live without vertical time, we have no meaning to lift us up, no significance that grows within. We then live in a horizontal time of length and breadth, but without height and depth. Perhaps a life without depths and without heights is a life without a meaning in time.

We Jews have known thankful time and wisdom's time. We have linked our small lives with the measured centuries—some fifty-seven of them. We have held time in our cupped hands, and we have counted the hours, dim as well as bright. We have known the time of death and the time of the world's hatred. We can mark our people's time on the slow swing of the arc of pain and torment.

But Jews need to look beyond the hour which is striking. We should listen to the larger rhythm of wisdom's time and thankful time. We should seek to attune ourselves to some steady pulse of the Eternal moving through the universe. We need to listen upward to the height of God's infinity, and at the same time we should look inward to our own heart's depth. We have trusted both: the height of God and the depth of humankind. We have learned to live in both dimensions of time: from eternity to eternity, from depth to height.

There is little we can control about what will happen around the globe. What about closer to home? What will the next twelve months be like for us? Where will the world be going during the coming year? There are those among us who would say at this time "Happy New Year." I would say this also, but I would say more.

I pray that it be a new year filled with thankful time and with wisdom's time. May the year bring happiness to those who know sadness; may it bring peace to those who know strife; may it bring comfort to those who have been experiencing pain and trouble; and may it bring each of us an understanding of what to do with our horizontal time that brings us into harmony with vertical time.

AMEN

# Judaism and Loneliness

## Rosh Hashanah Evening—1992

It hardly seems possible that another year is at hand, that time has come full circle. The wheel turns so swiftly and so noiselessly. While the tumult, pain and anguish of the world cry out, our time—the days, weeks and months—like running sand, slips through our fingers. A year is gone, and we meet again on Rosh Hashanah Eve. We greet each other with the beautiful Hebrew words, *"L'shanah tovah tikatevu"*—"May you be written for a good year."

A good year . . . . It seems like more than twelve months of events have occurred since we celebrated the beginning of the year 5752. Here we are together as 5753 begins, and we can look back at cataclysmic political events in Europe and the Middle East, truly heart-wrenching famine and violence in Africa and, closer to home, the unbelievable devastating hurricanes that swept through south Florida, Louisiana and Hawaii. These are the external events that we read about in the newspapers, listen to on the radio or watch with great ambivalence on television.

Since we were last together, the verdict about Rodney King triggered an urban riot; since we prayed as a congregation last year, Yugoslavia disintegrated. The centuries-old hatreds and antagonisms have erupted into a human tragedy of immense proportions that threatens peace throughout Europe, and the slogans of "ethnic cleansing" bring quickly to mind memories of the Holocaust a generation ago. Since we have meditated and shared our quiet space with one another last year, the scourge of fascism has intensified in Germany. The world that exists outside for all of us is one that intrudes upon my thoughts and, perhaps, upon yours as well—even at this time of year.

A holiday helps us measure and mark what has happened since its last occurrence, but a holy day asks us to take stock of who and what we are. So, like at other times when I have spoken to you, I want to try to communicate directly from my heart to yours. I want to try to overcome the physical and emotional distance that separates us and share my thoughts with you. Consider this part of our ongoing conversation, a dialog where I have the first opportunity to speak.

In addition to these events writ large upon the global marquee, there are other events—smaller ones—that do not make the news, are not seen by millions of others and are not recorded in the public consciousness. These other events are just as real, they can be just as troubling, and they sometimes are just as difficult. I am referring to the tumult of private problems, the strong stirring of personal pains and sufferings, the agony of individual tragedies that so affect everyone's life that each one of us face. Is it the illness of a parent? The failings of a child? The death of a loved relative? The pain of someone you love? These events touch our lives, and we have to account for them in order to meet the next day and the next year.

At this time we greet each other fervently, with a fervor touched by wistfulness and wishfulness. Indeed, may it be a good year. May it carry within itself only life-giving promises. May the year bring gladness, with health, good jobs, good classes, enough food and shelter for the millions who are in need, peace in your life, peace in the world and overflowing joy.

But even as we speak the words, our heart has its own reservations. What will the year 5753 truly bring? What will be with us a year from now? We move within a tiny spot of light, the illuminated present where we now stand—while all around us is darkness, the darkness out of which will be born the tomorrow that becomes a new today, the darkness that may bring not the joy we seek but the sorrow we would like to avoid.

Who can be sure? Is there one among us who does not know the weight of a deep sorrow? Who has been untouched by the death of a relative, friend or lover? Who has not felt the pain of illness, trouble or deepest resignation? How we would like to slow the swift-spinning wheel of time if we could and make sure that in its turning there is only the quiet hum of serenity and peace, unmarred by the whining noises of adversity, of suffering or of despair.

So we sit here together but solitary on Rosh Hashanah Eve in the universal awareness of loneliness, of aloneness. We all know this chilling blast that whistles across the dreary waste places of our hearts. None of us is a stranger to it. In a very real way, all the gatherings on this night are not a congregation of people but a gathering of individuals. We sit next to each other but not really close to each other. Aloneness creates a chasm across which our voices echo, and the sounds are lost before their meanings become clear.

People, all people, are lonely. I believe such loneliness is part of the human condition. We can be lonely in the midst of others, in the midst of our friends and families and sometimes in the midst of those who love us the most.

Pain is a lonely thing. No one can really and truly understand another's pain. Oh yes, we try. We say, "I had the same thing." But it is not so. There is not any "same thing." Each person's pain is his or her own. Their struggle with it and their battle with it is a lonely fight which others can watch from the periphery but not share from the center of the arena, try as we might.

A burden is a solitary thing. Nobody can carry the weight that I carry. I cannot carry anyone else's. My load fits my back. Its weight is molded to the grip of my hands. Its heaviness is the measure of my strength and my endurance. I have to carry my load alone. Because that is so, there is a particularly poignant kind of loneliness when a burden is placed not on us but on someone we love. Some burden or trouble dominates their lives, a burden we cannot carry for them, a burden they have to carry themselves. And we can only watch, with heartache.

All that I have suggested is here with us tonight on this Rosh Hashanah Eve. Here we have lonely children, puzzled young adults, heavily burdened men and women who face a difficult life and who walk alone bearing the load. Here are the sick who travel the solitary path of illness, buffeted by the winds of pain, tortured on every stone of adversity.

We are all here tonight—the young and the old, the well and the sick, the burdened and the worried. We are all here. We are together— and we are all alone. For some, the light shines through. For others, the darkness is very dark, and we are not sure that the new year will throw a light strong enough to pierce the lonely gloom.

What shall I do with my loneliness, then, and with my weight and my burden, with my sorrow and my pain? There is no easy answer. But there are answers—if we look across the walls that divide our loneliness from the loneliness of others and if we listen to what they have to say.

Primo Levi survived Auschwitz and lived long enough to write several volumes about the Holocaust. In one of his books, he describes the "shower" at the concentration camp and his friend who would wash himself there. Levi explains that the showers had no hot water or soap, and the water that came out of the shower head was filthy. Nonetheless, there was a man who would wash himself as often as he was permitted. When asked why he would subject himself to the wet cold treatment, he responded that to the effect that "If I did not wash myself, I would be unable to separate myself from the barbarians who had imprisoned me." In fact, this prisoner was desperately seeking normalcy and was trying to live that normalcy one day at a time. This death camp inmate spoke out of the great despair around him, but he did not despair. There was no self-pity. In his simple statement there was no railing against God and the world. There was no futile cry, "Why did this happen to me?" There is only the brave word from a lonely heart.

And there are other instances of great hope and courage in the face of difficult circumstances. Appropriate this year is to quote a single sentence from the log of Christopher Columbus, written during the journey that brought him to the discovery of the New World. The setting is: the ships had been at sea a long time. Morale was very low. There was the threat of mutiny. Columbus' own life was in danger. In that moment of despair, Columbus wrote in his log: "That day we sailed west."

So facing the setting sun and prospect of night—and sailing on. Courage and dogged resistance, fighting back and refusing to surrender or even to be defeated—that is part of the answer.

Another part of the answer is right here with us. If we are, each of us, alone, nevertheless we can share with one another. All of us, whatever it is we are carrying in our hearts, face the same new year. God will give to each of our days, one at a time, twenty-four hours of time, precisely measured. When those are gone, they will never be ours again.

Do you see one important meaning for this in a new year? Reach out your lonely hand in compassion and in understanding. It will find a hand that reaches toward your own. Lift up your lonely torch. It will cast a blessed light on someone else's bitter road. Open your heart. Let some love pour out to fill the emptiness of another's heart.

There is nothing else. The meaning of life is not only in the laughter and the bright lights and the music of the band. It is in the willingness of people to take their loneliness and with it strengthen the lives of others. It is sensitive hearts that alone can turn the world community of loneliness into a world community of brotherhood and sisterhood.

A strange kind of sermon for the beginning of Rosh Hashanah. Should this not be a time to speak only cheerfully concerning the days ahead? Is this not the hour for voicing again our faith in God? And I have hardly mentioned God's name.

Obviously, I do not really think it is strange. I have been talking about God. God can help bring light to the darkness within each one of us. God can help provide us the courage in adversity. God lives with us in the personal darkness that we carry.

How do I know? Because I see God in the lives and hearts of people. I see God in the compassionate and in the pitying. I see God in the silent, enduring courage of the heavy-laden. I see God in the trusting, uncomplaining faith of those who live with pain. I see God in Rosh Hashanah, in the eternal unfolding of time, in the measurelessness of the years.

There is a tale appropriate to this time.

> The ministering angels gathered around God's throne, and they asked God, "When is the New Year?" "Do you ask me?" responded God. "Let us go below, to those who dwell on earth and ask them."

When is the new year? It is not really on the calendar. The new year is within us. When we create it in the world of men and women out of the loneliness of our hearts. When we fashion it out of the strength to endure. When we fill each day with the life-giving waters of hope which are from God.

May it be God's will that we shall be written for a good year so that our loneliness will be transformed in the heat and fire of another person's need.

AMEN

# Judaism and Ecology

## Rosh Hashanah Morning—1992

We read throughout our liturgy on Rosh Hashanah that this is the birthday of the world. Judaism provides a Rosh Hashanah in which more than the year is renewed. All of creation is regenerated, ourselves included. We break out of the shackles of profane time and relive the possibility of starting completely afresh.

There is a centuries-old debate in the Talmud on the significance of various new years, similar to our modern fiscal year, calendar year, school year and so on. In the course of the debate, two second century rabbis introduce the thought that these purely calendrical realities also have mythic proportions, in that cosmic events are connected to them. In Tishrei, the Hebrew month that contains both Rosh Hashanah and Yom Kippur, Rabbi Eliezer says the world was created.

We normally read the Genesis story of the binding and near sacrifice of Isaac for the Torah portion on Rosh Hashanah morning. Instead, this morning we read an alternate passage from the book of Genesis— the biblical account of creation. I decided we should read this passage today because of the thoughts I want to share with you regarding Judaism, creation, our relationship to the environment and the natural world around us. (My appreciation and thanks to Rabbi Barry Schwartz for his "Eco-Genesis: Toward a Judaic Environmental Ethic" and Shomrei Adamah's "High School Curriculum on Judaism and Ecology".)

For a few minutes, I want you to enter with me into a world of myths, a world of legends and a world where we shall try to understand our human attempts of retelling how this world came to be. When we emerge from our primordial origins, we can decide what our responsibilities to this world we share should be.

We already heard the biblical account of creation. Here is another story of light and the seven days of creation. The light that was created on the first day was an awesome primordial light. It was seven times brighter than the light of the sun, which was not created until the fourth day. It was so bright that while the sun rose and set, there was never the sense of darkness or therefore of night. The sun must have appeared then like the moon by day. This primordial light shone uninterrupted over the seven days of creation and was not concealed until the close of the seventh day—the conclusion of the first Sabbath, on Saturday evening. But once the sun of that first Sabbath had set, and coincident with it the concealment of the primordial light of creation, then a great and terrible darkness descended.

Another tradition has fleshed out the idea in concrete imagery applicable to the Days of Awe. We are told, for example, that God began creation before Rosh Hashanah day so that the creation of Adam and Eve would occur precisely on the first day of the first year. It is as if the universe existed for a while with no humans to inhabit it, but the counting of days did not begin until Adam and Eve. Without them, historical time was impossible since there can be no history without humans to make it. Thus, exactly on the original new year's day, God created man and woman, and only then could it be said that the world was created.

Creation, beginnings, something out of nothing, our very origins and relationship with God. A world of mystery and amazement we read about in the biblical story of the universe's origins. A legend of wonder telling us a story of how things might have come to be, suggesting indeed that this wonder may be the root of knowledge.

Elsewhere in our biblical tradition, our text speaks about the human wonder of the transcendent, the human struggle with attempts to understand the mysterious and to do so with the humility of each of us alone under the canopy of the stars. In the Book of Psalms (8:4-5) we read:

> When I behold your heavens,
> the work of Your fingers,
> the moon and stars that You set in place,
> what are we that You have been mindful of us, mortals that you have taken note of us?

To find a place in this creation, to establish ourselves in that relationship with other beings created in the universe with whom we share limited resources—this is another of the tasks that our biblical story attempts.

How do we relate to the other creations and the other creatures? What is it that is expected of us in relationship with the swarms of creatures in the water, the birds above, creatures that crawl, reptiles and land animals? How do we understand our relationship to the atoms and molecules, the cells and organisms that comprise our universe?

Do we and can we understand our inter-connectedness? Is it too late to be taught about the necessity for reverence and the responsibility we have for sharing the creation with the next generation?

Nature has no pity. Animals destroy each other and live from the death of other animals. Carnivorous animals must kill. The stronger kills the weaker, and it is through this process that nature moves ahead.

But we think of ourselves as different, and our tradition teaches us that we are distinct.

Our biblical story informs us that there is an order, a progression and a responsibility. The immanence of God bids us to revere nature. The transcendence of God bids us to worship only God. We should revere nature but not worship it.

But are we so separate and so distinct? Are we so different and unique? Do we merely go our way in this world? Rabbi Shimon ben Yochai told the story of a group of people sailing on a ship. Suddenly, one took out a drill and began boring a hole beneath his own place on the boat. His fellow travelers saw him and exclaimed, "What are you doing?" He replied, "What does it matter to you? I am just drilling under my own place." But of course, the others exclaimed, "Don't you know the water will come up and flood the ship for us all?" (Leviticus Rabbah 4:6)

Those creatures that bother us, shall we exterminate them? Those animals that pester and sometimes scare us, shall we eliminate them? The rabbis said:

> Even those creatures you deem redundant in this world like flies, bugs and gnats, nevertheless have their allotted task in the scheme of creation as it says, "And God saw everything that God had made, and behold, it was very good." (Genesis 1:31)

> Rabbi Acha bar Hanina explained thus: Even those creatures deemed by you superfluous in the world, like serpents and scorpions, still have their definite place in the scheme of creation. (Genesis Rabbah)

So I believe we are taught to be caring of the earth's environment. I understand that we are taught to be respectful of what God has created and unless we treat it with care, we will, in the end, threaten our very own existence as well.

The Hebrew language has a way of expressing itself on this topic. In Hebrew there is no word for "possess" or "own." A theological statement perhaps? We have no way, like we do in English, of saying we own this land, that we own this earth.

Rabbinic Judaism has developed a concept of abstinence from wanton destruction which can inform the basic principle of eco justice that we are suggesting. It is called *bal tashchit*, which can be translated as "do not destroy." If we use things wisely, then we are acting as humans. If we cause damage and ruin, then we are no better than animals and have sinned.

Should our task not be forward-looking as well? How do we and how should we relate to the world we live in and the earth we live on? Is our task confined to the present? What is our role as stewards and conservers for the future? Listen to what our ancestors taught:

> While the sage Honi was walking along a road, he saw a man planting a carob tree. Honi asked him, "How many years will it take for this tree to bear fruit?" "Seventy years," replied the man. Honi then asked, "Are you so healthy a man that you expect to live that length of time and eat its fruit?" The man answered, "I found a fruitful world because my ancestors planted it for me. So, too, shall I plant for my children." (B. Talmud, Taanit 23)

For the future, for the next and successive generations . . . . Reverence and the humility to understand our fleeting place and role in these larger cosmic and universal creations. In the Book of Ecclesiastes (1:4-7), we are taught:

> One generation goes, another comes,
> But the earth remains the same forever.
> The sun rises, and the sun sets –
> And glides back to where it rises.
> Southward blowing, turning northward,
> Ever blows the wind;
> On its rounds the wind returns.
> All streams flow into the sea,
> Yet the sea is never full;
> To the place from which they flow
> The streams flow back again.

So we come full circle and return to where we began—the world's birthday. Today we celebrate the birth, the origin, the beginning. From nothing God created the world. Our story begins with the splendor and intensity of light to the commentary about where we humans fit into the larger scheme.

AMEN

# A Concise Blueprint for Living

## Rosh Hashanah Evening—1993

Each year I begin my first sermon of these holy days by reflecting upon how quickly the preceding twelve months seem to have passed. The course of world history moves quickly, the events in our own country have changed considerably and, for me—perhaps for you as well—this past year has hurried by.

The pace of change in the Middle East certainly has been nothing less than miraculous. These historic events present challenges, problems and opportunities hardly conceived of only a few weeks ago. In addition to these macro events, each one of us records and notes the micro events of our own lives and the lives of our loved ones. Tonight, I want to share with you more personal, more individual, more immediate concerns of the heart.

I am reminded of a description about time that I learned when our first child was an infant. At that time, someone more experienced in parenting told me that the days go slowly but the months go quickly. This seems true to me today as it did almost fifteen years ago. What makes time pass quickly? Of course we know that "time" moves at the same deliberate and consistent speed, but the perception of time passing, how each of us views and experiences the minutes, hours and days depends on what is going on in our lives. (I hope that the next fifteen minutes will pass quickly for every one of you.)

Some of you might have heard me say in the past that, for me, the hardest part of any sermon I prepare is deciding what I think is so important that other people should have to listen me. Of course I know that none of you are required to be here, that all of you decided with your own free will to be in this place, at this time, tonight. Nonetheless, most of you do not stand up and leave when it comes time for the rabbi to speak. Knowing that, I feel a significant burden of deciding what it is that I want to speak about and then preparing a sermon worthy of the topic.

This process takes me many months. Usually in the spring, I begin to make notes about what I think are worthy topics for High Holy Day

72

sermons. This year, the process was a little different. This past year, a terribly significant event occurred that was for me unlike any other. Last December my mother died. She was just short of her seventy-sixth birthday and had been sick during the previous twelve months. Nonetheless, her death came as a surprise to me and the rest of my family.

A few months after my mother's death, I prepared a sermon that I delivered to the students and faculty here at Hebrew Union College. I spoke about the most important lessons that I had learned from my parents. That experience of reducing and concentrating on the essential of life led me to a succinct yet powerful concept from the Talmud. We are taught that parents have the responsibility to teach their children three things: first, the study of Torah; second, a trade or profession; and third, how to swim in order to be physically safe.

More than ten years ago I utilized that quote to prepare an Ethical Will that I shared with this congregation at the time. But in preparing tonight's sermon, I have been looking for something more. I have sought to understand what our tradition teaches us about where we stand, what our purpose is in life and how we relate this to our belief in God. Not a simple task indeed and not one that I am likely to conclude in this one sermon or perhaps in any other. The challenge is one that is necessary for me to embark upon and one I hope you will conclude is worthwhile for you to hear.

The rabbis (Makkot 23b) teach that God communicated 613 commandments to Moses in the Torah. Such an arbitrary number has been discussed, researched and argued about for more than a thousand years. Some of you may be familiar with the discussion in the Talmud that there are 365 negative commandments, corresponding to the number of days in a year and 248 positive commandments corresponding to what our ancestors thought were the number of bones in the human body. Can we possibly relate to such a number? Is this what we can consider as the number of precepts that we should follow? This centuries-old discussion really rests on the struggle to find out what is expected of us in our relationship with God and our relationship with others.

The Talmud is concerned about the large and rather unwieldly number, and so the discussion goes further. We learn that King David reduced this large number to eleven principles. We read in a psalm, traditionally attribute to David (Psalm 15):

> God, who shall live in your tabernacle? Who shall dwell in Your holy mountain? 1) One who walks uprightly; 2) works righteousness; 3) speaks truth in their heart; 4) has no slander upon their tongue; 5) does no evil to their fellow; 6) does not take up a reproach against their neighbor; 7) in

whose eyes a vile person is despised; 8) honors those who fear God; 9) who stands by their oath even when it hurts; 10) who has never lent money at interest; 11) never accepted a bribe against the innocent.

The Talmud continues the discussion and notes that the prophet Isaiah reduced these principles to six. Isaiah said (Isaiah 33:15-16):

> 1) The person who walks in righteousness; 2) speaks uprightly; 3) spurns profits from fraudulent dealings; 4) waves away a bribe instead of grasping it; 5) stops their ears against listening to infamy; and 6) shuts their eyes against looking at evil. Such a person shall dwell in lofty security, with inaccessible cliffs for their stronghold, with food supplied and drink assured.

Then a later prophet, Micah, came and reduced these six principles to three, as it is written (Micah 6:8):

> It has been told you what is good and what the Eternal One requires of you: 1) only to do justly; 2) to love mercy, and 3) to walk humbly before your God.

We then learn that Isaiah reduced this number to two (Isaiah 56:1) and teaches us:

> 1) Observe what is right, and 2) do what is just.

Amos came and reduced them to one principle (Amos 5:4):

> Thus says Adonai to the House of Israel: Seek Me and you shall live.

The prophet Habakkuk came and taught that all of these principles, regardless of the number, are based upon one (Habakkuk 2:4):

> The righteous shall live by their faith.

In one important way, then, we learn in this extensive rabbinic discussion that the starting place is not how many precepts, principles or commandments we can distill from our tradition, not how handily we can reduce a large and complex way of looking at the world, but rather how we can learn to start on this journey. Our tradition teaches us that this notion of faith in God is a starting point, not a conclusion. From this starting point of faith many other things follow.

Upon continuing reflection regarding the impact that my mother's death has had on my faith and my relationship with God, I have more fully come to realize that one of the things that many of us lack in this secular society is the vocabulary to discuss our theological belief system.

My very first sermon as a rabbinic student struggled with this notion of belief in a transcendent being. I remember twenty-five years ago when I used the image of Jacob's ladder to discuss my personal theology, I struggled with the notion that the contract Jacob strikes with God suggests that God is limited in acting in human history. This rational notion of a limited deity proposed that we must be responsible for our actions and deeds, but even more than that, when bad things happened there was not much point in imploring God to intervene. My emerging understanding of a power greater than us suggested that this existence of ours was part of a partnership with God. The facts of free will and choice convinced me to believe in a God who had limited involvement in our world.

Such a belief served me well for a number of years, but it brought me up short more than a year ago when I hastened to California, hoping that my mother would recover from pneumonia and emerge from intensive care. I prayed to God for this recovery of my mother—but with very mixed emotions. Part of me felt that it was treating God like the "Doctor in the Sky." I was not seeking a relationship with God that would help determine my purpose as a Jew. I was not seeking closeness and was not trying to understand how I stood in a covenantal relationship between God and the Jewish people. All the things that I had believed and had preached about as a rabbi started slipping from my grasp.

I was seeking supernatural intervention, not the God of gradualness, of the slow natural cycle of earth. I wanted the God of splitting seas, of thunder and all-powerfulness. I wanted my mother to recover and live. Yet I did not believe that God worked that way.

For many years when I prayed silently in services, I pictured a series of concentric circles. The smallest one was our family; next came the community we live in, next the Jewish people, Israel and then came all of humanity. I thought about these circles when I closed my eyes and meditated on the meaning of love and peace. I did not pray that God would intervene and cure some particular circle in that constellation. Rather, I acknowledged these circles as part of the definition of who I was as an individual, as a Jew and as a member of the human race.

I have seen too many sick people who deserved to be cured, who prayed and hoped and still died to have confidence in God intervening in such matters. I believe that God has created a natural universe and, though malignancies occur in this natural order, God has given us humans the power, the ability and the curiosity to strive to continuously uncover the cures for such malignancies. God will not reach down and rearrange the development of the human body to accommodate me because of the fervency of my prayer—or the deservedness of my mother.

Still, I prayed. Part of my desperation—and now I realize even more, my understanding—is to take refuge in long shots. Who knows? I certainly don't have all the answers; I don't even know if I have all the questions. All these rational theological views could be wrong. Perhaps God not only listens but acts. Perhaps the heavens not only have ears but also arms.

So while sitting in the Dallas airport between planes that morning, I prayed. While in the ICU waiting room in California, I prayed. And who knows why my mother lived for another twelve months. My rational belief and certainty have been checked some. Now usually when I pray silently, I can only think about my mother.

Many think that we rabbis have fully worked through our belief systems, arrived at a definitive answer and are ready and able to articulate such beliefs to others. Long ago I realized that this is not the case. In fact, many rabbis are anxious and deeply suspicious of talking about their faith. We easily convince ourselves that everyone else knows with certainty about God, has developed a sound and systematic theology and, therefore, any admission that our own belief is in the process of "becoming" is withheld in the hopes that no one else will discover such shortcomings. This often successfully inhibits discussion of our own theological struggles.

My struggles go on daily. They go on when I see the sun rise or set, when I see my children smile or cry, when I see my love for my family blossom, when I see people I care about move closer to me. My struggles also go on when I close my eyes for a moment of reflection and almost always see my mother in sickness and in health. Thus, I learn more about the human condition and my faith every day.

In this process, I have learned one more thing. It is one key ingredient in the thoughts of the biblical prophets and in the thoughts of such present-day people of prophetic vision: we are not enough by ourselves. We do not see enough. We do not know enough nor understand enough. We do not have vision enough nor wisdom enough.

We need God. We need the hope which comes from God. We need God's wisdom for our hearts. We need God's eternal truths for our spirits.

We need God: for the sense of timelessness beyond our time, for the sense of eternity to cradle our brief hours.

We need God's arms to hold us up.

We need God's presence to know that the world eternally has a place for memory and for lives whose years are ended.

May it be a great and beautiful new year for you and for all of us. May every day be a time for the beauty of life and of the world, for God's blessing, deep and measureless.

Reach out to God in this newest year of our lives. Reach out to God, and may you find God in your reaching.

AMEN

# Behavioral Advice

## Yom Kippur Evening—1993

My message this time is going to be somewhat brief and simple because we are here to listen to the still small voice within ourselves, the voice that usually gets drowned out by the din around us. In addition, we come to listen for a few brief moments to the voices of those who have left us and not to me. First a few thoughts to share, and then you can return to your own.

I ask myself what is it I remember about different people? Sometimes my mind becomes like a television screen which is filled with the faces of people that I have not thought of for a long time. I sometimes see not just my family and relatives who are no longer living but the faces of other people whom I have known and loved. There is the camp director who I remember from the time I was in junior high school. Many of you, too, recall the important teacher or counselor of your youth. There is the face of my close friend who died when we were freshmen in college. His face is like the faces that many of you see when you close your eyes and think about those friends whose lives were cut off long before their time. And more recently, I see the faces of friends who are no longer able to laugh or smile with us. They fill the screens of our memories.

What we remember about who they were keeps their stories alive for us as we consider what they accomplished and why these memories matter to us. How do we know a person's worth? How do we measure what they accomplished? Listen to a passage from the Talmud (Erubin 65b) that tells us by three things is a person's character known: by their cup, by their pocket and by their anger. The Hebrew quote actually has a very nice rhyme and meter to it—"*B'shlosha d'varim adam nikar: b'coso, b'ciso uv'caaso.*"

What does this mean? Can we tell the character of another individual by what is in their pocket—*b'ciso*? How big is my pocket and with what would I fill it? What are the treasures I seek? What is truly precious in my sight? Is it money? Is it possessions—something to grasp

78

or to hold? Would it be sad to have a pocket so small that it is not big enough to hold heaven's glory nor a child's laughter? Hold this metaphor for a few minutes because I want to come back to it in just awhile!

A person is known by their cup—*b'coso*. What is one's cup? Is it the pleasures we seek? The wine of life that we would savor? The joys we would reckon as our own? Judaism is not opposed to pleasure and to joy. These are legitimate values in life.

Our text might suggest that we can be known for the pleasures we seek out for ourselves. Where do we stand in the continuum from moderation to excess? The difference between a drinker and a drunk is very little. The distance between a gourmet and a glutton is only a few mouthfuls. But this is not the cup that concerns us the most.

There is a symbolic cup, the cup of life itself. Into that cup, what do we pour? What do we drink out of that cup? Is our cup of life a cup of learning? Can we drink from it and then offer something meaningful with assurance and with pride to others? But more must be poured into the cup of life than learning. Our cup needs the precious essence of wisdom, the wisdom that gives life spaciousness, the wisdom of the simple things without which there truly is no life.

A life without courage is a defeat. A life without hope is a dead end. A life without grief is a life without love. A life without shadow is a life without dimension. A life without risk is a life without victory.

So we can fill our cup only with small and foolish things and be a small and foolish person, living in a small and foolish world. If we lift our cup only to satisfy the thirst of our lips and never try to quench the thirst of our hearts, our heads and our spirits, then we have not learned to separate the important from the unimportant, the real from the illusory, the permanent from the transitory. We may have gained knowledge, but wisdom will have escaped us. Our cup will be an empty one, and we will be poorer for it.

Then there is knowing a person by his anger—*b'ca'aso*. What makes us angry and how does that determine our character? There are those who go through life perpetually angry—angry at the clerk in the store who is berated for inattention; angry with the friend who is accused of passing us on the street without greeting; angry with children for acting like children; and angry at ourselves without understanding why.

To be angry at the right person, at the right time, for the right reason, that is an art. Moses was a very angry man. Angry with injustice and oppression. Angry with cruelty and with wrong. He was angry not with the unjust, but with injustice; not with the cruel, but with cruelty;

not with the unrighteous, but with unrighteousness. With the rest of us, sometimes our anger is trivial, sometimes demeaning and every once in a while unworthy. We tend to vent our anger upon the insignificant; and in the face of great wickedness we are silent. There is no righteous anger without pity and caring. If we do not care for others, we have no passion for life. If we have no empathy and are unable to understand another's pain, then we have a closed pocket, an empty cup and a forever angry heart.

Now I want to return to the first metaphor I mentioned in the Talmudic passage, the one about pockets. Pockets are for receiving as well as removing, for putting into and for taking out of. What we put in and, more significantly, what we take out tells a great deal about our character. And this brings me to a bit of financial advice. Yes, you may think it is strange on Yom Kippur for the rabbi to be giving financial advice, but please keep an open mind.

Here it is: That which you give away is your only permanent possession. That which you give away—that which you remove from your pocket—of your time or your money or your love, that no one can ever take away from you. That is your real legacy. That is what you will be remembered for, that and only that.

If you and I could only learn this truth, if we could really learn it, not only in our heads but in our hearts and guts as well, how different might our lives be.

So as you listen now to the still small voice within you, as you reflect on the lessons in the lives of those you have come here to communicate with, think about how they would wish you to spend your year. May you find contentment and satisfaction in your life.

AMEN

# Kaddish

## Rosh Hashanah Morning—1994

[Note: The sermon was delivered just prior to the reading of the Kaddish prayer. I am indebted to Rabbi Larry Hoffman for his invaluable assistance in providing me with excellent sources to study.]

Over the past few weeks I was organizing my thoughts and notes with the intention of speaking about the Shofar service, about the development of the selections of the Torah and Haftorah readings and about the Kaddish prayer. As my thinking and note-taking progressed, I realized that I was returning again and again to the Kaddish and putting the other ideas aside. Perhaps it was because I felt that the emotion and symbolism of the Kaddish prayer is often more powerful than any other part of the service; perhaps it was because I decided that the interruption should be kept to a minimum; perhaps it was because my own personal experience with the Kaddish prayer during the past almost two years during which time both of my parents have died has pushed me to focus on this experience.

So it is the Kaddish prayer I want us to turn our attention to this morning. Perhaps better known and more powerful than any other single Jewish prayer, I will present some of my thoughts about the origins, the secrets, the uses and the symbolic meanings which are contained in this prayer.

## Origins

Most authorities on Jewish worship agree that the Kaddish prayer as we know it originated about 1,500 years ago and began as a concluding prayer which praised God. It was to be recited following a sermon which would usually occur after reading from the Torah. Recited in Aramaic because that was the vernacular of the time, the prayer eventually expanded and then was used to conclude other parts of the worship service and in the house of study as well. We have indication from sources more than a thousand years old that when the prayer service would conclude, the leader would exit the synagogue, comfort the mourners and then recite the Kaddish. It appears that in this way the prayer grew to be associated more and more with mourners. The custom of having the mourners themselves recite the Kaddish at the end of the daily synagogue service for eleven months after the death of a near relative and then on every anniversary of the death seems to have originated at a time of intense persecution in medieval Germany after the twelfth century. While it is now a slightly different text, nonetheless today the Kaddish is recited by mourners around the world.

As noted, the Kaddish was not originally a prayer for the dead. A legend is told about Rabbi Akiba, however, which may have provided some of the impetus for its use by mourners. In one version (Sanhedrin 104a), Rabbi Akiba meets a deceased man who must atone for his sins with a severe punishment. Through the good deeds of his son, he could be relieved from this. The son was to read from the Torah, say the blessing "Praise God who is to be praised" and induce the community to utter God's praise. Therefore, Rabbi Akiba taught the orphan the Sh'ma, parts of the worship service, placed the child in front of the congregation and the child said, "Praise God." The congregation responded with "Praise be . . . " and thus the punishment was lifted from the deceased. One of the conclusions we can draw from this ancient story is the significance of uttering God's name in prayer, precisely what the Kaddish prayer contains.

So, why the tradition of reciting the prayer for eleven months? The Mishnah and the Talmud both state that the torture of Gehenna, the netherworld, is for twelve months, so originally the Kaddish was recited for that period of time. Then it was deemed inappropriate for children to suppose that the souls of their parents were in the netherworld, so the recitation time was reduced to eleven months.

## Secrets

There appears to have been another agenda at work in the development of the Kaddish prayer. The elaborate praise of God that appears in the text of the prayer is not just happenstance. Some scholars believe that there is direct influence of the early Jewish mystics. There are seven synonyms or adjectives for God's glory, and this corresponds to the seven heavens often found in the beliefs of the Hellenistic world. The notion of God on the throne of glory with angels around is a common one in this particular mystical tradition. The goal for us humans is to escape this world and break through the barriers that restrict us from seeing God's splendor. Incantations are necessary for this journey. Praise was key to enable us to ascend through heaven after heaven. It is not so much the literal meaning of the text that is important. In fact, content appears to be secondary to the effect, but the method is reciting the words of God's praise.

The central theme of the Kaddish is visualizing God as Ruler, sitting on the throne of glory, reigning over all creation. This prayer expresses the ultimate hope of seeing the divine vision and experiencing the coming of God's rule.

## Use

Once Kaddish became an established part of observance of mourning, it came to serve important psychological functions. It compels the mourner to reaffirm connections with the community through daily prayer precisely when despair and alienation are most profound. In its most abstract sense, Kaddish serves as a statement of the unknowability, though justification, of God's ways. Kaddish becomes a significant component—cathartic yet simultaneously self-affirming exercise—of the bereavement process.

For liberal Jews, where equality for both men and women in all aspects of ritual and religious life is the goal, Kaddish is an obligation and an opportunity. For some traditional Jews, this is a major concern. There is ample evidence over many centuries to demonstrate that within the traditional community women should be obligated to recite Kaddish. Indeed, women are obligated for all the laws of mourning, and Kaddish is an integral one of them. One of the reasons noted for reciting Kaddish is to give solace to the soul of the deceased and redeem the dead from Gehenna, and this applies to all.

## Symbolism

It is often noted that the Kaddish prayer sanctifies God's name and nowhere moves into the realm of the other world. The Kaddish does not step beyond the framework of the Jewish feeling for the this-worldly task of humankind. In the text of the Kaddish, the desire is expressed that the worshippers may still live to see salvation and that much good may come to those who occupy themselves with the commandments. In principle, Jewish prayer does not focus on the problems of humankind but on the cause of God. The worshipping community is again and again called upon to hallow God's name. In the most ancient sources, the Kaddish is not named as such but is referred to as "May God's great name be praised." It is clear that there exists a strong belief that the sanctification of the divine name will hasten the redemption of humankind and of the world.

Many Jews, alienated or not from their heritage, find in the Kaddish the historical connection of generations, a relationship between the present and the past. In the Kaddish there exists a tie with the deceased who were close to us and with the martyrs of all times who surround our history with a special aura. In fact, the Kaddish opens a more vigorous view on the future because it is a prayer of hope. The worshipper is united with the dead, with the time of sanctification. Sanctification, however, exists not only in dying but also in daily life.

Kaddish as a prayer for the dead is rooted in the Jewish consciousness more strongly today than ever before. We have left too many dead in the recent past in foreign lands and in Israel in cemeteries and in unknown graves where there is no marker for them. We cannot forget that. The thought of them we have encased within the Kaddish prayer, thus connecting the dead with the living.

The message for us is that we are not truly dead until we are forgotten.

# Faith and Love

## Yom Kippur Evening—1994

This is the retrospective hour of Kol Nidre when all the vows of yesterday, broken loose from the anchors of our faith, are recovered from the heaving seas and brought again to our noisy and restless harbor of self-evaluation and self-reflection.

Like a few years ago, I wish that we could talk about this as though we were but a few, a small company of friends, gathered in intimate conversation. Therefore, once again I am going to ask a favor of you. Will you try to forget that this is a large space, with hundreds of people present? Will you try to forget that this is a sermon and imagine that it is a friendly talk from my heart to yours about simple but desperately important matters? It will help me if you do.

Kol Nidre: when the night overflows with the echoes of used-up time.

Kol Nidre: when the heavens divide and the gates of prayer swing wide on the waiting, providing us with compassionate hinges of atonement and forgiveness; when memory wanders through the collection of our years, gathering up random recollections like coins falling out of a torn pocket.

Build a barrier around this hour. Start with a wall made out of the stones of regret and put the mortar between them with the muscle of failure. Set in place the windows of small joys and quiet gladness. Lock out today's time and the now. Time is more than this instant's ticking of the universal clock, more than this thin page of the new year. Time is the seal of endlessness on all things. It is the secret rhythm of the tides and the constellations of stars in the sky. Time is the slow separation of the day from the night, the parting of the shadowless and the shadowed. Time is the unceasing addition scribbled down in our everyday life.

Kol Nidre is all these: vows not kept, days ill-used, life and death, the antagonistic tides of time, incompletion.

Where is God's voice on this Kol Nidre Eve? It is above the roars of everyday life, the unbiased and unprejudiced noise which knows neither friend nor enemy, which simply supplies death's answers to life's questions.

Yesterday's friend is today's stranger, and yesterday's stranger is now our friend. We have called to You, O God, through centuries of Kol Nidres. You have talked with Abraham and Sarah, with Isaac and Rebekah, with Jacob and Leah and Rachel. We, the covenanted people, have emerged from their descendants.

We think of our history as a people, of the institutions and monuments constructed over the centuries. We think of our creations and God's creations, and we ponder them at Kol Nidre time. With our minds and our bodies, we think of them. We want to thank You, O God, who has made us a special people. Our ancestors were like all the others, and they could have remained so.

Others looked at Mount Sinai and saw only the mute stone and voiceless rock, a place of secrets and mystery. We looked at Sinai, and we saw flames and the divine presence and an overwhelming fire.

It sometimes has been lonely, O God, to walk this lighted way: to see a mountain peak no one else sees; to listen to words no one else hears; to say to us *na'aseh v'neshmah*—"act first and then listen." Listen, even if all the world is deaf. Act, even if no one else cares.

Where have You been, O God, on this Kol Nidre Eve? How many dreams have our people dreamed and then had them shattered? How many Sinais have we climbed and lost? How many stars extinguished, burned out matches of heaven? What perversity seizes hold of us so that we tear with angered teeth the words "brotherhood and sisterhood" and spit them out as though it were a terrible bitterness?

Why is the world an unending loud and louder scream? And the scream is red with the furnaces of Auschwitz, buried with the dead at Babi Yar, resurrected and sounding again in Bergen Belsen, the moan of ghosts lost in the shrouds of the innocent; a scream, until there is only the silence of death.

We ask, "Where were You, O God? Where are You?"

It is not our people alone, Adonai. Where are You, O God, when children lay dying in today's refugee camps, when tribal and ethnic hatreds spill over into the coldly calculated killings of young and old, strong and weak, soldier and civilian alike.

The questions are not irrelevant, but there are other questions which have precedence. Our brothers and sisters called, and their pleas died in the deaf air even as their bodies died in the graves commanded and by their own hands dug.

Where are we in our world? Too many of us have made ourselves bystanders, apart. Where are You, O God, we ask. But we do not ask the one hard, unyielding, unsilenceable question, "Where are we, O human spirit?" Where are we, with our clever fingers and our exploring minds and our soaring imaginations?

Some of us say, "You, O God are dead." Then we say, "Trust in our fellow passengers on this planet for they are our ultimate hope. Trust in the hands that have made the guns and bombs. Trust in the minds that have devised myriad ways for violent death. Trust the memories that already have forgotten the furnaces and the death camps. Put your highest, noblest faith in our kind."

We should not forget the old words that we will read tomorrow as we do each year on Yom Kippur morning: "I have set before you life and death, good and evil; therefore, choose life." You have given us the right to choose; to be human or beast; and You have decided to trust our final faith and choice. We decide: To see Sinai's fire or Sinai's desolation. We are the choosers, and You are the One who gives us the chance to choose.

We think we know what You desire. It is Your wish that we each be more than we presently are; to become bigger than we are; to reach beyond our own arm's length and see farther than our eye's vision. You are our choice, and we can choose to affirm You for life.

It is for us to affirm that the sin in the world is our sin and the hate in the world is our hate. Where there is evil, it is the evil that we have chosen and not the evil of an uncaring God.

The days of the new year begin to unroll, days of searching and questioning, days of children growing up and growing away, days enriched by our awareness of love, days by love's neglect made poorer.

O God let the joys ahead be many and the worries few. May growing up and growing older be through the more widely opened doorway. For the young, may growing older be the joyous miracle of maturing transformation. May it mean to become captive to the wonder of the world; to use time and not be used by it; to hear other voices beside your own. To recognize the validity of dependence as well as independence. To learn to listen as well as to speak. To be confident of your own strength and to recognize your limits. May these things make growing older an exciting adventure into tomorrow.

Kol Nidre holds open to us endless hope and give us the opportunity to risk our faith. Such risks can exact a very heavy toll. Such risks of faith can pull at the bottommost strings of our heart and soul. We can find ourselves with deeply held beliefs and faiths, some of which we think we can understand and others which we cannot. Take for example how often faith becomes love and love becomes faith. There is hope and happiness in the joy of new love and the satisfaction of continual loving relationships. There is pain, also, and the inscrutable mystery of death of those we love, whether it is sudden or lingering. The way is twisted; the path is uncertain and runs through dark places.

Love is a faith in the capacity of the other to return to us what we freely give. This love is faith. It can be confusing, and it can be incomprehensible. For love and faith require us to give up our total control and to sometimes place our destiny in something or someone else.

Kol Nidre comes every year, and it teaches us about what we don't know.

Kol Nidre comes and raises the ante for each one of us because it asks what is it we truly believe.

I know that the certain believers are wrong, those who have all the answers, those who know positively that life is a foolishness and a meaninglessness and that death is the bitter joke of an incredible deity; and equally wrong those who know positively that everything is all right and all the meanings are clear if only our faith is clear and unclouded.

We understand only partly. Some things are in focus, but some are still hazy. Some things make sense and other things do not. Some things have meaning; others do not.

Faith is a big word in what is bright and dark, clear and obscure, innocent and troubled, exultant and unsure. Love is a big word in what is joyous and fearful, wonderful and desperate, filling life and emptying life. Faith and love, Kol Nidre, solemn and exalted, tragic and lonely.

Let me conclude this conversation with you by admitting that I try to keep pushing ahead and make a path for this journey to understand where faith is and where love is. And I keep telling myself that faith is not bound either to blessings bestowed or to evils which befall. Love is not a reward nor is its loss a punishment.

Faith needs to be this big thing, beyond the reach of any single event in our lives. Faith is a way of life, seeking our path to God and living in conformity with our perception of that path. Faith is to walk in this world, which sometimes makes sense and which sometimes does not. Faith is not one thing when all is well and another when all is wrong. Faith has the courage and the strength to say, "I do not know why." And to say it without losing itself or letting sorrow turn it into something less than itself. Faith is in this Day of Atonement and is at the heart of our Jewish belief.

May it be our strength and our support in the year ahead.

AMEN

# Prayer

## Rosh Hashanah Evening—1995

A few weeks ago, I watched the movie *Apollo 13* with my family. We sat on the edge of our seats, gripped by the suspense and masterful acting. One part of the movie is worth repetition here. Shortly after an oxygen tank explodes, Mission Control is concerned about whether the astronauts can return to earth safely. The crew of the Apollo spaceship is commanded to rid themselves of all of their non-essentials. In order to survive, they must throw away every excess thing with which they are traveling.

Some of our travels through life are not as dramatic as a space trip, but some of them would probably make interesting movies. Obviously, the question for us at this time of the year, the time when we ponder the irreducible truths that we hope to live our lives by, is what is left for us when we rid ourselves of our non-essentials? I want to examine one of them with you tonight: the essential, the irreducible connection between us and our Creator—the communication link of prayer.

Prayer is the echo of God's voice within us, the remembered hope, the not-yet-lost aspiration. The best prayer, then, is not for our own concerns. The best prayer is when we forget ourselves and when we remember humankind; when we leave unremarked the need of our own hearts—when we remember God's holiness in all of us.

Prayer is not so much talking with God as it is making ourselves ready to listen. Prayer is to cast off and go beyond the words into the quiet and the wonder. Prayer is our answer to God's question, "What are you? Where are you?"

There are religious limits to prayer. We may not pray for just anything we desire. Our tradition teaches us about responsible prayer.

It is important to draw the distinction between magic and prayer. Let me put into words an explanation of the differences. A good example of magic is the story of Aladdin's lamp. Aladdin rubs the lamp in a certain way; he pronounces the right words, and the genie appears. The genie comes, not because he wants to, not because Aladdin deserves him to, but because the words have been said, the name has been uttered that makes him come.

In our tradition, God tells Moses, "I have no Name like that. I will come—not because you possess the Name that can make Me come—but because I care about you." That is the central difference between magic and prayer in the Jewish tradition. In Jewish prayer you can add words, delete words or even pray without words, for the words have no magical power in themselves. It is the intention of the heart that God cares about.

Thinking is prologue to prayer. For prayer is based on the knowledge of what is real. To understand what is real is essential for the realization of the ideal. We may not pray that an amputated limb should spring to life, but we may pray for the inner strength to deal with the loss. We may not pray for the resurrection of the limb, but we may give thanks for prosthetics. That we may not pray for a result that defies the laws of nature or contradicts the laws of logic does not reflect God's lack of power. It acknowledges the reality that God has created.

Prayer is no surrogate for medical attention. Prayer of its own will not cure cancer. It may alert the patient to curative powers and inspire the petitioner to devote his mind and heart to participate in the cure. Prayer ignites the fight for life.

We pray in relationship with God, as a partner in the covenant which we are trying to understand. That covenant between us and God began with Abraham. Our ancestors struggled with it for thousands of years, and we continue to struggle today. The covenant prayer is not modeled according to the relationship of ruler and subject, master to servant or shepherd to flock. Covenantal prayer is a two-sided relationship of co-creators and co-sanctifiers. I am not a passive recipient of an Other's will, judgment and act. I understand myself as an essential and active partner with the Divine Other.

Covenantal prayer is directed to God whose divine image informs the petitioner. The Hebrew word for prayer, *tefillah,* is derived from the verb *pallel,* which means "to judge." Prayer is a form of self-examination and self-judgment to correct one's ways.

The power of covenantal prayer derives from the basic biblical affirmation of the divine image implanted in the human being. The pivotal biblical verse is "And God created the human being in God's own image, male and female created God them." (Genesis 1:27) Prayer is a way of discovering who we are and what we must do to know God. Between us and God is a compact that enables prayers of dependence and acquiescence to become prayers of interdependence and mutual responsibility. Prayer is more than something to be asked for. Prayer is the constant search for the means of repair of the self and the world.

And we say to God through prayer that we are what we ought not be. We are the promise of what we can become. Prayer is the rim of our world; holiness is the hub of our world; and, from that center, holiness radiates out as spokes of meaning.

There are these clear shining spokes; and there is the dark terror of others; the spokes of pain and the fear of death; the sense of guilt and the knowledge of our own blindness and shortcomings; the spokes of torment and defeat and heartbreak.

Prayer may teach us that we cannot live only in the earth's dimensions. Our heart needs height, and our spirit needs the mountaintop and beyond. Prayer can lift us away from the focus on self and nearer to a relationship with God. The ladder of prayer, like Jacob's ladder, sets its base in the earth; it rests it's top on a ledge near God. On the ladder of prayer, our holiness ascending uncertainly meets God's holiness descending in welcome.

Prayer is not always words. Prayer is often silence. A Hasidic saying: "God loves what is left over at the bottom of the heart and cannot be expressed in words."

When prospectors went looking for gold, they used to swirl the gold-laden sand in a water-filled pan. The lighter sand particles were washed out, and at the bottom of the pan only the gold remained. The silence of prayer is not less golden. When the dross and valueless, the superficial and inconsequential are washed out of our hearts by the waters of life, then there is left over only the pure golden essence, the knowledge that we are not alone, never removed from the presence of the God who is ever seeking us.

So a person need not always talk to God with words. God translates our wordlessness, and God understand our unspoken outpourings.

A story is told about a peasant who came each day to the sanctuary and sat there motionless, for a long time, no word uttered, his lips still.

"What do you say to God during these longs visits?" he was asked. "I say nothing to God," the man replied. "I look at God, and God looks at me."

Prayer is the knowledge that we are never abandoned from God's sight. Prayer is our saying, "I see You, O God." Prayer is the end of the finite and the beginning of the eternal.

Some of us may have the habit of offering a prayer on a regular basis. My habits include doing so twice each morning. As I have grown older, I find that each time I awake, I sit there for minute and think about how fortunate I am to be able to physically function for another day. I thank God for the good health and proper functioning of all of my bodily parts.

As I go out into the world, I silently recite the *Sh'ma*. I have discovered that it reminds of where I come from and who I am. I find it valuable to think about me, the Jewish people and God before too much time has passed in the day.

In rabbinic Hebrew, prayer is called *"avodah,"* which means "work." The worshipper knows with what they have to work. Each one of us has choices to make and each one of us works at our own creation, our own ideal, in our own way.

Instead of praying for health of a loved one, we might pray for the insights of the physicians, for the strength and patience to assist our loved ones in their time of need. Our prayers could be to understand where we are in relationship to the Eternal.

The ideal of the divine image is the soul before it is touched by prayer.

Returning from prayer to the community of other people is part of our Jewish tradition as well. We need to find nourishment for our souls that can propel us to act in ways that work with God in "repairing creation," in *tikkun olam*. For when we only pray and do not try to act, our prayers can rarely sustain us.

This then becomes part of the irreducible, the fusion of prayer and action.

I know of nothing more essential, nothing more irreducible than the voice of prayer, no other way of reaching out beyond the measured to the measureless, the meaningless to the meaningful, the darkness of our deeds to the brightness of our hopes. Doing so helps me run my mind's eye down the spoke from the hub to the center and focus on what I will try to be. I hope to keep trying to do that every single day. I hope that you do as well.

AMEN

# Al Chet—
# For All These Sins

## Yom Kippur Evening—1996

A few minutes ago, we read the prayer, unique for Yom Kippur, *Al Chet*. The sentences of this prayer are traditionally arranged in alphabetical order, with two sins for each Hebrew letter. The editors of our prayer book have taken some liberty but generally follow this same format.

Notice what is not on this list. Read it through, and you will see that there is no mention of any ritual, no mention of Shabbat, Pesach, Purim, Chanukah. The sins that are on this list are the ethical sins between us and other people.

Why do all of us have to say all of these sins? Surely no one is so wicked as to have done them all. But we are all part of a community, and so we share some responsibility for what the others in our group have done. Sometimes we are indirectly responsible for the sins of others. What we condone, what we do not rebuke others for doing, what conditions we create that drive others to do things—these are our sins, too.

And there is another reason why all of us are asked to recite the whole list. It gives us each a measure of privacy. The person next to us cannot know which sins we are reciting because we really did them and which sins we are simply saying because they are in the book. This enables each of us to confess to God in private, even while we pray together in public.

We begin: "For the sin that we have committed against You— *b'ones uviratson*—under duress or by choice."

Why should the first of all the sins for which we confess be for the sin that we have committed "*b'ones*," under compulsion? Surely, if it was done under compulsion, if we had no choice, then it is not our fault and we should not be held accountable. It is easy to claim that we did it because of circumstances or environment or heredity or for some other reason outside our control. Repentance cannot really begin until and unless we face up to our deeds and say in all sincerity and in all honesty, "I did it and I was wrong, and I am sorry."

"I did it" is terribly hard to say. When the first person was confronted with his sin, he used an alibi, the same alibi that men have been using ever since.

Adam said, "She made me do it." And when the woman was confronted, Eve said, "The serpent made me do it." Perhaps it was for this—not so much for what they did, but for their denials and their futile efforts at covering up—that they were judged by God. Therefore, we begin our confessional with this sin—with facing up to those sins that we have claimed and rationalized and pretended were done "under compulsion" and admitting that we did them and we were wrong. Whoever cannot admit this sin cannot go on to the rest of the list.

Many of the *al chets* are sins of speech. Why? Because that is the part of the body with which we sin the most, isn't it? I don't think that I have hurt anyone with my fists even once during the past year. I don't think that I have hurt anyone with my foot even once during the past year. But I am sure that I have hurt many people with my tongue. Perhaps that is true for you as well?

Sometimes we end up saying some very hurtful things. Perhaps we were just very angry about something else and so we lashed out in a way that may have caused a pain that we never intended. This is part of being human.

But when we gossip, when we relate stories, when we tell tales, we usually end up hurting someone we did not mean to hurt. We might think that this is not particularly sinful, but our tale ends up creating something we never intended to create. Our slander ends up creating a life of its own, and you never know where it might end up. I tell you a little tidbit about someone else, and you tell someone else, and so on and so forth. Where might it end up? What it might turn into? Not just egg on our face, which is embarrassing, but truly hurting someone else.

The fifth line of *Al Chet* says *"b'deboor peh"*—"with our words." Our tradition understands this as not only an offense against the person we may have hurt, but that we should see that this behavior is a sin against God as well. It shows disrespect for God's creation. We have both offended God and we have hurt our friend or someone we do not know. Have we not also demeaned ourselves by this kind of talk? Our words can be used to destroy and injure. Our words can destroy a world. In other times and other places our words can create as well. We both create and destroy by the words we choose.

The world, described at the beginning of the Torah, was created by the word. How does the world come into being? By the words that God speaks.

> God said, "Let there be light, and there was light."
> God said, "Let there be water, let there be sky, heaven, earth, plants and trees and human beings."

Moses uses words when he relates the history and the covenant between God and the Jewish people. Moses addresses words to the new generation of Israelites who would inherit the land, but first they must hear his words before they can cross the Jordan and create a new world.

We create worlds when we speak. Have you ever learned something new? It is almost as if a new world is opened to you. Or when two people meet one another and begin a conversation. That experience can turn into a lifetime of conversations. A new world is created between these two people because they have found a way to speak to one another.

We create worlds with our words, mirroring others as we do so, echoing the words of the Ten Commandments—for in our tradition the Ten Commandments are described as *aseret ha'debroot,* "the ten words." One of these words is *kebud av v'aim*—honor your father and your mother. When we say these words, we create a world. When we say the things we should say to our families, when we pick up the phone and call parents, grandparents or relatives and share with them our words of love and concern, at these times we help create worlds with our words.

The prayer book reminds us that the tongue is a powerful and dangerous weapon. We must be careful in how we use it, and we must atone for how we abuse it.

Yet, I would suggest that there is one sin that is missing from the *al chet,* one sin that ought to be included in this list. If I had my way, if I were the editor of the prayer book, there is one sin we all commit that I think should be added to the *al chets* because it is at least as harmful, at least as destructive, as any of the sins of speech.

The sin that I would add to the list of *al chets* is the sin of silence.

The sin of silence is usually understood in a political sense. We usually think of it in connection with keeping quiet while evil is being done in our society. It is a phrase that is used, for example, in connection with the Holocaust, or in connection with the Jews of the former Soviet Union or the ethnic cleansing in Bosnia. It usually refers to people who sit on the sidelines and don't speak out as they should when evil is being done. But that is not what I have in mind tonight. That is an important sin to talk about; there is no denying that. There is an obligation on every human being to speak out when they see injustice being done. But I have something in addition in mind tonight.

What I have in mind tonight is much more insidious and much more widespread. It is the sin of silence that goes on within our homes and within our lives.

What I have in mind are the many homes in which couples sit side by side before the television set for hours and never say a word. Or, homes in which talking takes place but no words from the heart are communicated.

What I have in mind are the many homes in which kids come home from school and the parents say, "What did you do today?" and the kids say, "Nothing." And then the parents say, "What's new?" and the kids say, "Not much."

What I have in mind today is the invisible curtain that separates so many of us from each other as we go through life. For that kind of silence can warp and mar and strain and stain and spoil the growth of a soul. That kind of silence can hurt and harm at least as much as angry words can—and maybe more.

There are homes that are just as dead as those where people have officially gone their separate ways through divorce, separation or the dissolution of the relationship. For a home in which people do not speak at all or in which they can only talk about trivia is a cell or hell or a rest stop or something else, but it is not a home.

Do you remember the rhyme that kids sometimes sing?

Sticks and stones may break my bones, but words will never hurt me.

We know that this is not always true! Now that I am older, I realize that this is often inaccurate. Words CAN hurt, even more than sticks and stones. And silence can hurt even more than words.

Silence breaks the heart. Silence hurts a thousand times more than sticks or stones or even angry words. And, therefore, the sin that we ought to face up to on this holy day, the sin with which we hurt each other perhaps more than any other, is the sin of silence.

So I would like to make four specific suggestions. I think that if you want to measure the worthwhileness of your life, if you want to measure the amount of health that you have given to others during the past year, if you want a suggestion by which you can learn how to become more of a *mensch* in this coming year, you can do so in this simple way.

Resolve that in this coming year you will learn to say these four phrases more often than you have in the past.

"Thank you," "I love you," "How are you?" and "What do you need?"

These are four simple phrases. And I believe that it cannot be over-emphasized the difference that they can make in our lives and in the lives of the people with whom we live.

It does not matter how big your vocabulary is or how many languages you know. If you can't say these four phrases, you have some more growth to do during the coming year. If you can't say these four phrases, you impoverish the lives of those with whom you live.

"Thank you," "I love you," "How are you?" and "What do you need?" are phrases that have the power to transform lives; to give power and purpose, dignity, well-being and value to the people around us.

Our written prayers are filled with thanks to God, for health, for food, for peace and for well-being. Just as we say thank you to God, so we should say thank you to those with whom we live and through whom we live.

To say "I love you" can give you access to your own heart and to the heart of the other.

It is a *mitzvah* to say, "How are you?" To say it and then to listen to the answer, and not just say it in a perfunctory way, with half a heart or head, while your mind is somewhere else.

It is a great *mitzvah* to say to someone whom you love, "What do you need? What can I do to help you?" Perhaps if we said this phrase often enough and meant it when we said it, the walls that exist between us would sometimes be lowered a bit. Perhaps then when we ask, "Where did you go?" and "What did you do?" we won't be met with the answer, "Nothing."

So, when we recite the list of *al chets,* I see that some of the ones on the list speak to me. I find myself saying, "Yes, this is something I really want to work on this year." Some of them repel me and make me say, "I am not ready to deal with this one yet."

Part of our work is figuring out why some repel us and acknowledging that we may not be ready to do *teshuvah,* repentance, around this *mitzvah* yet. But there is a step I can take. Is there, for example, one person that I am going to stop gossiping with? Not everybody, but one? Is there one person to whom I am going to say, "I love you"? Is there one person who I am going to really listen to and not impatiently wait for them to leave?

Two final thoughts about *al chet* and words. The first comes from Hasidic sources and told by the late Rabbi Abraham Joshua Heschel.

Heschel notes that we Jews don't think much of asceticism. Don't torture your body. It is more important to discipline your tongue and thoughts than it is to deprive your body of its necessary fulfillment of needs. Therefore, Hasidim look askance at too much fasting. The founder of Hasidism, the Baal Shem Tov, wrote a famous letter to one of his disciples who was an ascetic. He wrote him and said, "Don't fast. The best way is to let the tongue fast—from talking, not from food."

The final thought is my attempt to bring this sermon full circle. I noted at the beginning that *Al Chet* is not filled with a list of sins against God but of those between one person and another. There are many possible reasons why. Perhaps it is because the sins between humans and God are beyond such straight-forward expression. Or, perhaps it is because we are taught there are some people who are more careful in observing ritual than they are in observing justice, mercy and compassion. So one of the central prayers, repeated several times in the course of Yom Kippur, comes to teach us to remember these qualities and experiences that exist in relationships. We are called upon to strive that much harder during the coming year to right the wrongs that exist.

May this be a year of successful insights into these concerns, and may each of us grow from the examination that this causes us to do.

AMEN

# Simple Blessings

## Rosh Hashanah Evening—1997

What has Rosh Hashanah to say to us, simple people with simple joys and simple sorrows? The simplest thing it says it: you are here. Whatever the year brought—illness, worry, trouble—you have survived them. You are alive. You are here. Maybe not with as much health or energy as you would like, but with enough to get you here for another Rosh Hashanah anyway.

We are here—and we are not alone. If we stretch out our hands, we will touch someone else. Recognize that we are here, and we are surrounded by others who are here for some of the same reasons of introspection and reflection.

But what about things, materials possessions? How about them? We work so hard all year to move ahead, to attain things—whether they be grades, promotions or possessions. This is the time of year when we need to ask not what we are, not what we have, but who we are.

There is a story I read not long ago, about a man who was told that he could have all the land he could encompass in a day's journey. At sunrise he set forth, walking briskly from his starting point. The sun moved higher in the heavens, and the man began to run. He could get around more land if he ran. Hurry, hurry, hurry! The afternoon waned. Run, run! Faster, faster! More land! More, more, more! You may guess what happened. At sundown, the man staggered toward the starting point, exhausted, his last bit of strength drained. And as he came to where he began, he fell over dead. So they buried him, and all he needed was six feet of earth.

Let us look about and look inside and see what is really important. It is Rosh Hashanah and we are in the synagogue, joined in the connection with others who are part of the people Israel.

Maybe God is here also, the God of our ancestors, of Abraham and Sarah, of Isaac and Rebekah, of Jacob and of Leah and Rachel. The God who has kept us alive and given us strength when we needed it. Tonight we see in this way not one Rosh Hashanah, nor even twenty-five nor even twenty-five hundred, but all the Rosh Hashanahs of all the ages and all the prayers crowding the air above us and all the voices rolling like a great tide.

This is another of the simple things that the beginning of the year says to us. We are here. The Jewish centuries are here. We might easily forget these simple central facts. The Holy Days can become only a kind of interruption in the routine of our lives. One sometimes hears people say, "After the holidays we will do so and so," or "We can't do that because the holidays come in between." It is as if these special and powerful hours of the year shrink into a narrow corridor through which we need to pass before the regular time of life and living can be attended to.

Occasionally I am invited to a meeting to deliver an invocation or to speak a word that is religious in character or to teach some text that might lend an insight into religious life. So I deliver my talk or prayer or teach my text, and then the chair will rise and say, "And now let us get down to business."

Some people do the same with Rosh Hashanah. It is something to finish—and then to get down to business. But a holy day like this may be the true business of life. To get the worries and the joys and the sorrows into perspective. To stand back and have a look at ourselves. To link with what is bigger. To tie our little today to the present of those who we are connected with and to project our little tomorrow into the endless future of the Jewish people.

Rosh Hashanah is not a night and a day to get through. It is a day to live by. This time and these acts are the regular business of being a Jew. Perhaps we could say that it is that the year interrupts Rosh Hashanah and not that Rosh Hashanah interrupts the year.

So, some among you are thinking, "I am not sure that I understand. This rabbi is saying that I am here, and God and the whole household of Israel is in one place. He says that I ought to get my life in perspective. He says it is the year that interrupts Rosh Hashanah and not Rosh Hashanah that interrupts the year. I certainly don't understand."

So, let me try again. Let me explain further.

Tomorrow morning, we read in the Torah of the willingness of Abraham to sacrifice his beloved son, Isaac, at God's command. God spoke and Abraham hearkened and obeyed with perfect faith and perfect trust.

When we read that story for ourselves and when we struggle with all our might to understand what was in Abraham's heart, then this struggle tells me that we want to have that connection to our people, our history, our tradition and our God.

Do you know when it is difficult to understand? When we don't care whether Isaac lived or died or whether God is here or not. When we don't feel that we really belong anywhere. When we say, "I am a Jew," and there is no sense of pride, understanding or satisfaction. That is when Rosh Hashanah is not really a new year but only an imperceptible pause in the rush of the same old days and the same old months.

Jews wish each other a good year, and I wish one for all of you and your loved ones. I pray that God will be with you. I pray for these simple things.

For our loved ones, I pray for a new year in which each day shall be like a shining coin we might find on the sidewalk, giving a new measure of joy. I hope that on each day happiness will be theirs without measure and renewed each night, renewed so generously that there will be room in their hearts for sorrow to enter. So, if in the days ahead a loved one cries, let it never be for an important reason; and may we be there to dry the tears and, with the magic of love, transform those tears into laughter and delight.

May the year not stand still for them. Let each day be a growing day, with strength for the body and growth of the spirit. May they learn to love words and sounds and come to understand the friendliness of books and the joys of music. Let them not be afraid, neither of their own weaknesses nor of the world's evil. With their dreams ever bigger than they are, let them hear God and trust in God.

And for you I pray that God gives your homes light, the light of love and of companionship. I pray that it will be a new year replenishing wells of affection, enabling waters of joy to flow clear and full. May each one of us recognize the difference between what we need and what we want; and may what we want not spoil the delight of what we have. Let us strive to be as rich as we can in generosity of spirit and not any poorer in envy and jealousy. I hope that our devotion to our loved ones, be they friends, lovers, parents or children will serve their needs and their abilities and not our ambitions.

Let us hope that we can help them to grow into what they have the capacity to become and not into what we think they ought to be.

Let us pray that we can assist them in finding the image of God in their lives and not their own image, nor only an image that is acceptable and approved by our friends.

These are some of my hopes as we begin this new year. These are some of my prayers as we begin these days of introspection and reflection.

May the new year find us filling our world with the simple blessings of brightness and hope.

AMEN

# Forgiveness and
# Then Perhaps Repentance?

## Yom Kippur Morning—1997

I have often felt that there is something strange about the order of the High Holy Days. Logically it seems that Yom Kippur should come before Rosh Hashanah. Yom Kippur is the day when we examine our sins and our errors in the past year. Rosh Hashanah is the day when we affirm the goodness of creation and begin a new year. Might we atone and repent for the sins of the past first and then turn to the future?

Logically that may be correct, but emotionally the order that is our tradition possibly works better. We begin to address the ultimate values in life and our own worth before we can go through the ordeal of considering all the things we have done wrong. We begin by expressing our faith in the future first, before we can face up to the mistakes we have made in the past.

If we did it the other way, if we began with the past, with counting up all our sins and all our shortcomings, perhaps we might never get beyond them. We might never get to the future. The risk is that once we start thinking of all that we have done wrong, we would become so depressed, so full of despair, that we would stop there, crippled by our guilt, unable to begin a new year. And so the Jewish calendar causes us to do it the other way. We begin by affirming life itself, by proclaiming the ultimate meaning of life, and then in the light of that affirmation, we are asked to examine our mistakes, the blunders, the missed opportunities and the wrongs we have done and to resolve that we will do better. The calendar bids us to begin with faith in God, in ourselves and in tomorrow. We seek a brand-new day, and then we set out to do the painful work of looking inside at all the guilt that has accumulated within us that needs to be shaken out, examined and cleaned off.

So last week's Rosh Hashanah service does not say a single word about sin or guilt or atonement. Instead all it talks about is glory and goodness and God. All it talks about is the wonder of new life and new beginnings. Only after these truths penetrate our consciousness, only after we really believe in tomorrow, can we begin the self-examination and the task of facing up to who we are, which is the agenda for Yom Kippur.

At the heart of this Yom Kippur agenda is the experience of repeating over and over a litany of sins, the repetition digging deeper into our souls each time and each year.

Yet the list of our sins to which the congregation has just confessed contains misdeeds not committed by most of us here. Why should we stand before God and ask for forgiveness for transgressions that we have never committed?

The first answer is that this acts as a shield for those who need to confess. When we as a congregation lift up our voices and say, "We have sinned by . . .," no one knows who is truly confessing to the misdeed.

There is another possible reason. We tend to split ourselves off from those who commit terrible crimes. They seem different in kind. Sometimes this protects us, sometimes it simply serves as an excuse. We turn criminals into monsters and therefore we need not share the sense that they, too, are people. Yet it is precisely the violation of what we share that is so horrible.

Judaism tries to teach us that those who commit terrible deeds are not monsters. They are human beings who have done monstrous things. If they were truly beasts, they would be blameless. They are human and responsible because they have betrayed their humanness.

We share humanity. It would be possible for us to commit those same terrible crimes in certain situations if we allowed ourselves to do them. Therefore, we are not allowed to say, "Well, given my character, I could never do such a thing." By confessing to sins we have not committed, we admit that such deeds are possible for us. We do not separate ourselves. We recognize the demonic potential that exists even in the most placid among us. We acknowledge the wisdom of our ancestors who taught that each one of us has an inclination to do good and an inclination to do evil. No one is totally pure who stands here this day.

We speak words to understand ourselves, sometimes the deepest pieces of ourselves. In the simple transition from "I" to "we" in the confessional, a world of insight is opened. The words of confession carry tremendous weights of meaning. We confess because confession sears the soul, it opens and exposes us.

All of the self-examination, and even self-flagellation, that occurs in the Yom Kippur confession seems strange at first. Why should we so deride and devalue ourselves? But of course, the point behind it all is that it is an exaltation of being human, not a devaluation, that is taking place. It is reminiscent of the joke about three scholars who stood in the synagogue during the confessional, beating their breasts and crying out, "I am nothing, I am nothing!" A humble unlearned man standing in the back of the synagogue saw the scholars debasing themselves and pleading before God. Seeing the great scholars behave like this, he decided that this was the proper way to pray. So he began beating his breast and screaming, "I am nothing, I am nothing!" With disdain, one of the scholars nudged the other, pointed to the man, and said, "Huh! Look who thinks he's nothing!"

The point of the joke is to underline the self-esteem that hides behind saying, "I am nothing." You do not say, "I am nothing" unless you think you are something. While in the joke self-esteem spills over into arrogance, in the confessional it is not arrogance but a healthy sense of value. Were we human beings not supremely worthwhile, there would be no point in confessing our sins. Sin would be expected. In Judaism, worthiness is the indispensable foundation for healthy self-blame.

Words sandblast the self. They reach toward truth, make their way inside us. What are we truly like? What is inside of us? To strip away the facades of self is the work of a lifetime.

Do words really possess the power to change reality? Can they truly atone for wrongs that have so profoundly affected so many people? The act of repentance, while seemingly humble, could possibly trivialize the very wrongs for which the wicked person has decided to atone—as if a few words could make up for all the suffering inflicted upon innocent people. Or is such an act, if freely done and truly meant, an act of contrition that is to be respected and an act of healing that can, in fact, help to heal past wounds?

Repentance is so extraordinary an act partly because it raises so many good questions. It seems to bear within itself such extraordinary possibilities: to change a person's sense of self; to clear an individual in others' eyes; to re-establish a harmonious relationship which had been destroyed because of someone's deeds. And yet, in the search for a morally appropriate response to wrongdoing, it is also true that repentance runs the danger of seeming puny—a lot of noise that really signifies nothing.

May our prayers this day enter our hearts, our minds and our bodies. May we, in seeking the way to make room for God in our lives, find a bridge to the hearts of others and seek a deep and abiding way to make love where there is indifference or hate, concern where there is indifference and peace where there is strife.

AMEN

# A Second Chance

## Rosh Hashanah Evening—1998

Some years ago, the late coach of the University of Alabama, Bear Bryant, was asked to do a television commercial for a regional telephone company. Coach Bryant's part was supposed to be just a single line at the end, ordering listeners as if they were his players to "Call your Mamma!" When filming his part, the Coach spoke from his heart. Unexpectedly, he turned to the camera and said, "Call your Mamma. I sure wish I could call mine."

The telephone company aired the commercial as filmed. The impact was overwhelming. Television stations were flooded with calls by those who had been touched by the sensitivity and tenderness of Coach Bryant. Many were prompted to speak to their own mothers or to another relative or friend they had been meaning to contact but never did. A man who expressed appreciation to the telephone company related that as soon as he saw the ad, he immediately called his mother with whom he had not spoken for several months because of a disagreement between them. They talked for nearly an hour. Whatever the source of their disagreement, neither could remember it by the time they had finished speaking. The telephone company representative thanked the man for his call but wondered why the caller was so effusive in his appreciation. The man explained that his mother had died the morning following that telephone call. He knew that if it had not been for Coach Bryant and that commercial, he would never have resolved his disagreement with his mother before she died.

I tell you this story on Rosh Hashanah because I think it reveals a great deal of truth about human life. We are not granted many second chances. As we live our lives, we must remember that human beings need each other. Each of us requires warmth, friendship, comradeship, love of family and the respect of the community.

In our Torah reading tomorrow morning, Abraham is asked to take his son, ascend the mountain and offer him as a sacrifice. Father and son travel with a unity of purpose, ready to meet great challenges—whatever they may be. Not once but twice the Torah tells us, "And the two of them walked on together." (Genesis 22:6,8) But what happened after the *Akeda,* the binding of Isaac? "Abraham then returned to his servants." (Genesis 22:19) Isaac is not mentioned. In fact, the two of them never are recorded as being together again. Abraham picks a wife for Isaac; the son inherits from the father, but never again do the two of them stand side by side.

So often in our lives we let little things get in the way of deep personal relationships. I don't think the *Akeda* is such a small matter. I'm not sure I would have ever spoken to my father again if he tried to sacrifice me. There are, however, many other types of sacrifices that lead to misunderstandings today.

How many times do people begin an argument, permit a wound to fester, allow estrangement to grow, and before they know it, forget what the original disagreement was all about? The reasons for alienation may be relatively minor: overlooking a family occasion, not offering an expected compliment, embarrassing a person, not keeping a confidence. But though the causes may be petty, the cessation of any meaningful relationship can be dramatic.

Few quarrels are as bitter as those between family members. I have sat with a family in mourning, quickly learned that the survivors have been feuding for years and recognized that this crisis will either bring out the best or worst in all concerned. There have been other times when I have been asked to officiate at family *simchas* (celebrations) with only a portion of the family present. The other members of the family either were not invited or did not wish to attend. A colleague pointed out that she has noticed something strange over the years. At a funeral for a parent, there is wailing, grieving and mourning among the children. But sometimes, when she officiates at the dedication of a tombstone many months later, she will see the children standing at opposite ends of the grave. Their body language speaks that they are not talking to one another. There has been a fight over some matter of the estate.

Rosh Hashanah reminds us that there is a need for reconciliation between human beings; that we must do *teshuvah,* repentance, and ask forgiveness for past misdeeds.

I understand that it was the social scientist Bruno Bettelheim who said that if you want to understand human behavior, you should study porcupines. They live in the forest where it is cold in the winter, and they are, therefore, forced to huddle together to keep warm. But when they crowd together, they hurt each other with their quills. So they recoil. But then they get cold again. So they alternate between being too far apart with the chill that results and being too close with the pain that stings. We dare not get too close to other human beings, yet we need their love, warmth, comfort and friendship.

Some of us seem to enjoy preserving a feud, even magnifying and exaggerating slights. There are children who harbor resentment for years against a parent because of something done. Husbands and wives have said things to each other that fester, irritate or wound. Siblings have destroyed their relationship because of a reluctance to forgive.

Tenderness, sensitivity and understanding go further than anger, frustration and revenge. We often miss chances to patch up meaningful relationships, to embrace those whom we really love and tell them how much we truly care.

Remember the film *Groundhog Day*? Bill Murray keeps getting another chance to have things turn out the way he wants them. But our lives are not a movie; we will not always get those second chances. Rosh Hashanah brings a message to us: "Reach out to your spouse, your lover, your parent, your child, your sibling or your friend." It may be difficult, and it may hurt—but it probably will be worth the risk. Don't wait to write, to call, to visit. Do it before it is too late.

There is another form of reconciliation needed on Rosh Hashanah. Not only must we reach out to our fellow human beings, but we must attempt to bring ourselves closer to God. And sometimes that is not easily done.

I have listened to bitterness expressed by those who have experienced pain and loss. At this time of the year, we can try to address the assertions that "It does not pay to be good. What is the use of prayer? What did I get out of worship services after all those years? I suffer so much, and God does not answer me."

It is important that we understand what prayer and faith can—and cannot—do. They cannot remove all barriers and sorrows in our lives. They can, however, bring ease to loneliness and heartache, comfort in hard times, hope for the future.

"Where is God?" asked Rabbi Menachem Mendl of Kotzk. "Wherever human beings let God in," was his answer.

Rosh Hashanah reminds us that after we seek reconciliation and forgiveness from others, then we can come back to God, to return and reconcile with the Divine Presence in our midst. Faith, in this world of skeptics, is unpopular. Belief in God is today often considered passé. And yet, in our personal life's crises we need faith more than ever. Even with all our advancements in scientific research and human knowledge, the sense of awe and mystery remains.

In the Book of Ecclesiastes, we learn that there is a God, but all we know is just that. We are unable to understand and comprehend the mysteries of the universe and even of our own lives. So much to understand and often there is so little that we can see.

This evening is the beginning of the Days of Awe. It is a time of the year when we each are given ten days to begin again and to ask others to forgive us. Let us be kind in our judgment of others, to forgive their weaknesses and to give ourselves and others another chance.

A final quote from a century ago. The British statesman Disraeli once wrote:

> Often we allow ourselves to be upset by small things we should despise and forget. Perhaps some man we helped has proved ungrateful . . . some woman we believed to be a friend has spoken ill of us . . . some reward we thought we deserved has been denied us. We feel such disappointments so strongly that we can no longer work or sleep. But isn't that absurd? Here we are on this earth, with only a few more decades to live, and we lost many irreplaceable hours brooding over grievances that, in a year's time, will be forgotten by us and by everybody. No, let us devote our life to worthwhile actions and feelings, to great thoughts, real affections, and enduring undertakings. For life is too short to be little.

So, Rosh Hashanah is here again. This time we should try to not make the same mistakes as we did last year for the chance may not come again. Unlike God, we don't have the opportunity to create a world. But we do have an even better and more important one—a second chance, an opportunity to begin again.

AMEN

# Why Be Jewish?

## Yom Kippur Evening—1998

For some of us the *Avinu Malkeinu* prayer that we just concluded is one of the highlights of these High Holy Days. We say this prayer five times between Rosh Hashanah and the end of Yom Kippur tomorrow. Though this prayer has become a lengthy petition today, it began as only one line—the last line of the prayer as we have it. Its author is said to be Rabbi Akiba of the second century, who composed his words on the occasion of a drought. It is told that his supplication for God's mercy, even in the face of humankind's apparent paucity of goodness, brought rain.

Tonight, we reacquaint ourselves with a central metaphor of these holy days: inscribing and sealing us in a book. We petition to be inscribed in the Book of Forgiveness; we seek to be inscribed for blessing in the Book of Life; and we ask to be inscribed in the Book of Deliverance and Redemption.

With little merit, we ask to be treated generously and with kindness. How can we possibly increase our merit? I submit to you that it is through our efforts of seeking justice in the world that we Jews have some chance of successful petition to the God of Justice. Through the seeking of a just and merciful world, we can hope to succeed in our quest.

Why should we—why must we—seek justice? Surely there is little need to begin with a recitation of the endless list of cruelties and miseries, of human pains and human sorrows in our world. From the land mines in Afghanistan to oppression in Tibet, from terrorism in the Middle East to poverty in these United States, and so on, injustice is our constant companion. No matter how insulated we ourselves may have become, we are altogether too sophisticated—and it is too late in the day for us—to require yet another rendition of the heartbreaking details of cruelty and indifference and of the pain that is their consequence.

We may not always know the precisely relevant statistics, but as every generation of Jews including our own has known, this world, our world, is badly fractured. Every generation of Jews, including our own, has understood that the heart of our Jewish enterprise here in the world is the repair of its fractures, its broken pieces.

Yet in every generation there have also been those who have questioned the propriety of that historic commitment, who have insisted that as Jews we have other priorities and other interests. That is, if it is justice we feel disposed to pursue, there is nothing distinctively Jewish about that pursuit and, therefore, it ought to be conducted under some other banner. And it follows that in every generation, including our own, it is necessary once again, and more than once, to make the case for a specifically Jewish devotion to the mending of our fractured planet.

So, why the Jews? The best way of answering this question is to tell Jewish stories, stories of where we have been and what we have done, stories that reach back to our earliest beginnings and stretch all the way to our own time. All those stories, from Abraham's dazzling and *chutzbadick* bargaining with God for the few righteous of Sodom and Gomorrah in order to save the world to the stories from our own time of the more modest interventions on behalf of the poor, the hungry and the dispossessed. They all are part of the important texts of the Jewish people that we need to hear over and over again.

Why at this time in our Jewish existence should a community so preoccupied with pressing internal problems raise its head above that fray and look to the urgent work, the larger challenge of repairing the world?

The answer to that question is that the Jewish community has no more urgent interest than the energetic pursuit of its values. For the central American Jewish problem of our time is not anti-Semitism nor is it intermarriage specifically or assimilation more generally. It is the problem of boredom, the fact that for very many American Jews, the experience of being Jewish does not seem to be about anything—not, at any rate, about anything that matters very much.

Many Jews are simply unable to fill in the blank in the sentence that begins with the words, "It is important that the Jews survive in order to____." In order to what? In order to survive? Lots of luck. Send out an invitation to the next generation that reads, "Please come survive with us," and see how many RSVP.

We do not need focus groups or questionnaires, much less gimmicks and slogans, to fill in the blank. We need only turn to the stories of our people, to which of life's many roads the Jewish people have most often chosen to walk down and which grand visions have most consistently inspired us. Perhaps there is only one statement to which more Jews through the centuries and even today would subscribe. One sen-

tence most accurately and comprehensively captures the most fundamental Jewish insight that this, our world, God's world, is not working
the way it was meant to—and that to be a Jew is to know that, somehow,
we are implicated in its repair.

Accordingly, the completed sentence reads, "It is important that
Jews survive in order to help repair this so-fractured world."

But if that sentence expresses the value we hold most dear, then
our overriding interest is to ensure its correspondence to our behavior. For if we persist in presenting ourselves as a community of
uniqueness and distinction, as a people with considerable ethical
achievement behind it and considerable ethical ambition before it,
as a people who seek God's mercy, others will want and deserve the
evidence to support our presentation. There must be truth in Jewish
self-advertising. Otherwise, it is not merely a misleading; it is an in-
dicting reminder of the gap between what we accomplished yesterday
and what compels us here today.

We come to this work at repairing the fractures from a specific perspective. Our Jewish world today labels, categorizes and assigns places
to each group of us. As Reform Jews, we hold certain principles central
to our definition of who we are and what motivates us uniquely.

Several of these guiding principles of Reform Judaism inform what
kind of Jew I am and how I act in the world. I wish to share four guiding
principles that are relevant here. I owe their organization to Rabbi Eric
Yoffie who recently inspired some of my thinking in this area.

First, we as Reform Jews are committed to a Judaism that changes
and adapts to the needs of the day. Judaism has always had an innovative character, and any attitude that resists continued change will make
Judaism an irrelevance. A Judaism frozen in time is an heirloom, not a
living fountain.

Second, we as Reform Jews are committed to the absolute equality
of men and women in all areas of Jewish life. A Judaism that diminishes
the equality of women is a Judaism that degrades our dignity.

Third, the commitment to social justice that I have been speaking
to is at the core of our beliefs. Like the prophets, we should never forget
that God is concerned about the everyday and that the blights of society
take precedence over the mysteries of heaven. In these self-indulgent
times, too many turn inward; but we know that there can be no future
for Reform Judaism without moral indignation.

Finally, there should be the principle that when we draw the boundaries of our Jewish community, we do so with the intention of being
inclusive rather than exclusive. There are boundaries, and they are ones

that need ongoing redefinition. That is self-evident, but they should not come in the way of full civil and religious rights for others.

Others, of different faiths and some of no faith, share our dream, and I am happy for them. The world's fractures are many and compound, and the work of mending requires a grand alliance. But we need to focus on what our special place is in the ranks of the menders. We are unique in that we have known slavery and freedom, election and rejection, exile and redemption; we have been both victor and vanquished, impotent and powerful, strangers and natives. And because of all that, our testimony on behalf of a world of dignity and decency may have some special weight.

For this is what we testify: Though we can still hear the hiss of the Egyptian slave master's whip and the canisters of Zyklon-B as the gas is released, God comes to us and we to God. This encounter is not in the wind and not in the earthquake and not in the fire, but in the still, small voice that echoes through time, asking us, like our ancestors were asked, "Where are you?" Then, just a handful of verses later, God asks, "Where is your brother?"

There is advocacy, there is direct service and there are deeds of lovingkindness. Many of them I have outlined and explained here in past years. Tonight, I am speaking of changes in attitude and perceptions, not of specific causes and calendar dates. There is no shortage of work to be done, and, as we are taught, the day is short. It is tempting in the extreme to evade the *henini* (the "here I am") that is expected of us. But there is a time when our energy and spirit flags, when we are tempted to ask, "Why the Jews? Why me?" The answer leaps out from the pages of our history.

Try to imagine these last hundred years of pursuing justice in an America without the Jews. If none of us had ever come to this country, you'd have to write a very different, a much-diminished history of our country and its efforts to redeem its promise. Try to imagine the Jews without a devotion bordering on obsession for social justice, and our heroic journey becomes a farce, our past and our future betrayed.

And if the effort should falter, what then happens to the downtrodden? And what then happens to us?

Although the work is endless and the day is short, we persist. We persist because mending the world is the authentic Jewish calling. We persist because those who have taken up the work of mending know that there is no greater joy, no deeper satisfaction than doing that work. We persist because we know that, though it is not incumbent upon us to complete the work, it is not right, it is not wise, and in the end we simply are not free to desist from it. We persist because we need to continue to be a proud and compassionate people.

We who seek blessing, who seek forgiveness and who seek to be written in the proper book, need whatever merit we can muster.

AMEN

# Four Things That Matter Most
## Rosh Hashanah Evening—2002

In some years, as individuals and as nations, survival is tantamount to victory. This past year, 5762, was one of them. Life is not a straight line in which we grow every year. Sometimes our stature is diminished. We regress. We fail. We lose our balance, and we fall. In the wisdom of the Jewish tradition and the rhythm of Jewish time, we are blessed with Rosh Hashanah, which begins a period of ten days when we can reassess the direction in which we are headed and change our course.

Rather than resign ourselves to repeating our errors and accepting the inevitability of disappointment and defeat, the beginning of the new year provides us with an opportunity to take to heart the verse that we read at the conclusion of each Torah service as we are closing the ark. We read from the last verse of the Book of Lamentations, *"Hashkivienu Adonai aleycha, v'nashuva; Chadesh yameinu k'kedem."* This can be translated as, "Take us back, Adonai, to Yourself, and let us come back; Renew our days as of old." (Lamentations 5:21)

In our own hearts and our own heads, we can decide what we hope to return to and what we hope to renew. On this night, many of us think of the things that mean the most in our lives. Tonight, there are hundreds of individual stories that we have brought into this space and this new year in each of us, in our hearts and minds and lives.

I will offer four thoughts about the themes of life and the new year, and it is my hope that one or more of them will provide you with the opportunity to go deeper into yourselves. (I am grateful to my colleague, Rabbi Harry Danziger, who shared with me this general concept some years ago.) After each of the four thoughts, I will leave some minutes of silence. In that silence, I invite you to let it take you wherever it will.

### Someone You Know Will Die This Year

For me, I will always remember as I say the prayer, *"Zochreinu l'chayim*—remember us unto life," that for a number of years my

114

parents were here with me at these services, and they are no longer. Next week at Yom Kippur, as in previous years at the *Yizkor* memorial service, each one of us will have the opportunity to recite the names of our loved ones whose prayer "Remember us unto life" was not answered. We will recall names of so many whose lives have ended.

Rosh Hashanah reminds us that none of us knows who will be here to give thanks next year for a new page in the Book of Life. None of us knows how many or how few will be our opportunities to share a moment with someone to whom we mean something and who means something to us.

Think of those people who are part of your life but from whom you have drifted away, not in anger but only in neglect. Bring them to mind and imagine that, God forbid, their names will be read next year at Yom Kippur—that their prayer *"Zochreinu l'chayim*—Remember us to life" will not be fulfilled. Imagine the phone call, the obituary in the paper that tells you of their death. Think of those about whom you would say, "I meant to call him—I meant to write to her." Think of those whom you might want to reach out to at the beginning of the new year. We pause . . . .

## What We Have and What We Need

We live in an affluent society. We are surrounded by advertisements telling us what we need, what we cannot possibly live full lives without. We are urged to acquire more, not to be satisfied with what we have. Instead we are often preoccupied and anxious over what we don't yet have. Someone has said, "People don't think of what they have but only what they're about to get." Too often, the present is not gift enough for us.

In his recent book, *Living A Life That Matters* (1986), Rabbi Harold Kushner writes about his experience of visiting people who are about to die. He observes that those who most feared death were those who felt that they had not done something meaningful while alive and that they would not be remembered.

On this night, take time to think about what you have and what you need, what is vital to your life and what is only peripheral. Take stock of the blessings you take for granted, not what new things may or may not be in your future. As a new year begins, turn your heart toward what you have as well as what you have done, and see if it is, in fact, what you need. We pause . . . .

## To Know What Is a Crisis and What is Not

We have many passing problems. Sometimes we make crises out of what are not. Some of us are so anxious over what school their child must go to—whether kindergarten or college—that we are convinced there is one right answer and all others will lead to tragedy. There are others among us who believe a test score or a particular paper will determine whether their life has meaning or not. Some people make decisions over a thousand things and torment themselves with the notion that any wrong turn will ruin their lives.

There are couples in conflict over arrangements for a wedding as though the menu and the color scheme will forever guarantee happiness or foreshadow disaster. There are people undergoing pain and inflicting pain because they magnify an incident into a crisis. And, so often, what seemed monumental is virtually forgotten within days or weeks.

On this night, when we turn to truly important things in our lives, think of those times in this past year that drained your spirit or sapped your soul with the worry that a single wrong decision or happening would ruin everything. Think of what did happen—of whether it was all worth it. Ask how many hours or days of this year you will lose in making a problem into a catastrophe. Look toward a year in which you can look with tranquility at life's stumbling blocks and say, " *Gam Zeh Ya'avor*—This Too Shall Pass." We pause . . . .

## Remembering What We Once Meant to Each Other

Each year, we hear of families that are broken or relationships shattered. People, once close, cut one another out of their lives or live in a state of hostility. There is estrangement between parents and children, brothers and sisters, husbands and wives. These are not casual acquaintances or distant family from whom we may have drifted apart. These were once loved ones but now people from whom we have cut ourselves off—perhaps physically, perhaps in spirit.

Sometimes it is inevitable, but most often it comes from people forgetting what they once meant to each other and why. Sometimes, it comes because we assume utter wrong on their part and no fault on ours.

How is that a child or a parent no longer speaks to the other? What leads a couple from the marriage *chuppah* to anger and bitterness, wanting to hurt and punish each other? Is it sometimes that they have forgotten that which they valued in each other? Is it sometimes that they have expected perfection in the other while demanding that their faults be ignored?

Are there broken relationships in which pride keeps us from taking the first step? Are there some in which we are afraid to be rejected? What is there to lose? If we have no contact, it has already been lost; we cannot lose more. Is it possible that two people separately are hurting, each wanting reconciliation, each afraid of the other's response? Will you be the one who waits or the one who acts?

If those words describe your life, think about the other person involved. Is it possible that you have taken your own disappointments and hurts and blamed them all on someone you once loved: a parent who made mistakes in rearing you? a spouse who cannot make you perfect? a child who does not fulfill your expectations? Do you expect them to be just as you want them to be, yet insist that your failings be understood and forgiven? Is it time for you to accept responsibility for your own actions, not simply blame them over what someone else is or is not, does or does not, did nor did not?

Or, if you have a relationship that is strong and loving with a parent or a child, a brother or sister, a husband or wife, consider it, give thanks for it, resolve to preserve it in this coming year by giving even more love and understanding. And to one another's prayers and hopes for this coming year, we say together "Amen."

# Finding Meaning
## Yom Kippur Evening—2002

What is at the heart of our personal story? What makes us whole, what reveals our uniqueness as humans and demonstrates some aspect of how we connect to others?

Just a few days ago I spent time reading the newspaper and a few minutes watching some of the events at Ground Zero. I was struck once again with the difficulty of expressing in words the emotions of the day. Though this did not stop the television commentators, it does pose a challenge to others. One of the articles I read on that day, September 11th, was an interview with Mayor Michael Bloomberg. In the article he noted that in Jewish tradition we raise a headstone after a year and that marks the time to stop mourning. What the mayor was referring to was the tradition of marking the first anniversary of the burial of a loved one with the unveiling of a stone. It is critical, however, to note that his quote was a bit misleading. Our tradition teaches us that this first *yahrzeit* can mark a change from one stage of mourning to another, not the end of our mourning.

It has become clearer to me as I grow older that relationships with the dead are not entombed in amber, fixed forever as they were at the moment of another's death. In fact, these relationships are like pieces of a puzzle except they are not fixed or solid. In fact, the puzzle piece can change over time with its size and edges changing like the liquid suspended in a glass container.

In our history there have been occasions where many have lost friends and family as a result of tragedies and have not yet recovered any of their remains. Thinking of them reminded me of the following story I read a few weeks ago about a woman at a burial who said how fortunate the deceased was to have had this funeral with family and friends gathered together. As a Holocaust survivor, she knew too well how many lie in unknown places, buried without a proper funeral and the comfort for loved ones.

118

This can help us to think about a grave and a burial as a blessing. As we remember in our hearts the brave firefighters who lost their lives rushing in to save others, the people who perished in the destruction of the Twin Towers as well as the planes that crashed and those whose remains are buried in the ashes and debris—we mourn their loss and understand this woman's words. For us, the living, as we continue to seek meaning during the Days of Awe, we are grateful for our blessings.

During these difficult times, with acts of terror so close to our homes, with friends or family suffering loss, with the daily threats to both people and hope in Israel, with the continued terror alert announced like a report card but with grades in color, only the naive or immature would disagree with the adage, "Life is not fair." But it is hard to accept this comment easily.

We dream dreams, and they are often broken. We make plans, and they may be shattered. We may think of new ventures only to realize that our strength has diminished, and we are advised to "slow down" or even worse, we are told "there will not be enough time." We may know that nowhere in the Good Book is it written that "life is fair," but we wonder. Life is filled with many challenges and many opportunities.

The Deuteronomy text that we will read tomorrow morning teaches us that when given the choice between light and darkness, we need to "choose life." Indeed, our Bible does document an unending effort to come to terms with unfairness and injustice, to discover what God asks of us. We face unexpected challenges, unanswerable questions, the very stuff of living. Immaturity is filled with blaming others. We all were adolescents once, and we each perfected, I am sure, placing blame into an art form. Life is messy. And the real question is: What shall we do about it? Nothing ever seems quite enough. But ours is always the choice of how we shall live our lives. Responding as best we can is perhaps what God has demanded of us all along.

We can be filled with the desire to blame others, rage, damn those around us, curse life itself, or like Job, even curse God. We can become obstinate, immovable, with a false sense of security, pretending that inertia will somehow protect us. Or we can choose to take the lemons and try to make lemonade.

The moment we stop changing and growing emotionally and spiritually is the moment we begin to die. The moment we let rage and anger control us is the moment we surrender the opportunity for renewal. The moment we fall into a rut, when everything new and different is uncomfortable and unacceptable, is the moment we let the spirit of death begin to shut the lid of the casket and remove our souls, our life force, from the possibility of what tomorrow might bring.

In the Book of Ecclesiastes we are taught, "How sweet is the light, what a delight for the eyes to behold the sun! Even if a person lives many years, let them enjoy themselves in all of them, remembering how many the days of darkness are going to be." (Eccl. 11:7-8)

A secret to finding comfort on life's journey, an answer to the question about the fairness of life, is written in our hearts and in the story of our unending search.

When a baby is born, we are instructed to pray for *chochmah, binah v'ha-sakel*—for wisdom, understanding and discernment. Of the three, discernment is the most valuable and rare. More than simple "smarts," it is the ability to look life's most serious challenges in the eye and find an understanding that is revelatory—what Martin Buber called "I and the Eternal Thou." Real life, meaningful living, is not simply found. It is the covenant of the search, a joint venture between the One who not only created us but who opens our eyes anew each day.

For many, tonight is one of the occasions in our year and in our lives when we measure time by the Jewish calendar. Yom Kippur is a scheduled pause as we seek the system of connectedness by which we make sense of our lives. This night and day can provide a template for our own personal time and space and relationship that is vastly greater than we know ourselves individually to be. It is a way to find out how we matter; how to connect our individual dots on the maps we use for things like history and destiny; the way we take a jumble of sensory data and shape it coherently into a picture.

Rabbi Larry Hoffman teaches us that this connectedness is one way of talking about dots that exist in our individual lives. To take stock of all our dots: our very existence depends on finding a pattern in the disparate events they represent. What have we made of ourselves, we wonder. Where do we go from here? How did we get this far? And why not farther?

So, too, we demand that the dots of our lives have some plan, some order, some direction. If not, we are living a tale of total unpredictability.

The shape of life is not a given; it is what we make of it. And we have no choice but to try and make something of it. The question is what that something will be. We come together as Jews, and part of our task is to inquire if our religious tradition can teach us anything about the meaning of our life into eternity.

What is the nature of existence, our own and eternity? The question is existential, not scientific. It is spiritual to its core. It has several possible answers but tonight I want to focus on one that speaks to me. The universe does not belong only to us. We share it with others, and we share it with a transcendent power that we struggle in our human language to describe, to whom we give the name God. We are its trusted keepers.

There is a centuries-old prayer, part of our daily liturgy, that acknowledges God and speaks of "daily miracles, morning, noon and night." A miracle by Jewish standards need not be the overturning of the natural order. On the contrary, a famous Talmudic passage describes one rabbi arguing with his peers and demonstrating his case by his ability to move water upstream and invoke voices from heaven. The rabbis reject his claims. These are inadmissible miracles precisely because God has arranged the world to be what it is, and that is the real miracle.

Some sins are not malevolent. To walk sightless among miracles in a state of blasé indifference to the miracle of being is itself such a sin. It is wrong in its own right because it squanders the preciousness of being. And it is wrong on a second count. Abraham Heschel spoke of the religious imperative of facing the world with "radical awe." To exist in the world is itself a miracle. That there should be a universe at all and that it should be ordered as it is—these are miracles that demand our attention. We know little or nothing about how we came to be or where we will ultimately go, but we are in charge of what we do while we are here. We can acknowledge the supreme gift of life and the willingness of God to share the universe with us to sustain us. We can see the reality of God breaking in on our existence with a gorgeous sunrise, the flow of the seasons, life itself (as long as we have it) and even death when it comes and when we are forced to confront it.

Religious thought struggles with issues of purpose and pattern. All the talk about God and salvation, reward and punishment, karma or nirvana is really about the way things fit together in time and space and the place we humans occupy in the chain of history or the purpose toward which that history is heading. Spiritual thinking takes these basic questions about the universe seriously, positing meaningful patterns in the face of randomness or pure blind fate. The most important question is whether humans really matter in the long run, and if so, how?

Meaning itself is the way one dot fits neatly with another. Think about what the word "seven" can mean: winning or losing at dice, the number of days in a week or other things with the meaning provided by context, without which the lone word seven means nothing at all.

Connecting diverse experiences is the way we manufacture a meaningful story of who we are. Also, it is the only way to make sense of
suffering. A question can be, from the personal perspective of tragedy,
what is the meaning of suffering? How, for instance, can people fit illness or pain into their lives so that they have biographies like everyone
else? Susan Sontag reminds us that while health is our home country,
we also hold citizenship in the land of illness. Most of us will spend
some time in each place.

Martin Buber, the great theologian of the twentieth century, dif-
ferentiated ways of knowing. We know most of the world scientifically.
It is a thing we measure, weigh, experiment with, or use for our own
ends. Another way of knowing, however, assumes we meet and treat
each other not as things to know objectively, but as primary consciousness that exist for no other purpose than to be there for each other, if
only for a brief moment. We are called upon to be distinctively human
in a sacred vein: to live the life of meeting—to see ourselves as a piece
of a large puzzle.

Especially in the ordeal of pain, illness or loss, we should remember the potential for meeting. Unable to cure disease, remove people's
pain, explain away great suffering, or bring back the dead, we can at
least deliver that shared moment of "being there," which is the way to
transform the exile of illness into at least the gateway to home; the way
also to identify with the suffering of others because we know we will
be where they are soon enough; and, in due course, the way we help
them (as we hope others will one day help us) make their way in peace
to a final home beyond the lifetime that we know. The importance of
meeting cannot deny the existence of suffering. But it can soften its
inevitable arrival.

The Jewish way of being in the world is, finally, a way of connecting with others because we are all part of the universe. I suppose some
solitary geniuses arrive at this conclusion and live it hourly as minori-
ties of one. But most of us need others on this human voyage that even
Jewish mystics described as dangerous to the psyche. The Talmud tells
of four who entered paradise, the rabbinic term for speculation about the
Ultimate such as we are now engaged in. Only one of the four escaped
alive. If ordinary mortals shun the lonely search for ultimates, who can
blame them? So, Judaism invents community, not market community
mind you, and something more than communities of truth, care and
virtue. The Jewish ideal is a sacred community in the image of God.

A Talmudic adage urges, "If you reach too far, you capture nothing." The successful beginning, then, is hardly a mission statement

announcing the need to find meaning in an instant or even a day or a month or a year. Sacred community begins with a modest but firm commitment to the journey and to finding the holy in such things as the ways we think, the blessings we say, the truths we discover, the homes we have or seek to find, and the relationships we build and sustain.

I pray that with God's help and the help of one another, we each will find the courage and faith to risk, to search, to see and to live life to its fullest.

AMEN

# The Difference Between Rosh Hashanah and Yom Kippur

## Yom Kippur Morning—2002

Like last night, I would like to begin with a reference to the events of this past Wednesday, September 11th. You will recall on that day the public officials invited to participate in the morning memorial service were assigned parts to read from "traditional" American texts. One read from the Declaration of Independence, one from the "Gettysburg Address" and one from Franklin Roosevelt's "Four Freedoms". There are probably a variety of reactions to this decision by Mayor Michael Bloomberg. It is not my intention to argue for or against the decision, but rather to note the historical similarities to our public recitation of the Torah and Haftorah.

For you see, Jews have been reading our traditional text of "teaching" or "law" for almost 2,000 years. It is believed by many historians that the introduction of regular readings of the Torah dates from about the first half of the third century of the Common Era and the selection from prophets shortly thereafter. Historians are not sure precisely what was read, how much of the text was recited, by whom and in what manner. For the purposes of this sermon, I want to call your attention to the notion that at important occasions there is ample precedent for reading texts that are not originally written by the speaker.

We Jews have been listening to the public reading of the Torah and Haftorah for almost two millennia. We turn to our tradition to give us a grounding in where we have come from, what are the eternal values that we should continue to hold dear and to ponder the implications of our text. It is customary to then use the occasion to amplify, apply, make references to, explicate and generally seek to find the relevance of our people's story from ancient times to the reality of today. Our Torah text this morning calls our attention to the importance of "choosing life," and then we hear from Isaiah in the Haftorah who questions whether "this is the fast that God wants us to observe." Reflecting upon these themes has led me to think about the contradiction between the ob-

124

servance of Rosh Hashanah and Yom Kippur. On Rosh Hashanah, our tradition teaches that we are supposed to feast. The authoritative Jewish law code, the *Shulchan Aruch,* says that you must eat and drink on this day in order to indicate through your rejoicing that you feel confident God has answered your prayers and given you a good year.

Ten days later, after we have shown our confidence in a good verdict by feasting, we are to return to synagogue again and this time feel frightened. To demonstrate this fear and anxiety, we are supposed to fast.

Is it feasting or fasting that leads a person to *teshuvah,* to the examination and reexamination of their life and their actions and seek to return to a better way? Rosh Hashanah says one, and Yom Kippur says the other. If we are supposed to feel confident that our verdict is a good one on Rosh Hashanah, why must we come back ten days later in fear?

Why are these two holidays so different in their moods if they are to accomplish the same goal, which is repentance? Let me suggest that it is because each of these two holy days deals with a different kind of sin and, therefore, a different kind of repentance.

Most holidays on the Jewish calendar are connected to some historical event. Pesach is connected to going out from Egypt; Shavuot is connected to the giving of the Torah; Chanukah is connected to the victory of the Maccabees. What are the stories or the events with which Rosh Hashanah and Yom Kippur are connected?

People think that Rosh Hashanah is connected to the creation of the world, but that is not so. That cannot be so here because Rosh Hashanah is a holiday that deals with sin and repentance, with being estranged from and coming back to God, and nothing of that is to be found in the story of creation. The story that is the source of the Rosh Hashanah observance is the story of what happened on the sixth day of creation. On that day, Adam was created; on that day Adam sinned; on that day Adam was judged, and on that day Adam repented.

What was the sin of Adam? There was only one thing that he was not allowed to do, and so that is what he did. His sin is understandable. Try telling children that they can sit on every chair in the house except one—and guess which chair they will want to sit on? Whatever a person is told not to do becomes the biggest challenge to them.

And so it was with Adam. God told him, "Don't"—and so he did. And afterwards he was sorry. He realized that he had committed a sin. He acknowledged it, and as a result, he was forgiven. We have Rosh Hashanah from that day to this in order to commemorate the truth that people can sin and atone and that, if they do, they will be forgiven.

What is the event of the story that is connected with Yom Kippur? It is the story of the sin of the golden calf. After the sin of worshipping this idol, Moses breaks the first set of tablets. Then he once again ascends Mount Sinai and returns forty days later with the second set, thereby renewing the covenant with God and the Israelites. Tradition associates this second forty-day period with the time between the first of the Hebrew month of Elul and Yom Kippur.

The biblical text explains that a total of 3,000 people worshipped the golden calf. This same text notes that there were 2,000,000 in the community of Israelites in the desert. Three thousand out of 2,000,000— not very many! What was all the fuss about if it only involved such a small group?

But it evidently was a big deal because our text tells us that God and Moses got very upset—so upset they nearly wiped out the whole people. The 3,000 who committed the sin, Moses executes. And then the text says, "On the next day, Moses said to the people, 'You have committed a great sin. I will go back up to God, and I will try to win atonement for your sin.'"

What is the sin? The people that he is talking to now did not do anything. Moses is accusing the survivors, the ones who did not worship the golden calf, of some terrible sin. What does he want from them? The atonement that he is seeking to win for them is for a sin that we cannot seem to identify.

The most well-known of biblical commentators, Rashi, helps us by explaining in a related passage that the sin the survivors were guilty of was turning their backs and ignoring the actions of those who built and worshipped the golden calf. Their sin was not what they did but what they did not do. It is the sin of being a bystander, the sin of standing by and doing nothing.

For the sins that we have committed we can atone easily enough. They are not so many, and they probably are not so severe. We have good reason to feel confident that God will accept our apologies for them, and so we are joyful on Rosh Hashanah. But for the things we did not do that we should have, for the sins where we stood by and watched and did not protest, these are the sins that have us anxious and concerned on Yom Kippur.

While this list may be countless—and we could elaborate on the many social ills which we are guilty of ignoring and minding our own business—I want to focus on another area of our lives where we commit the sin of omission. The sin of omission refers not only to what I did not do for others, but also to what I have not done for and to myself. It refers to the sin of not becoming what I am capable of becoming.

When God calls to Abraham in the Bible as we heard last week on Rosh Hashanah morning, God calls his name twice. Abraham! Abraham! The Midrash says that God did this because there were really two Abrahams, the Higher Abraham and the Lower Abraham. Each of us is composed of two selves as well—the self that we are and the self we could be, the self that we were meant to be. If we do not become all that we can be, what a sin of omission that is!

Before Yom Kippur concludes at the end of today, each one of us should look within. Which talent has been given to me? Which gifts are uniquely mine? Is it the ability to comfort? The ability to teach? The ability to give? Find out what your gift is and develop it. Look into your soul and ask, "What is my specialty?" For on Yom Kippur we are taught that God judges us. The judgment is based upon how we fulfill our task, our skill, our mission—that which no one else can fulfill.

On Rosh Hashanah we are judged by what we did right and what we did wrong. On Yom Kippur we are judged for what we have become and what we could have and should have become. It is a scarier day for more is at stake when we think of the sins of omission on our record.

May we atone for this kind of sin, too, and may we be forgiven.

AMEN

# Forgiveness

## Yom Kippur Evening —2003

Just a few minutes ago we read and then sang together the *Al Chet* prayer. This prayer is part of each service on Yom Kippur—evening, morning and afternoon. And the message of *Al Chet* goes to the heart of our work on Yom Kippur.

*Al Chet* has been part of the Yom Kippur liturgy for more than a millennium. In its present form, it dates back at least to the ninth century. An ancient ritual is to softly punctuate each line of the prayer by beating our breasts to demonstrate our atonement for the many sins listed in the prayer.

*Al Chet* asks us to confess to a long list of sins. The list is something of a poetic device. The first letter of each line is in alphabetical order—*aleph* for *onnes*, *bet* for *b'zadoon*, *gimmel* for *galouie*. And most of us are not guilty of these sins, at least in the literal sense. So why do we recite this long list aloud? It is a public confession. We stand together as a community to support each other and to be comforted by the knowledge that all of us, at one time or another, have failed to live up to our highest possibilities. In this way, we can more readily forgive others and ourselves. By doing it so publicly, we also are making a commitment to build on what we have acknowledged—to make a wholehearted effort to do at least some things differently in the year ahead. Singly and together we can take positive steps—even just a single step—to relieve some of the pain and suffering which human beings have wrought.

*Al Chet* sets before us a tall order of acknowledgement, forgiveness and renewal. The pivotal element, the quintessence, is forgiveness. Without the balm of forgiveness, it would be too difficult, too discouraging, to acknowledge our sins of omission and commission. Without the promise of renewal, forgiveness could not give hope for the future. The seeds of this hope, the heart of our *Al Chet* prayer, are contained in three simple phrases in the last line.

*V'al kulam eloha s'lichot, s'lach lanu, m'chal lanu, kapper lanu—* For all these sins, O God of forgiveness, bear with us, pardon us, forgive us. Why do we ask three times? Is it an accident? Another poetic device? An astute repetition for emphasis—to be sure we don't miss the point? Perhaps. But it seems to me that none of these explanations quite reaches the essence of *Al Chet* and Yom Kippur.

The rabbis taught us thousands of years ago that each written word is there for a reason, each word has a purpose, a message for us. So what is *Al Chet* telling us?

As many of you know, I'm a big fan of mystery fiction. I enjoy the detective work of figuring out "who dunnit" or why someone "dunnit." It is satisfying to see how clues fit together and how order can be restored to the messiness of daily life.

*Al Chet* gives all of us a chance to be detectives of a sort. We have three clues to the heart of Yom Kippur. As we've learned from famous detectives like Sherlock Holmes, Lieutenant Columbo and Adrian Monk, we should not be fooled by how the clues appear. We ought to pay close attention to a point that is made three times but with different terms. And we do not have to look at the clues in the order that they are laid out in the prayer.

Let's start with *m'chal lanu*. This word is the second rubric in the prayer, but it is Clue #1 for us tonight. What does *m'chal* tell us about forgiveness? *M'chal* comes from a Hebrew root which means "to erase." When it is used in rabbinic literature, it usually refers to a minor offense, one that can be erased with a simple apology. For example, being jostled on Muni at rush hour, forgetting a person's name or arriving late. These are minor discourtesies, '*michal*-able', erasable offenses. We offer an apology and are forgiven.

There is a Midrash which illustrates *m'chilah*, this most basic and simplest kind of forgiveness. As we learn in Genesis, Abraham felt deeply about the *mitzvah* of *hachnasat orchim*, welcoming guests and opening his home to strangers.

> One day, an old man came by. Abraham greeted him, invited him into his tent and brought him water to wash his hands and feet. Then the servants brought food and drink. Abraham said, "Before we eat, let us praise God who brings our bread from the earth." The old man didn't understand and picked up a piece of bread. Abraham was annoyed and said sharply, "In this house, we thank God before we eat." The old man understood no better and began to eat his bread. Abraham chased him out of the tent in anger.

> Almost immediately, the voice of God was heard. "Abraham, how could you? I've overlooked that old man's pagan ways for seventy-nine years. So can you. Go after him." Abraham chased after the old man, apologized to him, and brought him back to finish the meal.

That is *m'chilah*. It requires only that we recognize that a wrong has occurred. Repentance in the form of a straightforward apology—presumably well meant—is enough for *m'chilah,* for our sin to be erased. Then we can hope to go on about the business of daily life.

Now we turn to Clue #2 in understanding forgiveness. Number two is *kapper lanu*; it comes from the verb *kapper,* which means "to cover over." Yom Kippur derives its name from the same word. *Kapper lanu* applies to an offense that cannot be erased with a simple apology. Repentance must be deep, and restitution is required. Only then can one ask for and receive forgiveness. Both repentance and restitution are necessary for an offense to be "*kapper*ed," covered over.

*Kapparah* is important business, and it must be taken seriously. In contemporary terms, some offenses come with a standard form of punishment or restitution. We pay a fine for a parking ticket. Violations of civil law result in large financial settlements. Serious crimes bring jail time. And when one has not only repented but also made restitution, then presumably one's bill of sin has been paid in full. We are taught in the Talmud, "One who embarrasses a repentant sinner by mentioning their previous sins despises the presence of God, for in the place where a penitent stands even the fully righteous cannot stand." Then the offense is "*kapper*ed;" it is covered over, and life can go on. (At least that is the theory. Too often people are not allowed to escape their past and rebuild their lives. But that is subject for another time.)

So far, we have *m'chilah* and *kapparah*—forgiveness as erasing or covering over sins. Now for Clue #3: *s'lach lanu.* It comes from the verb that means "to forgive." It applies to offenses so serious that they cannot be erased or covered over. Neither apology nor restitution will suffice. At this point, Sherlock Holmes would light his pipe, Columbo would scratch his head, and Adrian Monk would obsess. And we can guess that we, too, are close to solving the mystery of *Al Chet.*

What do we do in the face of an offense so great that nothing the offender can do will make up for what happened? No words of apology are great enough, no amount of money is large enough, no punishment harsh enough, to restore life to what it was before. What can be done in the face of such pain, such loss?

We cannot afford to spend our lives hating. Only *s'lichah* can bring renewal. Forgiveness is the only choice we have, the quintessentially human thing to do. And in the moment of forgiveness, we are modeling ourselves on how God treats us.

One stirring example comes from the Book of Numbers. Moses commanded twelve tribal leaders to spy out the Promised Land. They knew what was expected of them. Two of them, Joshua and Caleb, were obedient. They returned and reported that it was a great land, a prosperous and fertile land and—most important—with God's help they could conquer it. The other ten leaders panicked. They said, "It's a good land, but the people! Like giants! We looked like grasshoppers next to them. There is no way to conquer that land." They forgot the difference that God's leadership was to make.

As often was the case in the Book of Numbers, God was angry. The Voice announced to Moses that the Covenant with the Jewish people that was only so recently established would be broken, the people destroyed and a new nation created out of Moses. Moses begged God saying, "*S'lach na*—please forgive them. They don't really deserve forgiveness. I can understand your anger. But *s'lach na*, because it is our only hope." And God answered, "*Salachti kidva-re'cha*—I pardon as you have asked."

And that is what we must do. We can forgive even if we cannot erase or cover over. What if the person I offended is no longer alive? Then what? The author Kate Wenner tells of her realization that the hardest work of atonement is not naming our transgressions but finding the courage to forgive ourselves for pain inflicted on others—an exercise that brings us face to face with shame.

During our *Yizkor* service tomorrow afternoon, we might wonder, "If this day is about forgiveness, why do we remember people whose lives are over? Hasn't their chance for forgiveness passed?" A Midrash tells us, "The dead have a new chance for forgiveness through us. We bring them into this day through our prayers, our memories. *Yizkor* is said on Yom Kippur because the dead, too, need atonement."

When we say *Yizkor* tomorrow, let us grant forgiveness to our dead. Try to grant it freely, grant it with love if you can. At the same time, forgive yourself for things done long ago or with someone you can no longer reach.

And so the mystery of *Al Chet* is solved. Three clues tell us that there are three kinds of offenses and three kinds of pardon: apology and erasing, repentance and restitution or covering over and forgiveness.

I wish for all of us this Yom Kippur that we have the honesty for *m'chilah*, the courage for *kapparah* and the blessing of *s'lichot*, of forgiveness. May we give *s'lichot* and receive it so that Yom Kippur can be a time of transformation and renewal.

# V'ahavtah, Viddui and Sh'ma Koleinu

## Yom Kippur Evening—2004

Ann Landers once received a letter something like this with a suggestion suitable for us today:

> Wouldn't it be terrific if a special day could be set aside to reach out and make amends? We could call it "Reconciliation Day." Everyone would vow to write a letter or make a phone call and mend a broken relationship. It would also be the day on which we would all agree to accept the olive branch extended by a former friend. This day could be the starting place. We could go from there to heal the wounds in our hearts and rejoice in a new beginning.

Ann Landers was really Esther Lederer, and she knew that Judaism has a "Reconciliation Day." It is called Yom Kippur. We are here for reconciliation with ourselves, with our family and friends, with God.

Our Yom Kippur liturgy guides us on a journey of reconciliation. Our liturgy has been shaped by centuries-old traditions and decisions that have led to the organization of the fixed order of the service as we see it in our prayer book. Though the early Reform Jews of almost two centuries ago made certain changes and deletions in the traditional prayers, we still follow an order in worship similar to that which has been part of synagogue prayers for many, many centuries. My sermon tonight is in three parts that will allow us to pause and reflect on three prayers that show us the way toward reconciliation.

### After V'ahavtah

The prayer we have just chanted in Hebrew and then read in English is *V'ahavtah*—"You shall love the Lord your God." What does it mean to be commanded to love God with all your mind, with all your strength, with all your being?

132

Our rabbinic tradition teaches that we have within us a duality—two inclinations—*yetzer hatov* and *yetzer harah*. We have the inclination to do good and the inclination to do bad. Both of these inclinations are needed to love and serve God. It is not enough to love God only with our inclination to create good. Rather, we also should use our inclination to hate, to hate evil. Both inclinations are called upon in our love of God.

What about the second part of the instruction—to love God "with all our being, with all our soul?" Our tradition teaches that we should be willing to defend the principles that we believe in with our very lives. From the deepest part of our soul, we are pledging to love Adonai, our God who alone is one.

These words that are set before us have been passed to us by our ancestors, sometimes through great adversity. And we are obligated, commanded, to pass them on to future generations through our thoughts, our teachings and our actions toward others. The essence of the *V'ahavtah* prayer should be ever-present in who we are as Jews.

Dr. Victor Frankl, a Viennese-born psychiatrist, survivor of Auschwitz, wrote about the moment he learned this within the horrors of the concentration camp. He had hidden the manuscript of his first book in his coat. The coat was taken away from him when he arrived at the camp and exchanged for an old ragged one belonging to an earlier victim. When he plunged his hands into the pockets of this second coat, what did he find? Instead of the many pages of his manuscript, he found a single page torn out of a Hebrew prayer book. And on that page? The words of the *Sh'ma*. Victor Frankel understood this moment as a challenge to live his thoughts instead of merely putting them on paper. So it should be for us.

The *V'ahavtah* can be a challenge for how we wish to live in the years ahead. The prayer continues, "And these words which I command you this day shall be upon your heart."

Why does it not say "in your heart?"

Because most of the time our hearts are tightly closed, and the words of God are unable to enter. But every so often, there is a rare, precious moment, a moment of joy or awe or insight when our heart opens a little bit. And if we pray regularly, then when the heart opens, the words are there and can enter.

But if we never pray, then when that rare moment comes and the heart opens, there will be no words available to express what we feel.

The late Abraham Joshua Heschel told a story about a small Jewish town in Poland. It had many kinds of crafts people to make and repair clothes and shoes, to construct buildings and furniture. There was no watchmaker. Over the years, many of the clocks no longer told the correct time, and there was no one who could fix them. Most of the owners stopped bothering to wind their clocks altogether. A few decided to keep on winding their clocks even though the time was not accurate. One day a watchmaker came to the town, and everyone rushed to him with their clocks. However, the only clocks that could be restored were those that had been kept running. Those that had been abandoned were too rusty to be repaired.

And this is why we pray—so that the words may be upon the heart, available, able to enter, if and when the heart ever opens.

### *After Veddui and Al Chet*

A few moments ago, we recited the confessional part of our Yom Kippur service with the *Veddui* and *Al Chet* prayers. These prayers were written more than a thousand years ago and offer a litany of sins. The prayers are in the form of an acrostic, making use of each of the twenty-two letters of the Hebrew alphabet: *Alef–ashamnu, bet–bagadnu*, and so on.

The longer confessional, the *Al Chet* prayer, was expanded over several centuries to become a complete double alphabetical acrostic containing forty-four lines. Our text tonight is an abridgement of that traditional source, and we will read a slightly longer form in tomorrow's services.

These prayers might strike us as a highly artificial literary device and even inconsistent with the deep seriousness of their theme. Yes, there is little doubt that those who composed these prayers were displaying their verbal inventiveness and literary skill. It is likely that the acrostic device was adopted before printed prayer books came into existence or when they were still quite expensive and scarce as an aid to the worshipper's memory. Most important, however, to Jews then and now is the content, not form, of the prayers.

In fact, it is the content with which many of us modern Jews take issue. Should not a confession be personal, reflecting our own experiences, our own shortcomings and failures? Here, however, are impersonal and general formulas, speaking of sins of which we may or may not be guilty. This notion of silent confession misunderstands the true nature and purpose of these prayers. There are other times for personal and private confession on Yom Kippur. The *Viddui* and *Al Chet* are the collective confession of the community. Notice that they use the word "we." "We have committed offenses, we have transgressed . . . . " Each one of us when reciting these prayers associates ourselves with the community and acknowledges the collective guilt we share. And if we are honest with ourselves, there are probably very few of us who will not see in at least some of these mentioned a truth about our own lives and our own deeds.

There is another reason why all of us recite the entire list. It gives us each a measure of privacy. The person next to us cannot know which sins we are reciting because we really did them and which sins we are simply saying because they are in the book. This enables each of us to confess to God in the privacy of our hearts even while we pray together in public.

When we look closely at the *Viddui* and *Al Chet*, we see that they only deal with moral violations, offenses against other persons and against one's self, not with infractions of Jewish ceremonial or ritual law. These are the moral commandments—between people— and so perhaps weightier than the ritual commandments that are between us and God. On these holy days, it is the infractions between one person and another which we seek to acknowledge and name, for which we seek forgiveness from our families, friends and neighbors.

A central word and concept in these confessions is the Hebrew word *chet*, which does not have the same overtones as the English word "sin." *Chet*, which is really a term from archery, meaning "missing the mark." This concept of sin suggests a straying from the correct ways— a *chet*. It is possible that every mistake or failure is the wrong amount of a good quality.

A rabbinic student told the story about coming back from officiating at a synagogue during the High Holy Days and complained to his teacher.

Professor, I simply cannot take the *Al Chet* anymore! All these sins, repeated so many times—it is just too much!

And the Professor said to him, "Of course it is. I haven't said them all in years." The student was taken aback. Could it be that his teacher, who was such a genuinely pious person, had not recited the *Al Chet* in years? "What do you mean?" he asked.

"It is very simple," said the Professor. "What I do each time is I choose one of the sins on the list, one that applies to me. And I think about its implications and meditate on how and why I committed it. By the time I am finished with that one sin—the rest of the people have finished reciting the whole list.

We have missed the mark—individually and collectively—at some time during the past year. Tonight we acknowledge our *"chet"* so we can renew ourselves and our community.

### After Sh'ma Koleinu

We just sang *Sh'ma Koleinu*, "Hear our voice, Adonai, our God." It begins in a manner similar to the usual *Sh'ma* prayer that is part of every service. But to that usual beginning we add, "Have compassion upon us, and accept our prayer. Help us to return to You." What does returning mean to us?

Our ancient Jewish tradition offers the following story:

> An angel was sent down from heaven to bring back the most precious thing in the world. When the angel reached earth, the angel came upon a wounded soldier who had given his life for his people and his country. The angel brought back to heaven the soldier's last drop of blood. In heaven the angel was told, "This blood is precious, but it is not the most precious thing in the world."
>
> So the angel descended to earth a second time. This time the angel brought back the soul of a person who had given her life to save another. They said to the angel in heaven, "This soul is precious, but this too is not the most precious thing in the world."
>
> Again the angel returned to earth in search of the most precious thing in the world. The angel saw a robber enter the home of a very rich couple. The robber planned to kill the rich man and take all his money. Just as the robber was about to do this, he noticed the rich man's wife in another room of the house. She was saying a bedtime prayer with her small daughter. Suddenly the robber remembered how his mother used to say the same prayer with him. A tear fell from the robber's eyes, and he ran from the house.
>
> It was this tear that the angel brought back to heaven, and everyone there said to the angel, "This tear is the most precious thing in the world, because there is no one greater than one who decides to return and repent."

So it is with us. Yom Kippur comes every year and gives us another opportunity to return, to repent, to not run from the presence of God. Being human, we sometimes err and go astray. Therefore, Judaism includes the confessional on Yom Kippur. We need no priest to intercede for us when we confess. United with others in prayer, we raise our voices together directly to God, and we thus reestablish the relationships that makes us one with God.

We have come full circle in our journey of reconciliation—from reflecting upon what it means to love God to asking God to pardon our iniquity, remember God's mercy and accept our prayers. MAY IT BE SO

# Editing the Story of Our Lives

## Rosh Hashanah Evening—2006

I want to share with you some of my past. I graduated from high school in Los Angeles in 1963. That summer and the next I worked at MGM studios. My uncle, a well-known and successful film editor, arranged for me to have a summer job. I learned a bit as that summer and the next progressed about the craft of film editing.

When silent movies began, all the editing was done from the film of one camera. Everything proceeded from the story line of that single camera and emphasized the linear progression of events. Then the technology improved, and two separate cameras filmed events. The editor spliced frames from two perspectives into a single sequence. The result was more complete and more dynamic. Later, multiple cameras were used concurrently to shoot footage from several angles. The editor artistically combined the different angles and events along with the soundtrack, frame by frame, creating livelier action and sometimes surprising visual effects. Today's digital editing gives film editors hundreds, even thousands, of clips that they are able to interweave and relate—cutting and pasting images into a composite product.

But the essence of every movie is the story, the editing a process that gives a coherent direction and meaning to the finished product. Maybe you feel the same way I do. How I wish I could tell my story like a film editor does—to edit it like a movie. Have you thought about being able to take out the bad parts, speed up the slow parts and look deeper into the good parts? What would our edited life stories be like?

Our biblical stories often combine bad episodes with good ones, some that are boring with ambiguities and shadings along with the clear story lines. Tomorrow morning, we will read of Abraham and his journey with Isaac up a mountain. This is the same Abraham who many years before heard God's command to leave all that was known and familiar and embark on a journey that led him to become the patriarch of a great nation. Not a smooth process—one with some very difficult times and glorious moments—rather like our lives, if a bit more dramatic.

Each one of us is also on a journey, and our life stories have drama, tension, tears and joy. What do we do with the parts we would like to forget? The parts we are proud of? The parts yet to be written? The reality is that we can't edit out the parts we don't like nor fast-forward to get to the ones we most enjoy. So we're stuck with them, all of them, to find the meaning and make sense out of them. That is our challenge—our opportunity—for these High Holy Days, to piece together parts of our lives.

We are here together in the synagogue at this time for reflection, for critical self-examination and for confession of failure. A central part of our prayers for the High Holy Days is when we recite together these words, "For these sins, O God of mercy, forgive us, pardon us, grant us atonement."

We do not say these words publicly because we have committed heinous crimes. We are not terrible people either in our eyes or in the eyes of others. On balance, we might even claim to live reasonably decent lives. Yet if we open ourselves to honest self-scrutiny, we know we are not all that God—or we ourselves—would want us to be. Rabbi Sam Karff reminds us that spiritual progress often is uneven. For most of us, we sense a mismatch between how we live and how we think we should be conducting our lives. And yet it is possible to turn, to return.

So, we are together again for another High Holy Day season. What good does it really do for us? What will we make of it this time? Yes, it is wonderful to see family and friends, see the roundness of apples and taste the sweetness of honey, remember perhaps with new understanding or longing Rosh Hashanahs past. But we want more.

Perhaps you are like me. I vow each year to be different. I want to be more spiritually mature, to be less dependent upon peer approval, to be free of jealousy and envy, to truly delight in the attainments of others. This is what I wish for.

Each of us has an idealized image of how we would like to be, but there are gaps and inconsistencies that stubbornly mar our personal story. We are like broken vessels aspiring to an ethical wholeness that eludes us. Sooner or later, we discover that the absence of wholeness is not just part of our story. It is inherent in the human condition.

Consider this moment from our tradition. About 2,400 years ago, Ezra, the scribe, and Nehemiah, the Jewish governor of Judea, assembled a small congregation of Israelites in an outdoor sanctuary. This convocation took place on the first day of the Hebrew month of Tishrei. It was Rosh Hashanah. The people offered prayers of praise to God. Ezra unrolled the Torah scroll that contains God's commandments. He read a story that related how in the wilderness the Israelites had often failed to abide by those commandments. When the people measured their own lives against the teachings of the Torah, they broke down and wept. They felt so worthless. Then Nehemiah made this remarkable statement: "Don't weep. This day is holy to the Lord. Dress up and eat and send portions to those who are in need [so that they can eat too] because the delight of the Lord is your strength." (Nehemiah 8:10)

On the Day of Judgment Nehemiah preached to the public: Don't torture yourselves because you haven't perfectly fulfilled the covenant. Let God's acceptance of you in your humanness be your strength. By all means strive to grow and move toward spiritual wholeness. You can make significant changes for the better—but keep perspective. God respects the rough edges, the bad parts, of your life. God doesn't expect you to have a perfect story; neither should you. God accepts you in your brokenness, your imperfections; therefore, you can accept yourself. God's delight in your humanness is your strength.

Tonight is the beginning of our new year. There are a few important things we can do. As the year begins, I am going to work on improving the good parts of my story. I will try to use every opportunity to extend kindness to others, and I will seek wholeness while admitting my imperfections. I hope you will join with me.

Tomorrow morning when I open my eyes, I will thank God that I have another day. Every day, every minute, every breath truly is a gift. As the new year begins, may we strive to see that and make something of the small opportunities that come our way each day.

Our life's journey so far may not be the story we hoped for. There is brokenness and there are holes, but there are sparks of light also. We need all the parts for our own stories to be complete—and, as one community, join our stories into a greater narrative. At these High Holy Days and in the months to come, we can support each other—balancing strengths and weaknesses, moving individually and communally toward wholeness.

I pray that we find a way to strengthen each other and to work on improving our imperfections that are part of the human condition. God's delight in our humanness is our strength. Let your humanness be your strength.

AMEN

# Forgiveness is Not Forgetting

## Yom Kippur Evening—2006

Do you realize that it's just four weeks until Halloween? It's more than just a quirk of the calendar, for I believe that there's a connection between Yom Kippur and Halloween. On first glance, it seems a bit far-fetched. After all, there is no place for candy, costumes or pranks in our holy day observance. Rabbi Harold Kushner reminds us that on Yom Kippur we are connected in a special way to the spirits of people now gone who were important in our lives.

Now we all know that Halloween is not part of the Jewish tradition. But there's a subtle and significant relationship. Halloween is short for All Hallows Eve or what we might describe as *Erev* All Hallows Day. All Hallows Day was a special time of religious festivities in some European pre-Christian traditions when people believed that the spiritual world could make contact with the physical world. It was a solemn period, a liminal state—a period of openness when thoughts and behavior are relaxed, opening the way to something new.

So there's a connection for us between Halloween and Yom Kippur. We might think of it as a time when our thoughts are open in special ways—open to the tangible world around us and also to the world of the spirit and of memories.

Jewish tradition teaches that the month before the High Holy Days—the month of Elul—is when we ask the people in our lives for forgiveness. And just a few moments ago, before we chanted the Kol Nidre prayer, we asked God for forgiveness. Many of the prayers we read together tonight and tomorrow will remind us to ask forgiveness.

Most of the time we think about forgiving other people or asking them to forgive us. But we rarely think about asking forgiveness from the people we love who are no longer with us . . . and that's very important to do. If we can listen to the voices of those who we can no longer reach out and touch, we can give and receive a special kind of forgiveness. There are voices lodged deep in our hearts and memories. We need to pay close attention to these voices.

For some of us, being here in this sanctuary makes it very easy to hear the voices of loved ones—those who once sat nearby or even in the very seats where we sit right now. Some of us remember other synagogues, other holiday tables, other special places that connect us fast and sure to the voices that once loomed so large in our lives. In the quiet of this moment, our memories become vivid and real enough to touch.

We can draw wisdom and strength from those who have gone before us if we turn inward on this holy day. We can transform the fullness of memory into forgiveness that lights a path for us into the new year.

The voices that we can hear in the quiet of Yom Kippur set before us a challenge: to look both backward and inward. Backward: so that we can look forward to honor the past in all of its complexity so that we build for the future. Inward: so we can recall memories that are among our most precious possessions. They last for a lifetime and beyond. They tell us how we came to be, who we are today. They give hope, comfort . . . and pain. Memories of love and memories of loss come together, and we can't have one without the other.

Naomi Shemer, the beloved Israeli composer, wrote a song "*Al Kol Eileh, Al HaD'vash v'al Ha-Oketz*"—"For the Honey and the Sting" that speaks to the heart of Yom Kippur. The title comes from a story in the Talmud about a man who sticks his hand into a beehive to take the honeycomb and is stung by the bees. He walks away muttering, "I can do without the honey and without the sting." Here is a hard truth. If we welcome the sweet and the good and the joy in our lives, then we are vulnerable to the bitter and the harsh and the sorrow. The honey comes with the sting.

And it's the same with the voices that we hear on Yom Kippur if we let them in. They say to us, "We bring you memories of joy and sorrow, memories of days that warm your heart and days that make you cry. And we come to remind you that you can't have one without the other."

Let's listen to what these voices can teach us.

They say, "Remember us. Remember us because we live on through your stories and your actions. We don't live in the cemetery. Our picture may exist in a photo album, and our name may be on a memorial plaque—but the only place we live in this world is in your heart. Pass on our names and our stories, the good that we wanted to do and our hopes for the future."

And they say, "Remember us because you need us. You can't understand who you are, where you come from, why you behave as you do, if you forget the people who shaped your world."

And the voices that visit us here tonight are saying, "Remember us. Remember us even if some of the memories are difficult, memories of illness and helplessness, memories of words unspoken that should have been spoken, and words spoken in haste, because you can't hold on to the good memories, the golden hours, without the sad memories tagging along as well. You won't have the opportunity to taste the sweetness of the honey without some of the sting of the bee."

And they say, these voices that have joined us for Yom Kippur, they say, "Remember us with love. Let the good memories prevail. And let's draw hope and comfort from them. And the other memories—the bitterness and disappointments, the anguish and regrets—for these memories, now is time for forgiveness."

We can—indeed, we are commanded—to forgive. And for forgiveness to be complete, we must seek out and say in our hearts, "I forgive you . . . for deeds of omission and for deeds of commission." And we can ask that they forgive us, too. Yom Kippur gives us the opportunity to acknowledge what was and how it might have been, to look backward and inward and then go forward into the new year with hope and strength and courage.

In his book, *Aging Well* (2002), George Vaillant of Harvard University talks about the traits of personality that seem to forecast a happy and successful life. One of the qualities that he identifies is the willingness to forgive people we're upset with or angry at. Dr. Vaillant also reminds us that forgiveness means recognizing that it's too late to have a better past. All we have is today.

And our tradition gives us Yom Kippur as a moment when we stand between yesterday and tomorrow, a liminal time, one of transition when we step outside of our normal routines to listen, to think, to heal. It is an opportunity to take stock, take a long hard look at where we have been and then commit ourselves to making the most of tomorrow.

Nelson Mandela, years after he left Robben Island, South Africa, following a long time of painful imprisonment, was asked, "How did you forgive your jailers?" And Mandela responded, "When I walked out of the gate, I knew that if I continued to hate these people I was still in prison."

To forgive does not mean to forget. Indeed, we should not forget. Rather, forgiveness means that we can live more fully. It gives us deeper understanding, greater compassion, richer appreciation for all that is good in our lives and the potential to make the most of this new year. With forgiveness comes gratitude and the opportunity to make the world a better place in some small way.

There will be moments during the Yom Kippur service when the voices you hear will not be my voice or the cantor's or the hundreds of people chanting around us. They will be voices from our past, asking to be remembered, speaking of pain and courage, speaking of and love and thanks, speaking of memory and forgiveness.

On this Yom Kippur, I pray that we can forgive those whose memories live deep inside our hearts, thereby transforming the fullness of memory into forgiveness that lights a path for us. Then will we truly be ready for the new year 5767.

# The Power of *Tzedakah*

## Yom Kippur Morning—2006

The great American philosopher and psychologist John Dewey was a champion for progressive education. He believed that the classroom was a place to prepare new members of society with an understanding of the core values of the culture and skills like critical thinking and problem-solving to help society improve itself. Dewey knew that the challenges of contemporary society could not be solved with rote memorization and the unthinking acceptance of the status quo. He firmly believed that each person could—with the proper foundation in life—contribute to repairing social ills.

A story is told—perhaps apocryphal, but it doesn't really matter—that the late Al Shanker, who was president of the American Federation of Teachers for many years, went to see John Dewey and asked for his advice.

Shanker asked John Dewey the question that was most on his mind, "Is it possible, really, to fix America's schools?"

Dewey said, "Yes. Yes. There are two ways you can do it. You can do it the miraculous way, or you can do it the natural way."

And Shanker asked, "What is the natural way?"

Dewey said, "Well, the natural way would be if a band of angels descended from heaven, scattered across the landscape, went into every school in the land, waved their hands and fixed the schools."

Shanker said, "My God! What's the miraculous way?"

And Dewey replied, "The miraculous way would be if the people did it themselves."

We can perform miracles, too. And this is what our tradition teaches us on this Yom Kippur morning.

A few minutes ago, we read the *Unetanah Tokef* prayer. It begins: On Rosh Hashanah it is written, on Yom Kippur it is sealed. Who shall live and who shall die?

This seems to speak of fate . . . of the inevitable.

But the ending—ah, here we find a reason to hope, guidelines about what we can do to take control of fate. The prayer ends "*U'teshuvah, u'tefilah u'tzedakah ma'avirin et roa hagzeirah*—Repentance, prayer, and *tzedakah* avert the severity of the decree."

Today, we are repenting—here and together this day. And we are praying as one community and each of us in the solitude of our hearts. But what about *tzedakah*? How does that affect our fate?

*Tzedakah* is one of those Hebrew words that is hard to translate accurately. We often say that *tzedakah* means "charity." The word "charity" comes from the Greek word "caritas" meaning love. In this sense, a charitable act happens when I, of my own free will, give to another out of my sheer openhearted, unencumbered love. That is a wonderful concept—but it is different from the essence of *tzedakah*.

The word *tzedakah* is derived from the Hebrew root *tzade-dalet-kuf*, meaning righteousness, justice or fairness. The Torah teaches us, "*tzedek, tzedek, tirdof*—justice, justice, shall you pursue." (Deuteronomy 16:20)

In Jewish tradition, giving to the poor is not viewed as a generous, magnanimous act. It is an obligation, an act of justice and righteousness—yes, our duty. We are commanded to perform acts of *tzedakah* with our resources or our time. Love for the other is irrelevant. We give because it is just.

Judaism teaches that a certain amount of what we have doesn't belong to us. It belongs to the needy, and we have been entrusted to make sure it gets there. *Tzedakah* is rooted in obligation, not love—although it is wonderful if love can be part of it. The Hebrew prophet Isaiah spoke to this very issue in today's *Haftorah* portion—the well-being of the neediest members is the measure of the health of that society. Frankly, this communal well-being is too important to be dependent upon other people's feelings of love and generosity.

Our tradition reminds us over and over again how important *tzedakah* is. In the Talmud we read, "*Tzedakah* is as important as all the other commandments put together." (*Baba Batra* 9a)

There is a story told in the name of the sage Hillel from 1,900 years ago. He once asked his students,

> "If I have 1,000 *dinars*, and I give away 300 of them to the needy, how much do I have?" The students answered, "Obviously, you have 700 left." To which the teacher responded, "Your math is good, but you don't understand *tzedakah*. I don't really have the 700 *dinars*. I could lose it by accident or in a business venture, or, with luck, I might be able to leave

it to my children. But—for the rest of my life—I KNOW I have the 300 *dinars*. I can always, even at the moment of my death, look back on those *dinars* that I contributed to *tzedakah* and know that it was something that I did that really helped the world. So the answer to the question is: If of 1,000 *dinars* I give away 300 *dinars*, the amount that I most truly have is 300 *dinars*."

Our community has its fair share of major league *tzedakah* heroes. Many members of our congregation are very generous in helping others—with their time, their expertise, their resources. And our local communal agencies, like Jewish Vocational Service and Jewish Family and Children Services among others, are dedicated to fulfilling obligations of *tzedakah* for Jews and non-Jews alike.

I think—I hope—that each of us has at least one special place where we fulfill the obligation of *tzedakah*. And I ask that you consider increasing your efforts by adding another one or redoubling your efforts in this new year. There are many, many worthy destinations for our *tzedakah*. I ask that you consider four that have special relevance for our community.

I ask you to think about four opportunities for *tzedakah*: one that is deeply rooted in our home at Sherith Israel, two that are part of the ties that bind us to our people's home in Israel, and one that addresses terrible injustices in the world.

The first is the program established at Sherith Israel thirteen years ago in response to a sermon from Rabbi Alice Goldfinger. *Hamotzi* has been preparing food for the hungry and the homeless every week. On Sundays, in the Newman Hall kitchen, teams cook and package food which is then distributed to shelters. We need new volunteers to be part of this program, and we need donations to help pay for the costs of this endeavor. You can shop, chop, stir, wrap, deliver, pay. The work awaits more helping hands.

A second destination for *tzedakah* is our local Jewish Community Federation's Israel Emergency Campaign. The Federation has targeted relief to those living in the north of Israel which bore a particularly large burden of the war last month.

The third opportunity for *tzedakah* is supporting the efforts of the Leo Baeck High School in Haifa, Israel. Part of the World Union for Progressive Judaism's efforts in Israel, the Leo Baeck School provides assistance to the entire community in Haifa—Jew and Arab alike.

A fourth opportunity is the American Jewish World Service's efforts to turn the tide of genocide in the Darfur region of the Sudan.

Do we take literally the words of the *Unetanah Tokef* prayer that *tzedakah,* along with repentance and prayer, literally can change our fate for the new year? That is a matter of personal belief. What I am sure about is that we do have control over how we experience what life brings us and what we do with the time we have.

Death is inevitable, but the tragedy of a meaningless life is up to us. *Tzedakah* makes a difference—not because it necessarily changes the day of our death, but because it changes how we live each day and, in so doing, it changes us.

*Tzedakah* is not a miracle. It is an obligation. It can be a grand and public contribution or a small, quiet act of giving with a full and open heart. And it has the power to transform our fate.

May your new year be blessed with prosperity, together with the joy of giving and the blessing of generosity. And in partnership with God, may your *tzedakah* help to heal some of the brokenness of our world.

# Small Changes, Big Results

## Yom Kippur Evening—2007

Think about the width of your cell phone, your credit card or the distance from your index finger to your pinky. All are approximately three inches long. Three inches may be small enough to comfortably fit into your pocket, but they can be very significant.

Paul owns a hardware store in Chicago, you know the kind we all like to wander around in and find things that we really don't need. His family suffers a tragic accident, and as a result God gives him a special power to change lives by three inches. This is the plot of a movie titled *Dimension*. Screenwriter and director Matthew Scott Harris notes how many times lives have been altered by the smallest event. To change a life by three inches, he decided, is the exact distance to demonstrate how so little can mean so much. In the movie, a woman adds three inches of zeros to the amount of money in her bank account; a man decides to retroactively become young again by three inches of calendar years (without losing the hard-won wisdom of age); another woman moves her husband by three inches when a brick tumbles from the rooftop

What if Yom Kippur gave each of us the power to create three inches of change? Could we imagine changing something basic about our lives if we had a gift of three inches? What you would like to change? Your waistline? Or your height? Add three inches to your kitchen or the space in front of your airline seat? What would you choose? Maybe it would be the focus of your life? Or we could use one inch to look forward, one inch to look deeper and one inch to turn ourselves in a new direction.

Each of these changes—pragmatic or metaphorical—point to the potential of even the smallest alteration to achieve major and lasting influence on the course of our lives.

This same idea of change informs the central concept of Yom Kippur, the power of *teshuvah*. *Teshuvah* is a hard idea to translate into English. It is usually rendered as "repentance," but that is inadequate.

Repentance is such a gloomy, unappealing word. It has connotations of regret and self-reproach. But *teshuvah* is more than that. It is more than apologizing, more than saying "I'm sorry." It is certainly more than the half-hearted pseudo-apology that we hear so often from public figures: "If something I said or did offended you, I apologize." In essence, that's just a way of saying that any hurt feelings are really your fault, not mine. Have you ever been on the receiving end of such apologies?

So what is *teshuvah*? Its basic Hebrew meaning comes from *la-shoov*, to turn, turn inside for reflection, turn to face the people who matter in our lives, turn to the future, turn to God. When we understand *teshuvah* as "turning," then we can say, "I don't like the person I was when I did that. I don't like being someone who could do such a thing, and I don't want to be that person anymore." When we say *teshuvah*, we accept responsibility. *Teshuvah* can be a pivot—a point of redirection, a new understanding of who we are, what we can do.

Six weeks from today, each of us will have the opportunity to do something we may have often wanted to do. For many of us, it will be something we have prayed for during the past year, something we thought might make our lives significantly happier. In six weeks, we will be invited to do something about which we may have said, "If I could only do that, it would mean so much to me." And almost without exception, we won't lift a finger or our heads to seize the opportunity.

Six weeks from now, as Saturday night November 3rd becomes Sunday morning November 4th, we will change from daylight savings to standard time. Once again, we will move the clock back and we will gain an hour. Can you imagine how our lives might be different if we did more than enjoy an extra hour of sleep? What if we could take that added hour—when 2 A.M. to 3 A.M. repeats itself—and live an hour of the past year differently, a "do-over." Even imagine cutting and pasting it into another hour of our lives. Yet most of us will sleep right through it.

What do you think this small change would be worth to Don Imus, Mel Gibson, Michael Richards, Senator George Allen or Larry Craig—to be able to live one infamous hour of their lives over again? Or other public figures who saw their careers damaged by words they wish they had not spoken, things they wish they had not done. What would they give to go back in time and have a chance to do it again? And what about us? I know I've wished that I could have a "do-over." What about you?

Yom Kippur is that time to contemplate moments in our lives we wish we could take back and act differently—take back words spoken in haste or say aloud thoughts we did not share.

It is the audacious claim of Yom Kippur that we can use the future to change the past—that is, the future can change the meaning of the past. Rabbi Yosef Soloveitchik recognized that our understanding of the past is based on what we choose to do today. Because we are free to shape our future, thereby do we determine what the past really means. His message can be summarized in one sentence: We are not prisoners of our past; we are architects of our future—yes, architects of our future.

The psychologist Carl Jung has written about what he calls "the shadow." He explains that we all have parts of our personality that we are embarrassed by, that we wish were not there. So we put them behind us, like a shadow. But like a shadow, they keep following us wherever we go. *Teshuvah* is the surgical procedure for removing our shadow. It involves saying, "I'm tired of wrestling with that particular demon," whether it's our eating or drinking habits, our passivity, impatience, selfishness or self-sacrificing. Whatever troubles us on Yom Kippur with *teshuvah*, we can say, "I'm tired of wrestling with that particular demon because I lose too often, so I'm going to change by just a little bit," and see what happens.

The way to change, the way forward, is to choose to renew and be renewed; to make our vision of the future guide our understanding of the past and so free ourselves from repeating what we regret. And that is why we have Yom Kippur.

If we are serious about Yom Kippur, it can't just be a day of skipping lunch, sitting through a long service and then saying to God, "I did that for You. What are You going to do for me?" But there is another aspect to this day. It can help liberate us from our shadow, from the parts of our past that we regret, the things that we wish we had done differently and let our new self emerge. It can give us the new year as a brand-new start, no longer a prisoner of our past but the architect of our future.

There is a story about Abraham that really solidifies this message.

One day an old man wandered into Abraham and Sarah's camp, tired and dusty from his long trek through the wilderness. As a gracious host, Abraham invited him inside the tent to eat and get warm, but the old man refused, saying he preferred to sleep outside. But Abraham pleaded with him until he changed his mind.

When they finished the meal, Abraham offered up a simple prayer of thanksgiving to God. The old man watched curiously. "What is this *Adonai* that you speak of?" he asked Abraham. "I have not heard of this god in my travels." "Not heard of *Adonai*? Why this is the one true God, Creator of heaven and earth, unseen but seeing all."

The old man shook his head. "I know only the gods of my youth. I am too old to believe in such things as invisible gods." Abraham became angry and pointed a shaking finger at his guest. "Then out with you, old man! I will not have such a stubborn fool under my tent. Slowly the old man gathered up his few belongings and headed out into the desert night.

As soon as he was out of sight, God spoke to Abraham. "Where is the old man who I sent to you, who came for shelter under your tent?" "I have chased him away for he denied You." God said, "Abraham, all these years I have been patient with this old man. I have not minded that he doesn't worship Me. But you—you, however, lost patience in only one night!"

Abraham felt overcome by a terrible sadness, for he had disappointed God. "Forgive me for my impatience." "It is not I who deserve your apology, Abraham, but the old man," answered God. "Go find him and beg his forgiveness." So Abraham hurried out into the desert night and found the old man shivering from the cold. "Forgive me," begged Abraham. "I was wrong. Please return to my tent."

The old man forgave Abraham and followed him back to the tent, where he spent a peaceful night.

Abraham said, "I was wrong." A perfect example of *teshuvah*, of changing one's present by altering one's past with three small words that mean so much—like three inches of change.

On November 3rd, we change our clocks, but now, tonight and tomorrow on Yom Kippur, the 10th of Tishrei, we can change ourselves. Do it right, and we will walk out of here at the end of Neilah tomorrow a little bit different.

Let us each look deep inside ourselves to commit to small changes—as small as three inches—that we can make stick this year. We can strive to become the person we have always wanted to be rather than the person we have too often settled for being, the person God has wanted us to be all along. And we will have reason to thank God for the new year and for the new direction in our life.

Think again about the width of your cell phone or credit card or the distance from your index finger to your pinky. It can be a reminder of what three inches can do for you.

May we find the focus, the courage and the hope to change—and may it be for good.

# God is Like a Mirror

## Yom Kippur Morning—2007

How are you doing on your homework from Rosh Hashanah—to make a life list of things you want to do and be? Finished? Congratulations. Started? That's good. Still thinking? That's good, too. Not to worry. We have several good hours left before the end of Yom Kippur, and there is a Jewish tradition that teaches the Book of Life is not closed until the end of *Sukkot*. (That means you have another twelve days, still time—but so don't put off until tomorrow what you can do today.)

Does your list include anything about faith, about God? Figure out what you believe? Read what scholars say? Feel comfortable with the poetry of the infinite? My list includes working on my Israel problem—no, not solving the problems of the small homeland of the Jewish people in the Middle East. I mean my struggles to find God. (We are named Israel because Jacob was given that name as he wrestled with God.) I return to a question that occupies me a good deal: how do we sense God's presence in our lives?

In the opening pages of the Bible, God is all there is. Nothing else exists, and nothing happens until God makes it happen. As the story progresses, God remains an active presence, indeed a dominating presence, pulling strings, telling people what to do, raining plagues on Egypt.

Then, by the time we get to the prophets, God's role has changed. Now God is no longer in control. Now God urges, God scolds, occasionally God complains, "Why don't people listen to me?" Yes, God complains! No longer an all-powerful Master of the Universe.

And finally, by the time we reach the last books of the Bible, God's name isn't mentioned at all. What we are left with is a God who created the world and then gradually withdrew from it—until today, God is a vague memory. God's absence is more conspicuous than God's presence.

Some biblical scholars use the analogy of the relationship of human parents to their child. The parents create the child; they give it life. In the beginning, the child is completely helpless and dependent on its parents. The child begins to grow up, but the parents are still in charge. They set the rules; they pay the bills. When the child becomes a teenager, the parents realize they have less control. Their tone becomes much like that of the biblical prophets, teaching, warning and sometimes complaining. As the adolescent grows up and takes responsibility for his or her own life, the parents recede into the background, ultimately die and become memories. Is this the story of the relationship between God and the Jewish people?

Why doesn't God speak to us the way God spoke to previous generations? How can anyone tell when an invisible God has disappeared? Maybe God is still there, still active but working in more subtle ways. Perhaps we lost the art of recognizing where God is.

In truth, no matter how many years pass or what happens to them or us, our parents don't disappear from our lives. They remain with us: their advice, their values and example, even their criticism continues to echo in our hearts—even after they are no longer alive. And I think something similar happens to God's relationship to our world. God hasn't disappeared. God doesn't have to be splitting seas or making the sun stand still every day to have a defining impact on our world and on our lives. Rather, God seems invisible to us because we rarely know how to recognize God's presence in our lives.

As with our parents and others who have shaped our lives, we need to know how and where to look for their lasting lessons. So, too, do we need to know how and where to look so that we may recognize when God is present. The philosopher Martin Buber has taught that God is found in relationships between people. Buber means that when you and I are truly attuned to each other, God comes and fills the space between us so that we are connected, not separated. Both love and true friendship are more than a way of knowing that we matter to someone else. They are a way of mattering to the world, bringing God into a world that would otherwise be a vale of selfishness and loneliness.

How does God come into our lives, sometimes without our realizing it? The Midrash teaches that, "God appears as a mirror. The mirror never changes but everyone who looks in it sees a different face." Each of us has our own understanding, our own awareness of God. And they may be very different. Yours doesn't have to be wrong for mine to be right. And more—our understanding of God's presence, God's support and love may evolve as we go through life.

Viktor Frankl was an eminent Viennese psychiatrist in the 1930's who was sent to Auschwitz, miraculously survived and wrote a book about his experience there called *Man's Search for Meaning* (1946). He recounts a critical moment after Hitler had invaded Austria when he had to decide if he should accept a visa to America and leave his elderly parents behind. Visiting them one evening after their synagogue had been vandalized, Frankl read the single word *"Kabed*—honor" on a small fragment from the damaged building that his father had brought home. This was the beginning of the Fifth Commandment: *Kabed et Avecha v'et E'mehcha*—Honor your Father and Mother. He understood this as a message from God to stay with his parents.

Did God inspire those young vandals to desecrate the synagogue and throw pieces of the Ten Commandments in the street so that Frankl's father would bring home that particular piece of marble? If not, then how was God present for Viktor Frankl that he could make so momentous a decision. I don't believe that God literally told Viktor Frankl what to do with his life. Rather, the broken tablet was a reminder of his personal values. In that moment, he knew with great clarity that he could not leave his loved ones to seek his own safety. And so he stayed.

Not long ago a mother came to ask me a question, "My son says he doesn't believe in God, Rabbi. How do I get him to believe?" I answered her by saying, "One good question deserves another. How do you recognize the invisible hand of God? What are the times that you might find God's presence in your life? Let's explore this together and see what you can answer your son." Our conversation is still continuing.

What are the times that we might find God's presence in our lives? Where do we look? What do we see? When we find someone with whom we share love? When we are fully present in the moment of a relationship with another person? When we do something wrong and are forgiven? When we find ourselves capable of forgiving someone who has hurt us? Whether we are a child or an adult, then we are in the presence of God.

When we have a major decision to make and are confused and uncertain about what to do and the uncertainty is driving us crazy, and suddenly the fog lifts and we understand what the right thing to do is, we have just looked into God's mirror and found our answer there. Yom Kippur is a day for looking into this mirror. When we cast our glance, we need to realize that no one of us is the same. Every one of us will find a different message there, and each one of us will be correct.

When he was a child, a great master lived near a forest. Almost daily the young boy ventured off into the woods by himself. His father, who was basically a tolerant and understanding man, didn't want to interfere with his son's daily excursions, but he was concerned because he knew that forests could be dangerous.

One day the father pulled his son aside. "I notice that every day you go off into the forest," he said. "I don't want to forbid you to go there, but I want you to know I'm concerned about your safety. Why is it that you go there, and what is it that you do?"

"I go into the forest to find God," was the boy's simple response.

His father was deeply moved. "That's beautiful," he said. "And I'm pleased to hear you're doing that. But don't you know? God is the same everywhere."

"God is," the boy answered, "but I'm not."

We are like the boy who knows that he is not the same at every point in his life. Today we are here—together in prayer and song, alone in the silence of our hearts. May we look deep into God's mirror. May we recognize the signs of God's presence in our lives. I pray that each of us will take another step on our own struggle, wrestling, our journey of faith—and find comfort, courage and confidence for the year ahead.

# If I Am Only for Myself, Who Am I?

## Rosh Hashanah Evening —2008

This is the time of year we come together and work at seeing our way through any false information and confusion to figure out how to stay close to our friends and our values.

One way that may help comes from William Phelps, a Yale University English Professor, who years ago began each semester's classes with the following message: Pretend, when you rise from bed in the morning, that this is the first day of your life. You are overwhelmed with awe and wonder of all that you see for the first time. Your heart is filled with gratitude. Now pretend that this is the last day of your life, never to be repeated, never to experience it again.

This is a very difficult assignment for anyone, regardless of our age, living so fully in the present and yet focusing on what really matters. At the new year, we are reminded of how unpredictable life really is and what we'd like to have accomplished when our end comes. Perhaps it is it is the very fact of uncertainty—if we can acknowledge it, tolerate it, embrace it—that gives us the strength to live in the present for we never know from day to day what may happen.

Did 5768, the year that ended as we came together tonight, turn out as we hoped or planned? Better, I hope for all of us! What does 5769 hold? Over these High Holy Days, we have a special opportunity to reflect, prepare and imagine. Yet we know that there will be surprises— that the unexpected will find us. It always does. And this insight is a great teacher if only we pay attention, very close attention—if we are careful to look and also to see; if we listen and also hear; if we can touch and also feel in the present moment.

It is very hard to live with either our first or our last days as our regular perspective. Our normal lives, however, are filled with times of great joy, surprise and satisfaction as well as with routines, repetition and, sometimes, even boredom. Many of the true miracles of life are nearly invisible and so we fail to treasure them, to be grateful for them … except when they disappear.

You've been listening to me for a few minutes now, and you may not be particularly aware of one small miracle—the miracle of breath. An adult takes in average twelve to twenty breaths a minute. For the sake of conversation, let's use the measure of eighteen breaths per minute. After all, eighteen = *chai* = life. Using this calculation means that we breathe 1,080 times an hour and 25,920 times a day. If we are in reasonably good health, we barely notice the fact that we are taking breaths. By the age of forty, we will have taken 378,000,000 breaths; by the age of 60, more than 500,000,000. (My 98-year old father-in-law has already breathed more than 927,000,000 times.) With so many breaths as a normal part of our existence, it is possible to overlook that each breath is a measured gift of our lives.

It is so easy to forget to pay attention to everyday miracles—our friends, our loved ones, even our breath. It's easy to be distracted, preoccupied multi-taskers—consumed with all the kinds of busy that tempt us into self-importance and shortsightedness.

The biblical story of Moses and the Israelites in Egypt presents an example of people being too busy. The Israelite slaves hear Moses preach that God will aid them in their quest for liberty. But they show no enthusiasm, no joy, no gladness, and they tell Moses that they are too busy with other things.

The Exodus text says, "They would not listen to Moses because of *kotzer ruach* and hard labor." (Exodus 6:9) *Kotzer ruach*: literally it means "their shortness of spirit." As slaves, our ancestors had much to occupy their time and their energy and perhaps their hopes. *Kotzer ruach*, shortness of spirit, a self-absorption, can affect any one of us, rich or poor, enslaved or free. Shortness of spirit is for those of us who think we are too busy to make the hours count, and we run the risk of losing clarity and confidence and commitment to that which we value most.

What is it that gives meaning to your life? Have you ever asked yourself the question? Is it particular people? Is it the work that you do? Is it a sense of the community that grows out of meaningful encounters? Is it our Jewish tradition that provides connection to a transcendent power in the universe?

How do we find meaning if we are totally self-absorbed? So much in our own immediate experience supports our deep belief that we are the absolute center of the universe, the most important person in existence.

We rarely talk about this sort of natural, basic self-centeredness because it's politically incorrect, even socially repulsive, but I suspect that it's pretty much the same for all of us deep down. It's our default setting, hard-wired into us at birth. Think about it: There is no experience we've had that we were not at the absolute center. The world as we experience it is right there in front of us, or behind us, to the left or right of us, on our TV, or our computer monitor or whatever. Other people's thoughts and feelings have to be communicated to us somehow, but our own are so immediate, urgent, so real.

If we're automatically sure that we know what reality is and who and what is really important, then we are not likely to consider possibilities that aren't pointless or annoying or just different from our own. But if we've really learned how to think, how to pay attention, then we have other options. It actually will be within our power to experience many situations in our daily lives as meaningful and even sacred, filled with the possibility of compassion and love.

Central to this perspective is that we must be serious and also enthusiastic about examining our lives and reflecting upon them in such a way as to find out where the meaning is for each one of us. It is about simple awareness—awareness of what is so real and essential, so hidden in plain sight all around us, that we have to keep reminding ourselves, over and over, "If I am only for myself, who am I?"

From the novelist David Foster Wallace comes the following vignette: Two young fish swimming along meet an older fish going in the other direction. The older fish politely asks, "Morning, children, how's the water?" The young ones look at each other in puzzlement and say, "What the hell is water?" The fish remind us that water—just like the air we breathe—is one of those ubiquitous and simultaneously important miracles of life. These miracles are often the ones that we are in the midst of and are the hardest to see and talk about.

Water has no taste, no smell, no color—and yet it is among the elements most necessary for life as we know it. In Jewish tradition, water symbolizes ultimate meaning and connectedness. It is water that saves the Israelites in the desert. Water is used to cleanse us, and yet it does more. We refer to living waters because they help us move from one realm of life to another. It is water in the *mikveh* that we use to finalize the choice for those who take the step of becoming Jews; it is water at our doorstep that we use to make the transition into a home following a burial; it is the salt water that we use to acknowledge the bitterness of slavery at our Passover Seder.

Water can be our enemy if we are overwhelmed by it and drown. It can be our life-support when we are parched and thirsty in our bodies—and in our souls.

How is it we want to be remembered after we die? Not the words written about us but the memories that live in others beyond our years. The rabbis of old taught that during our lifetime we are sustained by three things: by our possessions, by those we love and by our good name. And when we die, they leave us in exactly the reverse order in which we created them. No sooner does our soul leave our body than all of our wealth flees with it as well. Friends and families are more faithful. They accompany us to the cemetery and shovel dirt to cover our graves. Then they, too, leave us to go on with their lives. It is only our name, the good deeds we performed for others and the influence we may have had upon them, that outlive us and offer us a share of immortality.

Strange then, isn't it, that we spend most of our lives chasing after money, spending far less of our time than we might with our loved ones and spending so little of our efforts to accomplish those things by which we will be remembered.

As this year begins, none of us can be certain about how much time we are allotted and what will happen in the days between now and next Rosh Hashanah. But however much time we have, I hope that all of us will pay attention to what brings value and meaning to our lives. Rather than suffering from shortness of spirit, I pray that each of us will know that we are enriched by the small miracles of life—of breath and water and love.

And let us remember what the sage Hillel said: "If not now— when?" We should make our moment now. We can do it by taking a few minutes to think about what we would want to do with each day as if it were our last. Between now and Yom Kippur, think about the small miracles in our lives and what it is that truly matters to each one of us.

AMEN

# How Do We Decide as Modern Jews?

## Yom Kippur Evening—2008

With apologies to Charles Dickens, we live in the best of times and the worst of times. We live in a country where just a short time ago it seemed that anything would be possible, and today it appears that much is not. In these troubling times, Rabbi Bernard Mandelbaum reminds us that it is all too easy to think that we can't do anything about the troubles of the world. Not so. Either we do something to make things better or, doing nothing, we add to the woes of the world. (*Choose Life*, 1968)

But how might we begin to do something about any of the problems we read about in the newspaper or experience in our personal lives? We have options! Solutions can be curative or they can be preventative or, best of all, perfective. A medical metaphor to illustrate what I mean might be helpful. Let's consider for a moment how we deal with illness.

When we are sick, naturally we turn to a doctor to cure what is wrong: to stop an infection or to repair an injury. It's the most common and familiar way to treat an illness—after it has occurred. This is curative. And yet there are people who chose to ignore the signs of illness until a cure is no longer possible.

There is another level of medicine—vaccines to prevent polio, cervical cancer and other diseases. And science continues to find new ways to protect us from disease after disease. This is the preventive approach.

There remains a third level for the care of our bodies. Medical science seeks not only to cure and prevent illness but also to perfect our health—to bring new strength and energy into our daily life through fullness of exercise, diet and healthy living. This is striving toward the perfective solution of life.

Surely, whoever we are—whether we find the problem in ourselves, in our family, in our work, in our city or nation—we can work towards a solution at one of these levels.

How do we go about finding our way and discovering the perfective level? Let's turn to our Jewish history and tradition for some guidance. We begin by understanding a bit about San Francisco. Our city has the smallest percentage of people under the age of eighteen in North America, with Jews part of the fabric of San Francisco since it became a city in the 1850s. Since the vast majority of Jews here are not affiliated with any synagogue, we need to examine what it means to choose to be Jewish today.

We live in a time of great mobility and in communities where personal boundaries are very permeable. Last spring the Pew Forum on Religion and Public Life reported on religious change in America. The study indicated what a strong hold Judaism has on its members. Seventy-five percent of us who are raised as Jews say they have remained Jewish as adults (the second highest rate of any religious group in America). A further statistic: fifteen percent of today's Jews were not born Jews but have joined the community.

Judaism is basically a system of doing. Judaism has principles but no dogmas. There are a few core concepts that constitute the spiritual, moral and communal foundation for our people. There is, of course, a covenantal relationship between God and humanity, and, therefore, life is worth living. Judaism looks to belief not as an end to the salvation of the soul but as a means to make life better on this earth. Instead of stressing belief, we stress the quality of right living.

What about our own congregation? This sanctuary building was constructed when the membership numbered two hundred households. Sherith Israel, now celebrating its 157th year, was not always a Reform congregation. From its beginning in 1851 to 1895, this was an Orthodox congregation with separate seating. Prayers, music and the style of worship came from Posen, that area of Poland from where most of the founding families had emigrated.

A gradual movement away from orthodoxy began during the time of Rabbi Henry Vidaver (1870s) and culminated under the leadership of Rabbi Jacob Nieto when Sherith Israel became a Reform synagogue in 1895. Why? Why did we move away in 1895 to what we are today? A new generation of Jews had grown up in San Francisco interested in the social justice concerns of the time—fighting the white slave trade, assisting the city's poor, participating in progressive politics as well as discovering the new science of evolution. Our predecessors here embraced this perspective on Judaism 113 years ago, and we are the inheritors of this change.

What does that mean for us today? There are three guiding principles for us Reform Jews that I want to focus on. (My thanks to Rabbis Eric Yoffie and Janet Marder for inspiring these insights.)

First, all of us are created *"b'tzelem elohim*—in God's image." This is true regardless of our gender, our race, our sexual orientation. This teaches us that the individual varieties of humankind are all deserving of our love. A Judaism that diminishes the equality of some is a Judaism that degrades our dignity and besmirches our soul.

Second, even as Reform Jews have embraced ritual, prayer and ceremony more than ever, we continue to see social justice as a central tenet of Reform Judaism. The biblical prophets remind us that God is concerned about the everyday and that the blights of society take precedence over the mysteries of heaven. Our congregation, like most Reform synagogues, directs a good deal of its energy to alleviating the anguish of the suffering.

Third, we need to remember that "reform" is a verb, and we are committed to a Judaism that changes and adapts. We understand the difference between central, core beliefs that endure through time and social attitudes that may change from generation to generation.

For example, *"tzedek, tzedek, tirdof*—justice, justice shall you pursue" is an eternal truth taught in the Torah. In contrast, the laws that permit us to own slaves or to stone to death someone who violates the laws of Shabbat is a vestige of ancient times best abandoned today.

There are contemporary issues that call upon us to apply all three of these principles. One such issue is same-sex marriages. How do the Jewish values of us all being created in God's image, the pursuit of justice and the need to change apply?

This Spring the California Supreme Court ruled that a categorical ban on marriage was unconstitutional. The first time the court did so was 1948, when we became the first state in the nation to strike down the law preventing interracial marriage. In May, the Court stated that sexual orientation, like race or gender, "does not constitute a legitimate basis upon which to deny or withhold legal rights." Chief Justice Ronald George, writing for the majority (which included our own congregant, Judge Kaye Werdeger), said that "the ability to responsibly care for and raise children does not depend upon the individual's sexual orientation.... We therefore conclude that the California Constitution properly must be interpreted to guarantee the basic civil right of marriage to all Californians, whether gay or heterosexual, and to same-sex couples as well as to opposite-sex couples."

Let's imagine the culture of 4,000 years ago. In the time of Abraham and Sarah, wives were the property of their husbands, and marriage has changed since then. Four thousand years ago in the time of Bible, it was legal to stone wives for adultery. Marriage has changed since then. Four thousand years ago, in the time of Jacob, a man's wealth was measured in how many sheep and wives he had. Marriage has changed since then. Over the course of the past 4,000 years, people of different races as well as people of different religions were prevented by law from marrying each other. Marriage has changed. (My thanks to Rabbi Ken Chasen for this idea.) Rabbis for Marriage Equality, a group that I am a member of, reminds us of our core Jewish value that every human being is created in the image of God. Each one of us is different in some special way from others. As Jews, we have a religious obligation to speak out, to educate and to defend the civil rights and human dignity of our gay and lesbian brothers and sisters, mothers and fathers, sons and daughters.

As Reform Jews, we should apply the values of equality and social justice to the circumstances of the present day. What does this mean for marriage? It means that we Jews can uphold our tradition's essential definition of marriage as the covenantal commitment of two adults under the *chuppah*, freely joined in mutual love, respect, faithfulness and responsibility while letting go of the tradition's stipulation that those two adults be a man and a woman. And here on November 4th, the choice is before us once again.

A century ago, Hasidic teacher Rabbi Levi taught that there are six parts of our daily existence: three are in our control and three are not. Eyes, nose and ear are not. Our sense of sight, sense of smell and our sense of hearing don't always depend upon our actions. That may be true. However, it's hard not to see the TV, the newspapers or listen on the radio and not be bombarded by the events of our day. And when we do, we discover that there is a stench that comes from greed and deceit.

Rabbi Levi says, "Mouth, hand and foot are in our power." What we say, what we create with our hands and whether we walk the walk are in our control. We can choose whether or not to follow after the desires of our mouth to consume without limits or to remember that our bounty is a delicate balance between God's natural creation and our human efforts. We can use our hands to create or to destroy, to tear down or to build up. We can walk in the path of righteousness, not steal or covet and fulfill the commandments that we have inherited. With our feet we decide which building we walk into and where to spend our time.

We can choose to use our abilities—our hands, our voices, our feet—to do something about the problems of the world, even if it is just one problem in the place where we live. And our Jewish tradition can help us make choices, speak up, take action so that when we die a small place in this world will be better because we were here.

AMEN

# New Runs and Continuous Creation

## Rosh Hashanah Evening—2009

Growing up in Los Angeles, my brother and sister and I often competed with our father for who would be the first to read the comics in the *Los Angeles Times*. (I won't tell you who won—or what shape the paper was in when we were done.) One of my favorites today is "For Better or For Worse." It is written by Lynn Johnston, the first woman to be named Cartoonist of the Year by the National Cartoonists Society. Johnston's creation centered on the life of a young mother and her family. However, unlike other comics, Johnston chose not to freeze her characters in time. Rather, she showed the lives of her characters as they grew up, encountered life decisions, moved out and started families of their own. After thirty years of creating this strip, she decided to retell the story from the beginning with updated drawings and story lines that she calls "new runs"—new runs to retell the story with a fresh and wiser perspective.

Have you, like me, wished sometimes that we could just start over, wanted a "do-over?" If only we had the power, if only I had the power, what stories would we rewrite based on the clarity of 20/20 hindsight? Confronted with the same situations that we have had, would we make the same choices? What would our lives be like if we could change our past experiences and move our lives in different directions? This is the allure of the road not taken. It is the stuff of fantasy, of alternate universes—and it can happen in the comics. It is also the message of Rosh Hashanah. Yes, it is the message of Rosh Hashanah.

Beginning tonight, we are blessed to have the opportunity to reflect upon who we were and who we have become. Some of us may carry the physical and emotional scars from our mistakes or we may have some grey hairs, bruises, tender spots or calluses from doing the same thing over and over—as well as the badges of pride from our successes. What do these marks tell us? What do they say? They are our history, and they add strength and wisdom to our lives.

165

At the Smithsonian Museum in Washington, D.C., there is an exhibit that tells a story of scars and bruises. It began in late fifteenth century Japan, when a shogun sent a damaged Chinese tea bowl back to China to be fixed. The bowl returned held together with ugly metal staples, launching Japanese craftsmen on a quest for a new form of repair that could make a broken piece look as good as new or better. Clay vessels are remarkably durable, yet they are vulnerable to breakage if mishandled or dropped. The craftsmen drew on the longstanding practice of using plant resin lacquer as an adhesive to rejoin broken ceramics but transformed the appearance of the repair by sprinkling the lacquer with powdered gold, thereby creating a new component for appreciation. The most interesting part is that it is not meant to hide the damage of the piece. Rather, the gold lacquer repair of a treasured ceramic recognizes the flaw. It adds strength to the history and mends what was broken into something new and richer.

And so it is with us. So it is with us. The marks of the lived life—the bruises, the regrets, the mistakes—they are how we learn and the source of wisdom and energy for renewal and good deeds. Mending what has been damaged is at the heart of the High Holy Days.

Søren Kierkegaard, the nineteenth century Danish philosopher, believed that we understand our lives only retrospectively, by looking back. Yet life must be lived prospectively, by looking forward. We can understand our lives by looking at the past, but we live in the present by looking forward. Central to these days is the Hebrew word *teshuvah*, which not only means "repentance" but "to turn." *Teshuvah* comes from the word *la-shuv*—to turn and return. We can use our life experience to make the best possible choices in similar situations that we will encounter in the year ahead.

Instead of calling the High Holy Days the "Ten Days of Repentance," we might call them the "Ten Days of Turning." For ten days we review our year, searching our hearts and our memories, taking stock with a severity that we can only endure once a year—looking backward so that we can live forward.

At the end of these ten days, we can stand together on Yom Kippur as part of a community and claim our failures and seek to move forward. We turn to ourselves, to the scenes of our regrets—in our memories if not in actual fact—and turn to God. Each of us must turn alone and look deep, with eyes and heart fully open. And then we can enter the New Year together in wholeness and in community. Although we do this hard work individually, we gather here collectively. The strength to turn and return by ourselves is supported by the ritual of doing it together.

On Rosh Hashanah, we read in our prayerbook *"Hayom hara'at haolam"*—today is the birthday of the world, the anniversary of creation. The great Hasidic teacher Rabbi Nachman of Bratzlav said, "God created the world in a state of beginning." The universe is always in an uncompleted state. In the form of its beginning, it is not like a vessel at which the master works for a while and then finishes. Rather, it requires continuous labor and unceasing renewal by creative forces." *Chadesh yameinu.* We ask that our days may be renewed. *Chadesh yameinu.*

This anniversary of creation, this Rosh Hashanah, gives us the opportunity to look back and then move forward. We can pick one moment, one relationship, one action and look at it from all sides. Turn it over; turn it around in our mind and heart. Consider where the cracks are and what the story tells us about the complexity of living and living well. We can repair it. When we do the repairing, we take strength and wisdom from the effort.

As we prepare to think about our regrets, the mistakes of omission and commission, let me tell you about a wealthy person who lived not so long ago and not too far away.

> Now this person had great power, great wealth and great landholdings. He was very rich. His palatial home was filled with treasures beyond count, and the most precious of his treasures was a large, perfect gemstone. He loved his stone; he loved to look at it every day and to show it off to his friends. But one day the gem slipped from his hands, fell to the ground, made a terrible sound and cracked right up the middle.
>
> He called all around, promising any amount to whoever could fix it. Many came and examined the gem but to no avail. One day, from a very distant corner of the country, came a famous artisan to see what she could do. She had heard about the gemstone and promised to fix the crack. She locked herself in a workroom, and there she labored for ten days. She eventually emerged with the gem, holding it up for all to see.
>
> The owner of the gem took it with great anxiety and anticipation. His excitement was quickly dashed when he saw that the crack was still there. "Look closer," the artisan said, "and see the big picture." The wealthy man looked again and saw that though the crack was still there, it had been artfully transformed from a mere crack into the stem of a rose that had been carved into the gem.

I wish for us that we will see the rose, the beauty, the wisdom in the imperfection that is part of each one of us. Like the gem, as God's prized possession, we humans contain cracks and imperfections. But it is not the fact that these cracks exist. Rather, it is how we embrace them, understand them and become stronger, wiser and kinder to ourselves and others.

May each of us, in the quiet and power of these Ten Days of Turning, look inside to find the beauty and wisdom that lies beneath the imperfections in our lives and be strengthened.

AMEN

# Our Club

## Yom Kippur Morning—2009

*(I am grateful to Rabbi Misha Zinkow for inspiring this sermon.)*

What is in your wallet? In my wallet are photos of my children, bank credit cards, my driver's license and membership cards—auto club card, health club card—and most of us are members of several clubs. Each club comes with certain privileges and requires us to follow certain rules. Some clubs are very strict in who they admit, and others are more welcoming.

Today we are at the annual celebration of our club, the Jewish club. We have club songs, club traditions, and on this day each year we review the guidelines of our club. We also renew our commitment to those guidelines, so we can continue to be members in good standing. That is what we did when we heard chanted the three key words from the Torah.

*"Atem nitzavim ha-yom,"* which we translate as "You are standing here together this day." How is this relevant to our Yom Kippur observance? Let's look at each word one by one. First is *"atem,* which is "you" in the plural." All of us—past, present and future Jews—are said to have participated in the revelation of Torah. We all were standing at Sinai when the thunder and lightning occurred, and the Ten Commandments were given to Moses.

Now the ancient rabbis knew that none of us were literally there, but we are familiar with similar language about a timeless and continuing present. For example, in the *Haggadah* that we read every year at the Passover Seder, we are instructed to celebrate Passover "as if we were slaves in Egypt." And it is the same way we are to feel—that we have a part in what happened at Sinai many thousands of years ago. So, on this day, we who are here now are part of a community that reaches back—almost to the beginning of Jewish time and forward into the Jewish future.

Let's look at the second word, *"nitzavim"* in *atem nitzavim ha-yom.* *Nitzavim* means "standing together." Standing is an active process, as you know from standing up many times during our club meeting today. So it is with Torah: we engage actively when we participate in the life of our Jewish club. Some of us are legacy members, born of Jewish parents. Some of us are FOJs, Friends of Jews—and we just blessed and thanked you this morning. Some of us have applied and have been accepted into the club as "members by choice." The Torah makes it clear—regardless of how we came to the club—we all have the opportunity to belong.

The third word in our special phrase is "*ha-yom*," which means "today." What "today" is this? Is it part of an ancient moment when Moses gathered the Jewish people before him to remind them of the giving of the Ten Commandments on Sinai?

A story is told that Moses stood before them and said, "You are all here to enter into the covenant which Adonai, your God, is making with you *ha-yom*, today." What did Moses have in mind when he repeated *ha-yom*, "today?" A child came up to Moses and asked that very question. "Why do you keep saying '*ha-yom*?'" Moses embraced the child and said, "Every day is *ha-yom*. Today is the most important day of your life, the day you stand in the presence of God. But tomorrow and the next day and the next day and the next day will also be *ha-yom*. Your challenge is to know that wherever you are and whatever you are doing, the only day that really matters is *ha-yom*, today."

What about our *ha-yom* this Yom Kippur Morning 5770? Why are we standing together today? We live in an era in which every one of us must actively choose Judaism. Why do people choose to be part of this club? And why do we renew our membership each year at the High Holy Days?

Important clues come from those among us who formally and publicly chose to become Jews. We have heard their stories, and they tell us that being part of the Jewish club matters for a few central reasons. One reason is the sense of belonging to the community of the synagogue and the Jewish people. A second reason is the worship experience that brings peace and connectedness with God. A third reason is the opportunity to question, argue and struggle with profound issues. And the fourth reason for being Jewish is the framework for pursuing justice and social change.

Today is the time to ask ourselves, "Why we are here?" Some of us are here for our children, for our partners, for our parents, for ourselves or for God. Some of us are here to find answers or to ask questions, to seek forgiveness or to be comforted. We are here freely, most of us anyway; that is, we are here by choice. I believe every

Jew is a Jew by choice, however we come to be affiliated with the great big club of Jews.

If you are considering formally becoming a Jew or know someone who is, let me say this now: The door is open—please come in—we welcome you here! I invite you to explore placing your future with the Jewish people by choosing Judaism. A journey of learning and living awaits you. At Congregation Sherith Israel, we offer a variety of classes, one-on-one mentoring by a wonderful group of volunteers, many ways to see what synagogue life is like and opportunities to study and talk with our clergy and our outreach coordinator. I recognize and appreciate how many personal questions you may have. I invite you to explore them with us. Perhaps this is your time to choose making an eternal bond with Judaism, a sacred covenant, a *brit*.

Happily, our worship space is crowded with people all around us: our friends and family and people that we do not yet know. We have arranged the chairs in our clubhouse so that there is room for all of us—and for all of our prayers and hopes.

A story is told about the great Hasidic master, the Baal Shem Tov, who came to a town and stayed for a while.

> When the time for worship came, the townspeople asked if he would walk over to the synagogue to lead them in prayer. He was happy to oblige. He stopped, however, at the door of the synagogue and stood outside for a long time, so long that people started to get anxious. Finally, a little boy asked him, "Why aren't we going inside?"
>
> The Baal Shem Tov replied, "We can't go in because the room is full." Now everyone in town was standing around outside the synagogue, and so the child was puzzled. Who else could there be around here? Who might be *inside* the sanctuary? The boy looked inside but, to his continued puzzlement, there was no one inside, no one at all. He turned to the rabbi and asked, "What do you mean, the synagogue is full?"
>
> This is how the teacher answered the boy. "It is true that there are no people inside the synagogue, but the room is full of the prayers and hopes that came before us. So we can't go in and dream another dream, hope another hope, pray another prayer, until we give life to the dreams and hopes and prayers that are already in that space."

And that is why we say, *"atem nitzavim ha-yom"*—"we are standing here together today." It is up to us to fulfill our hopes and prayers to make room for learning and doing and growing in the new year. May we choose well!!

Amen

# A "Third Place" and the
# Three Sounds of the *Shofar*

## Rosh Hashanah Evening—2010

Sometime in the 1970s, a Russian Communist commandant comes to America to visit a factory. He takes a tour and closely examines the factory product, the height of American ingenuity. Suddenly he hears an industrial whistle, and the workers start to leave. The Russian guest gets upset. "Hurry, stop them, don't let them escape." The factory owner smiles and responds, "Don't worry, it's only the lunch whistle. They'll be back." An hour later, the whistle sounds again and, sure enough, the workers return. The Russian commandant is amazed. At the end of day, the factory owner turns to the Russian, "So what about our product?" "Never mind the product," he responds, "I'll take one of those whistles."

We Jews have such a whistle. A whistle that reminds us of who we are, reminds us of our community and calls us to action. It is the *shofar*, and when it sounds, as it will tomorrow morning, we come together. We return to worship here. The sound of the *shofar* calls us every year. It challenges us to "*sh'ma*," to listen, to listen deeply—to listen to a sound that connects us with all the generations of Jewish people. We who are fortunate to be together at this time, we will hear the sound of the *shofar*—making it easy for us to connect with what is most important.

Most of the time we work hard to be connected. We carry our cell phones with us at all times—in our pockets or our handbags like a wireless umbilical cord—so we can talk or text or email to each other from Pacific Heights to Noe Valley, from California to Massachusetts, from the United States to Israel and even to someone who is sitting right next to us. We go online and instant message each other, engaging in multiple conversations at once. We take photos of our surroundings and send them wirelessly through the air. We create blogs to get our ideas out to the world. Smart phones accompany us on every vacation. Are we ever offline anymore?

The *shofar* is perhaps the world's first device for social networking. It is the only instrument from the biblical period that has remained unchanged in its use in worship for thousands of years. While it no longer is used in time of war, the *shofar*'s use in ritual and worship continues to the present day. Made of any animal with horns except for a cow (we don't use a cow or a calf because it would remind us of the "Sin of the Golden Calf"), it connects us to history, to tradition, to values, to each other. The sounds of the *shofar* create what sociologists describe as a third place in the midst of our busy lives. In contrast to first places (home) and second places (work), third places allow us to put aside our concerns and simply enjoy the company and conversation of those around us. (Roy Oldenburg, *The Great Good Place: Cafes, Coffee Shops, Bookstores, Bars, Hair Salons, and Other Hangouts at the Heart of a Community*, 1999)

Starbucks is one such place for people to gather. At Starbucks—we can add Peets or Royal Ground or wherever we order our fair-trade, shade-covered and sustainably grown, organic, just-roasted, half caf, half decaf, extra hot, no foam, soymilk cup of coffee—this is where we might work or study, relax or chat. These places offer the prospect of being part of a community but without necessarily engaging with others. (Lori Chalk, "Starbucks: The Third Place." *Annual Meeting of the American Sociological Association,* August 12, 2005)

Our special third place is created by the *shofar* sounds that demand we be engaged. The horn is capable of producing tones that evoke a wide range of emotional responses. They can be quivering trumpeting sounds of alarm, shouts of jubilation or sobbing and moaning. The magical and transformative experience of hearing the *shofar* is defined not by walls or food or activities but by three sounds. *Tekiah, shevarim, teruah.* We hear these sounds only on Rosh Hashanah, but we know them well.

Scholars have struggled for centuries about what to say concerning the *shofar*'s sounds. (Joachim Braun, *Music in Ancient Israel/ Palestine*, 2003) While the Dead Sea Scrolls describe a mighty war alarm, it is the first prayer book, edited more than a thousand years ago, that gives us details of the *shofar* sounding in worship. The first sound, *tekiah,* has been the sound used to gather everyone together on meaningful occasions for the community of the Jewish nation. The word *tekiah* comes from the same Hebrew verb that is used to "seal an agreement" and "to clap hands" and "to drive home a point." *Tekiah*, the blast that is uninterrupted, calls us to eliminate complacency in our lives.

*Tekiah* commands action and courage. It tells us that this is the time to determine what we will devote the efforts of our hearts to in the coming year. What will be the sound of opening our hearts to those we care about? What will it sound like to us? Let the *tekiah* note remind us to take action, to reach out, to be courageous.

The second *shofar* sound asks something completely different. *Shevarim* is one long note broken into three. It is a cry that comes from the Hebrew verb meaning "to break" or "to be shattered." Used many centuries ago to warn of danger, it commands us to look beyond self-absorption to see the pain of a broken world that it is our task as Jews to help repair. It is the clarion call that reminds us that we can use our hands to help fix that which is broken. There are meals to be cooked, calls to be made, letters to be written, places to be built, causes that can use our sweat and our financial support. *Shevarim* reminds us to reach those in need here in our community, those in distant lands and our cousins and family in Israel.

And there is the third sound, *teruah*. This word means not only to "sound the horn" but also "to protest" or "to cry out against injustice." When the Israelites in the desert heard the sharp short *teruah* notes, they knew to break camp and prepare to move forward toward the Promised Land. Today a *teruah* directs us listeners to shake up our behaviors and habits that constitute the status quo.

> Two hundred years ago the Dubner Magid tells of a naïve villager who came to the big city for the first time. He was awakened in the middle of the night by the loud beating of drums. He inquired what all the fuss was about. He was told that a fire had broken out and that the drum beating was the city's fire alarm.
>
> On his return to the village he reported back to the village elders. "They have a wonderful system in the city! When a fire breaks out the people beat their drums and, before long, the fire subsides."
>
> The city officials immediately acquired a supply of drums and distributed them to the population. When a fire broke out, there was a deafening explosion of beating drums, and while the people waited for the fire to die out, several homes burned to the ground.
>
> A visitor to the village chastised the people. "Don't think that beating a drum will put out a fire! You beat the drums as an alarm, but you also have to do the work together to extinguish the flames."

The *shofar* blasts alone will not improve our lives. The *shofar* is the alarm, as Maimonides puts it. "Awake you sleepers from your slumber and rouse you from your lethargy. Scrutinize your deeds and return in repentance."

We are commanded to listen. "*Sh'ma*—listen," to listen closely to the sounds of the *shofar* this High Holy Day season. Hear the cries and the calm and the urgency. The *shofar* sounds not only like tears, but it also sounds like laughter. Yes: The *shofar* sounds not only like tears, but it also sounds like laughter. I find that dichotomy fascinating—such opposites that make up the human condition.

*Tekiah, shevarim, teruah*: wholeness, followed by brokenness, followed by wholeness. We all start out from a place of wholeness. Along the way we are anxious, we are wounded, disappointed, lost, and cry out in pain or loneliness or sorrow. We hope and pray that we can move towards wholeness again.

During these Ten Days of Awe, let us each take the *shofar* sounds into a special third place deep inside us. It calls us here, together as community, to understand why we are here, what we want to do and where we want to be in our lives for this new year 5771.

And then, at the conclusion of all the *shofar* sounds, we hear the one great blast of the *shofar*—the *tekiah gedolah*. We will hear it soon. We need to get ready to go forward into the future that we want to make for ourselves, our loved ones and our community.

I wish that each of us will find a good third place this High Holy Day season, one that can be a place for reflection, hopes and action. May it nurture us during the Days of Awe and into the new year of 5771.

Shanah Tovah

# Bad Calls, Apologies, and *Teshuvah*

## Yom Kippur Morning—2010

Who saw the Indians play the Tigers last June and the nearly perfect game that wasn't? Tigers pitcher Armando Galarraga had retired the first twenty-six batters he faced and was about to become the twenty-first pitcher in Major League history to throw a perfect game. Then first-base umpire Jim Joyce called a runner safe on a ground ball. Yes, the Tigers won the game, thanks to Galarraga. When the umpire reviewed slow-motion replays, he saw that the runner had, in fact, been out because the pitcher had his foot on the bag before the runner reached it. After the game, the umpire asked to meet with the pitcher and offered a profound apology for his bad call. Jim Joyce took full and humble responsibility for his mistake.

I am indebted to Rabbi Aaron Gaber who spoke about this issue and reminds us that neither pitcher nor umpire is Jewish—but they modeled for us an important step in *teshuvah* or repentance, a heart-felt apology. Compare that to how Tony Hayward, Chief Executive of BP, handled his apology about the Gulf of Mexico oil spill a few months ago. As reported in the *New York Times* (June 6, 2010), at a Congressional hearing he said, "I was not part of the decision-making process." He was not at fault. And in other remarks about the disaster, he observed that it was not BP's fault either. Yes, they set up a compensation fund and have worked at trying to clean up the mess, but the results of the oil spill will be with us for many, many years, if not decades, to come.

It's a non-apology apology, the kind that enables hurt to fester and embitter. Apologies don't make things all better, as we might want to say to our children. Real apologies enable those who have been hurt and those who made the error to move forward, wiser if they are sincere and less likely to do it again. Perhaps this spill might result in different techniques and methods used to extract oil from deep-sea wells. Only time will tell, but I don't think this horrendous accident will change much in the off-shore oil-drilling industry.

But what does Jewish tradition reveal about what happens when a mistake is made? In the Talmud (*Horayot*), there is a large section devoted to answering the question of when a *beit din*, a Jewish court, makes a mistake. Who's responsible? And if people follow the mistaken ruling and find out, what are their responsibilities? The conclusion is that the court is responsible. It must make proper restitution and pay the penalty. If the people who followed rulings made in error didn't know they were wrong, then they are exempt. But if they followed knowingly, they are required to make appropriate restitution. In other words, there is both accountability as well as making it whole. There is a rule of law.

Moses Maimonides writes about repentance (*Hilchot Teshuvah*) and reminds us that there are three types of people in this world: those who have more sins than good deeds (the wicked); those who have more good deeds than sins (the righteous); and finally, the rest of us whose good and evil deeds balance out as the average person. Standing on the edge between salvation and destruction, each action has the potential of tipping the scales one way or another—not just for us personally but for the entire world.

Rabbi Nachman of Bratzlav teaches that we all have some good in-side—flotsam and jetsam—random bits of goodness floating in the vast sea of our lives. As we find these bits of goodness, however small they may be, we can string them together in a *niggun* of life. This *niggun* is not the wordless melody we know best at Shabbat worship. Rather, it is the elements of goodness that make a song of life. In this sense, a *niggun* is a way to begin work on a *heshbon hanefesh*, the accounting of our souls.

This taking stock on Yom Kippur is the work we have the opportunity to do. The apologies we make are important—if they are sincere. An apology is a way we can respond to those who have been wronged, to help them feel understood and to reduce their pain. In fact, an act of repentance can do more than soothe the hurt person: it can change the person who has performed *teshuvah*.

It was once told that after a long, hard climb up the mountain, some spiritual seekers finally found themselves in front of a great teacher. Bowing deeply, they asked the question that had been burning inside them for so long: "How do we become wise?"

There was a long pause until the teacher emerged from meditation. Finally the reply came: "Good choices."

"But, teacher, how do we make good choices?"

"From experience," responded the wise one.

"And how do we get experience?"

The teacher smiled, "Bad choices."

Making good choices is not easy. Sometimes we are lucky and do the right thing the first time. More often, we are lucky if we have the opportunity to try again—and again and again—growing in understanding as we go.

May the process of *teshuvah* enable us to make good calls and better choices in the new year.

# Walls, Illusions and Change

## Rosh Hashanah Morning—2012

*(My thanks to Rabbi Jory Lang for several ideas in this sermon.)*

Allow me, if you will, to paint the scene of the crime: a father sneaking away with his son in the middle of the night; doing this early enough and quietly enough that the boy's mother doesn't hear them; secretly taking a knife with him while his wife is sound asleep. This is ripe for investigation by one of the very best detectives. Maybe it's Sam Spade, perhaps it's Monk or Columbo, or, I think it could even be Lieutenant Briscoe. What would the most skilled detective deduce?

We know who the characters are in the drama, but what was the motive behind this? What was this father thinking? Why would the son be so willing to go along? What would the mother say to the detective when he questioned her? None of these characters wanted change. Isaac was happy, Sarah was pleased, and Abraham was content—but each person was profoundly changed by these events.

Change is a central theme for the holy days. It's not easy, not easy at all. You all have heard that you can't teach an old dog new tricks or that a leopard can't change its spots. Yet, on close inspection I believe it isn't necessarily so.

The founder of modern Hasidism, the Baal Shem Tov, gives us a Jewish perspective. He used to tell the following story about the challenge of change before the blowing of the shofar on Rosh Hashanah.

> Once there was a great king with magical powers. With his magic he created an illusion—a hologram of sorts—that gave the appearance of a mighty palace fortress with high walls, locked gates and a series of moats surrounding them. Then he invited his subjects to come visit him in the palace. The people came from far and wide, delighted that the king had invited them. When they approached the imposing walls of the palace, with its locked gates and elaborate moats, they saw no way to enter. The people were dejected because they had struggled so hard to get there and now entrance seemed impossible. So they turned back and returned from

179

whence they had come. Only one subject—the king's son—figured out that the obstacles before him were just an illusion. Taking a breath, he walked forward into the walls and found himself standing before his father, who embraced him.

This is a classic story, one that follows a paradigm often used in the Talmud and by the Baal Shem Tov. Here is the format: God is portrayed as the King, humanity as His subjects and the people of Israel as the King's son. So, too, here in our story about the fortress, the King is God. The subjects are all humanity yearning to draw close to God, to live holy lives, to find comfort and inspiration, guidance and strength, and most of all a sense of peace and harmony with God, with ourselves and with our world. Do you think this is easy?

Like the King's subjects in this story, we face obstacles in our path, barriers that seem to block our way. Like the subjects in the Baal Shem Tov's story, we turn back. We give up. We stop trying. We retreat to who we are comfortable being rather than striving toward who we could become. We allow those obstacles to block our way.

But the message of the story is that those obstacles, all of our obstacles, are surmountable. The Baal Shem Tov is urging us to look beyond them, to move past them, to see—as the King's son saw—a way to achieve a life of meaning.

We know that change, turning, is not so easy. Every time we seek to turn, we run up against our own metaphorical fortress walls that seem to stand in our way, barriers that prevent us from doing what we know we should do, being who we should be, barriers that separate us from our truest selves.

Every year at Rosh Hashanah we start out with a set of goals. We might say, "This year I'm going to treat my family and friends better. I am going to be a better listener and a better person. I am going to spend more time with my parents, my spouse or my children. I am going to be more patient, gossip less, be more forgiving, more honest, more compassionate, less jealous. I will give more *tzedakah*, attend worship services more frequently, make time to study, get more involved in the synagogue, share my expertise, paying it forward since I already am a recipient of generosity."

It's a great list. Yes, it's a great list. But for most of us, it might sound a lot like last year's list. To many of you this might seem a lot like last year's sermon as well, and it might sound a lot like next year's, too. No matter how sincere we are when the year begins, no matter how hard we try, too often we end up right back here, making some of the same plans over and over again. Why? Because we come up against those barriers—like those fortress walls. And our barriers are real.

But it is illusion, a conviction, that we cannot do anything about them. The illusion is that we are stuck with who we are, that we cannot do real *teshuvah*, real turning and achieve real change. And caught up in that illusion, we stay in our old ways. Why? Perhaps because we are comforted by them, finding comfort in our daily routine.

Let's examine some possible barriers to *teshuvah,* real turning. First is that we try to change too much at one time. It is a little intimidating to think about all the changes we want to make. We tend to become overwhelmed and to give up. Yet imperfection is human. When the Amish make their beautiful quilts, they have a tradition that the quilter deliberately puts some flaw into the design of the quilt as an artistic representation of an important theological truth. Things human beings do are never perfect. Perfection only belongs to God.

Judaism teaches that if we try to grasp too much, we end up not grasping anything at all. So let's not try to change everything in one year. Instead, I'd like to propose that we choose one area in which to focus our efforts to change. Try making one *mitzvah* choice this year. It can be an ethical or ritual one. What might it be? Maybe the ethical *mitzvah* would be controlling our anger, giving *tzedakah* more generously, taking the time and spending the energy helping someone less fortunate than we are, honoring our parents (in life or memory) or another person who has been important in our life. Maybe the ritual *mitzvah* is examining what we want our observance of Shabbat to become, how we make choices about the food we eat or our approach to prayer. The point is that God embraces us for every individual change we make. The rabbis taught "*mitzvah goreret mitzvah*—every *mitzvah* leads to another." In the same way, we can say every little change leads to another little change. It's about habits, one step at a time. Rather than being overwhelmed with all those changes, just make one. And in that one we can find ourselves closer to God.

Another way we resist *teshuvah,* real turning, real change, is the fear of failure. We have all been in the position where we must start again. Sometimes we lose our confidence, and we worry about the future. Will we be treated differently? Will we be embarrassed? Will we be judged? And all the other thoughts that go through our minds, causing us to stay where we are—not allowing us to go forward and live life. These impediments and the way we struggle affect us in every aspect of life where we would like to change or improve.

In the Talmud (Berachot 34b) it says, "*Makom she'ba'aleiy t'shuvah om-deem, tzaddikim g'morim aiy-no om-deem.*" Translated, this teaches that "even a totally righteous person who has never sinned doesn't merit standing in the place of one who has sinned and repented." Only knowing the power of temptation and the reality of failure prepares us to improve. When we make the decision to move forward despite our slips, we begin to know our true selves—and that makes it easier to turn, to change.

A third barrier is that we are overly concerned with what others think of us. We fear asking forgiveness or admitting a mistake because it makes us feel vulnerable. It's true that we shouldn't worry about what others think about us, because they don't. We are afraid that revealing our flaws will chase away those we love and respect, that we will be judged only by our mistakes or that someone malicious will use our failures to harm us.

A highly respected faculty member at Carnegie Mellon University, Randy Pausch, gave a now famous lecture which included a wise observation about metaphorical brick walls. These may seem to come between us and our goals. Rather than keeping us out, as literal walls could do, metaphorical walls can tell us how much we want something. And today, in Pittsburgh, Pennsylvania, there is a very special footbridge, built in memory of Professor Pausch. The bridge was built in such a way that those crossing it perceive there is a brick wall ahead, and yet as you approach, you realize you can walk right through it.

Let's not let the walls deter us. The obstacles are an opportunity for us to prove how badly we want to be better, how much we desire to be connected to the ones we love, to community, to the world and, most importantly, to God.

Find a place here—on one of these walls, one of the windows, up on the dome—and visualize the *mitzvah* you are choosing this year. Take a moment. Find a special place, a place you like to look at, somewhere that your eye is attracted to regularly. Each time we return to this sanctuary, we can look and be reminded of what our *mitzvah* is for this year.

When we see those walls looming ahead, when we see that bridge ahead of us—think about what it takes within us to get to the other side and how we can help one another get there.

# Looking Up or Down? Keeping Our Eye on What's Important

## Rosh Hashanah Morning—2014

Last summer I took a photography workshop in the Eastern Sierras. While I was there, our teacher shared photos and stories of a place some miles south of where we were. The place is known as "Dante's View," overlooking Death Valley. If you have been there, you know how spectacular it is. You can go online and see amazing photographs of the place.

It was named after the author of the Divine Comedy because standing there you can imagine the nine circles of Hell, the seven terraces of Purgatory and the nine spheres of Paradise. At this lookout point you can either look down or up. Looking down, you see the lowest spot in the United States—a place called Black Water. Looking up you see Mt. Whitney—the highest spot in the continental United States.

So it can be for us. We can look at the lowest or the highest—the regrets or the love, the sorrow or the joy, what we fear to do and what we hope to attain. Deciding which way to look gives us a very specific perspective on life. Figuring out what to see makes a difference, a big difference, on how we live our lives—and we have a choice.

Picture the desert location in the hills around Jerusalem. Abraham is there, lifting up his knife and ready to do what he understood God asked of him. And suddenly an angel cries out, "Abraham, Abraham … don't lift up your hand against your son." (Genesis 22:12ff) And what happens then? Abraham turns, looks up and sees a ram caught by his horns in the bush. And he sacrifices the ram instead of his child.

Why didn't Abraham see the ram right from the start? Rams have been part of this hilly desert landscape for thousands of years. Imagine what is not stated in the text. If a ram were caught in the bushes, wouldn't he make some noise? It shouldn't have been difficult to see and hear. Even a young ram can weigh over 100 pounds, a mature one several hundred. If the ram is stuck by its horns, he would make quite a lot of noise trying to get away. But Abraham didn't see the ram. He was so focused on what he was doing that he didn't see anything else that was going on at the time.

That's our job—every day—and especially on Rosh Hashanah. We have to figure out what direction to look and what we need to focus on. What is important and what should we pay attention to and really see— even if it might be difficult to discern, to name, to acknowledge? Do we see the threats and what is missing or failing in our lives? Or do we see the joys and satisfaction we might find in our world?

We live in an age of multi-tasking and to-do lists. We have apps that prioritize our apps; we have technology that helps us learn new technology; we have remote controls that seemingly help us find and use the other remote controls. The challenges we face in keeping a focus on what's really important in life is enormous. George Orwell said, "To see what is in front of one's nose needs a constant struggle." ("*In Front of Your Nose, 1945–1950," Collected Essays, Journalism and Letters of George Orwell,* vol. 4)

How do we do this? How do we go about looking and deciding about what's important in our lives, what we want to pay attention to, to see, to really see? Consider two paradigms. One says there is a limited supply of satisfaction in the world, like the limited number of places in a select college or like a trip to the World Series that only two of the thirty major league baseball teams will attain and everybody else goes home. If so, we have to work every day and hustle to get our share before someone else can claim it. This perspective says that life, like sports, like politics, is a game of winners and losers. In politics, if you get 47% of the votes, you don't get 47% of the power. At best, you get your name in small print in the history books.

A second paradigm says there is something for each of us and for all of us, for it is like a puzzle. We find a piece that fits so that the final result is something gratifying for everyone, and no one goes home a loser. We shouldn't be looking for the perfect college, the perfect job, the perfect home to live in, even the perfect marriage partner. We should be looking for the right one, the best one for each one of us, even if it isn't right for everyone.

The paradigm of life as competition rather than cooperation—life as a contest rather than a jigsaw puzzle—creates many more losers than winners. It increases the amount of unhappiness in the world. And it teaches us to see everyone else as threats to our happiness, people who want to get more of the limited amount of satisfaction in life so there won't be any left for us. It makes us compare ourselves to others—what they have and what we don't. They must be happy because they have more than we have. This perspective leaves even the winners wondering what they have won and if it was worth it to push aside all the people to get there. What is it that's so important?

What does Judaism say about this? A text in the Talmud can give us guidance. It says in five words "*Kol Yisrael arayvim zeh ba zeh*—All Jews are responsible for one another." (Shavuot 39a) Judaism requires us to care about other people. When we are selfish—when we are self-centered, when we think that there is not enough to go around—we build walls to insulate ourselves from other people's problems. We need to break out of the alonenesses we have created. I believe it is part of who we are as a people to care about others with *mitzvot*, deeds and with *tzedekah*, righteousness. We are connected to each other and encouraged to create circles of friendship and caring.

The longest continuous narrative in the Hebrew Bible is the story of Joseph and his brothers. Joseph dreams about his family bowing down before him. Twice he tells his family about his visions of superiority. The brothers are hurt and enraged by Joseph's arrogance. They sell him into slavery. Joseph experiences the depths of loneliness and despair as an Egyptian slave and as a prisoner in jail. But in prison Joseph learns to sympathize. There he accepts a principle basic to our Jewish tradition: all of us are responsible for one another. Imprisoned with the royal butler and baker, he helps them gain their freedom. In doing so, Joseph learns that arrogance isolates, but helping others can bring redemption.

Our Jewish faith also speaks with the words of another text. In *Pirke Avot: The Sayings of our Ancestors* (2:4) it says, "*Al tifrosh min hatzibor*—Do not separate yourself from the community." This can be a recipe to cure our self-absorption, this lack of concern for others and the notion that we are not able to do better.

Today and through these holy days—during the moments of communal celebration and reflection and in silent private contemplation—we can admit, "Yes, I did a lot of things wrong this past year, things I knew at the time I should have done differently. I let people down, people I genuinely care about. All too often I hid from the truth rather than admit that I was wrong."

But Judaism says, "This is part of being human. Of course, we did those things, and so did every one of the hundreds of people sitting around us, not because we're bad but because it's part of the human condition."

We welcome everyone to gather and pray together—especially imperfect people. Ours is a religion for imperfect people, for people who, when we are being honest with ourselves, can't help wondering if we're good enough for what we yearn to do. Imperfect people are good enough for God. This is what the Talmud teaches about imperfection: "Even a totally righteous person who has never sinned doesn't merit standing in the place of one who has sinned and repented." (*Berachot* 34b) This teaches that we are not perfect, but we have the capacity to do better.

As we learn from Dennis Prager (www.prageru.com), we are quite good at sabotaging our own happiness. It is all too easy to be preoccupied by a flaw, something broken or missing, instead of the big picture, something beautiful or important. For example, right here in our synagogue with its domed ceiling and hundreds of lights, it is all too easy to focus on the burnt-out bulbs instead of the grandeur of the setting.

Sometimes it is essential to pay attention to what is missing. We don't want a physician to overlook the slightest medical detail or a builder to overlook a single brick. And, indeed, if there were no burnt light bulbs here, what would everyone spend their time looking at or thinking about—the rabbi's sermon? Perhaps. But what is desirable or even necessary in the physical world can be very self-destructive when applied to the emotional world.

Ceilings can be perfect; all 1,100 light bulbs in our ceiling should illuminate. But in life there will always be pieces missing, bulbs out. And even when they aren't, we can always imagine a more perfect life and therefore imagine that something is missing. And yes, for some, something is always missing, something is always going wrong and spoiling the experience!

I was told about a fiftieth wedding anniversary party for Harry and Shirley held at the couple's home and arranged by the family. The festivities moved along smoothly until two things went wrong. The first thing that went wrong was that the bakery somehow forgot to deliver the wedding cake. When they realized what had happened, Harry stood up and said, "Ladies and gentlemen, we have a problem. The wedding cake has not arrived. So I am going to ask one of my grandchildren to drive to the bakery and pick up the cake. And meantime, I want everyone here to be patient and continue singing and dancing and telling stories."

And then, the second crisis occurred. When the cake arrived, they opened the box and saw that the inscription on the cake was "Happy Anniversary Fred and Louise." Shirley, without batting an eye, reached for the knife to cut the cake. And before she cut it, she said, "Ladies and gentlemen, we want to wish Fred and Louise—whoever they are—as much joy at their anniversary party as we are having at ours. We hope that they feel as surrounded by love as we do at this moment."

Today is a good time to start focusing on how we're going to make it together in this crazy mixed-up world. Let's look up and focus on the important things: being receptive and understanding and giving and caring—the things that we should really prize.

When we go home, let's try to focus on what is really important. Let's tell those who are here with us, those who are at our homes, those across the country or elsewhere in the world, how much we love them and how much they mean to us.

# The Book of Life

## Yom Kippur Evening—2014

Our tradition teaches that what we do is recorded, part of the Book of Life. The Talmud says, "Three books are opened on Rosh Hashanah: one for the totally wicked (who might they be?), one for the totally righteous (anyone here volunteer?) and one for those in between (where most of us might place ourselves). The totally righteous are at once inscribed and sealed for life, the totally wicked are at once inscribed and sealed for death, and the in-between, well, we're left in suspension (until Yom Kippur)." (*Rosh Hashanah* 16b)

The language of our prayers presents God metaphorically, right? When it comes to the Book of Life imagine this: God as the judge and ruler, sitting in the divine court on the divine throne of justice, reviewing our deeds. On a table before God sits a large book with many pages, as many pages as there are people in the world. Each of us has our own page, only one. We don't get more than one. Written on that page, by our own actions, in our own hand, in our own writing, are all the things we have done during the past year.

The prayer text we recite in both our Rosh Hashanah and Yom Kippur morning services says that *tzedakah* (righteousness), *tefillah* (prayer) and *teshuvah* (repentance) can mitigate the awful fact of our human vulnerability. We know those three practices won't send cancer into remission or keep the drunk driver off the road on a particular night or keep the hurricane or earthquake from striking those we love. But attention to these three things creates a world that shines a little brighter—and that's enough, because it has to be enough.

Take for example *tzedakah*, acting righteously—choosing opportunities every day for *tzedakah* because it is the right thing to do. If *tzedakah* is an abstract concept, it is doing the act, the *mitzvah,* that is the right thing.

Here are two opportunities to act righteously at Sherith Israel. The first is an opportunity to save lives on Yom Kippur. I can tell you that members of our congregation are alive today because of this. Tomorrow, if you are between the ages of eighteen and sixty, you can do something very concrete, very positive, very simple and potentially very lifesaving. This *mitzvah* opportunity can potentially save the lives of patients suffering from leukemia, lymphoma, other cancers and genetic disorders. With a simple and painless swab of the inner cheek, your information will be entered into a database for bone marrow transplants for people in need all over the country. This is in partnership with the Religious Action Center of Reform Judaism and the Gift of Life Foundation and will take place tomorrow from 11:00 to 3:00. You will have the opportunity to seal your name for good in the Book of Life.

Here in San Francisco and all over the country, there are many children and adults who go to bed hungry every day. Their sheer numbers can overwhelm us, and there is much as a nation we need to do to improve the safety net that has been largely removed from the needy in our very affluent nation. Yet there is one thing we can do here, with our own hands, our own feet and our own hearts. Many, but not all of you, know about our *mitzvah* program of providing nourishing and delicious meals to homeless shelters and to people unable to leave their homes. For more than twenty-five years, our Chicken Soupers (in cooperation with Jewish Family and Children Services) has been preparing meals for shut-ins, and our *Hamotzi* program cooks for shelters. You can find an informational flyer downstairs at the table. Sign up, and a coordinator will talk to you about volunteering to cook, to shop or to deliver. There are many members in this congregation who do this *mitzvah* work, and you can join them.

Not enough choices, not enough opportunities, to make better additions on our page in the Book of Life? These are just two. Come to us and propose other ways we as a Jewish community can make a difference in peoples' lives. We three clergy, staff and board members will listen and see what we can do together with you.

God will not prevent the lives of friends and loved ones and decent strangers from clashing headlong and meaninglessly into the plans of those who would destroy. When people decide, in darkness and hate, to kill, God's hand is not likely to descend, protecting any of us. The laws of nature operate, and some people will die. Not because they deserved to, but because our stories are intertwined, sometimes for bad, sometimes for good, sometimes randomly and sometimes with purpose.

We will all someday die. That is our fate as human beings. Unfortunately, some of us will die before our time, some of violence and others of neglect, some in pain and others in need. What is left to us is our response.

Picture the *Sefer ha-Chayim*, the Book of Life, which lies open in heaven. There are two types of inscriptions. The first are those that we write about ourselves. We write about all the good we have done, the kindness we have shown, the *mitzvot* we have fulfilled—as well as about our sins where we have missed the mark and need to try again. The second type of inscription is what is written about us by others. These are our reference letters, written by those whose lives we have touched. What do we want to have written about us? These two types of inscriptions about our lives are what God reads today.

The image of these inscriptions in the Book of Life is compelling because it reminds us of something we know but often wish to forget. Everything we do and say—plus everything we neglect doing and fail to say—does make a difference. We know the difference a complimentary word or kind gesture from someone else has made in our lives. So, too, a disapproving look, being snubbed or ignored, a critical or caustic comment flung our way. Nothing simply hovers in the air. All those looks, gestures, words, comments—all find a landing spot in our heads and hearts.

Let's now re-imagine this *Sefer ha-Chayim,* the Book of Life. Perhaps these pages look less like a journal with an entry each year and more like a page of traditional Jewish text. Our entries are in the center, and all around the edges, all around the margins, are commentaries from others. We're responsible for both kinds of inscriptions: those that reflect how we've lived during the past year and also the potential blessings and curses for those we know and love.

The flip side of saying that everything we do and say makes a difference is that we are writing not only onto the page of the ledger that has our name at the top but also onto pages of others. On our own pages we write with own deeds and words. On the pages of others, we also write with deeds and hopes and with kindness or cruelty.

What if we only write on other's pages with kindness and affirmation? What if this year we begin anew by acknowledging our capacity and responsibility to bless the lives of others? What if this year, instead of sitting back passively and begging God to bless our lives, we understand *Avinu Malkeinu* not as a laundry list for God but as a "memo to self"? What if this year we pick up the pen of our lives and start writing the text we want God to read next Rosh Hashanah?

Let us take this time to think about ourselves and how we can build together with our lives and with mitzvot. The Book of Life is open until the gates close at the conclusion of Yom Kippur. But it stays open in our hearts and the hearts of those we love every day. May we inscribe it with the traditions, the values, the focus, the caring and the training that are worth trusting in.

*G'mar hatimah tovah*—May we be sealed well.

# Whatever Became of the Permanent Record?

## Rosh Hashanah Evening—2015

Many years at our High Holy Day services I have shared with you a perspective from the imagery of the prayer book. You have heard me ask, "When you were in third grade and you misbehaved, what did the teacher say?" Who remembers? Anyone?

My third-grade teacher at Crescent Heights Elementary School in Los Angeles said, "You better behave, because if you don't, it will go on your Permanent Record." Did any of you have a teacher say that to you?

When the teacher said the words "Permanent Record," we straightened up and stopped fooling around immediately. None of us had ever seen a Permanent Record, but we had no doubt that it existed. We pictured the teacher taking mental notes of what we had done wrong all day, and then, when school was over, we pictured her taking the notes about our misbehaviors down to the principal's office—which is where we assumed the Permanent Records were kept—and recording them there.

No doubt there was a gray file cabinet in the principal's office where the Permanent Records were kept, one for each and every student in the school. And we sort of assumed that when we graduated elementary school and went on to high school, the Permanent Record would follow us there. And we assumed that when we graduated high school and went to college, the Permanent Record would be sent there as well. And we believed that when we graduated college and started a job, the Permanent Record was sent to our employer, perhaps with a carbon copy sent to the government. We thought that when you went down to City Hall or to the Department of Motor Vehicles in order to apply for a marriage license or for a driver's license, they looked up your Permanent Record. If your record showed that you had misbehaved in third grade, they might not give it to you.

Our morning prayers for the Holy Days say, *"B'rosh Hashanah yikateyvun, u'v'yom tzom kippur yechateymun.* On Rosh Hashanah it is written, and on Yom Kippur it is sealed."

Who is the "they"? In the conventional reading of the prayer, God is imagined as Judge, Auditor, Grand Inquisitor. The great Book of Life is opened, and our actions for the year are examined. God is the One who decides if it will be a year of plenty or poverty, of sickness or health. God decides, and God's decision is recorded in the Permanent Record of the Book of Life.

Many of us read the prayer this way. After all, we all were once small children, completely dependent upon the goodwill of all-powerful adults. That sense of being judged for life and death still lives deep inside us.

But this reading is quite upsetting and disturbing. It connects our fate to our behavior, and it puts our destiny in God's hands. Was our loved one's cancer really God's decision? Was it punishment for some infraction? What about the victims of earthquake, fire, plague or even the Holocaust? Were they victims of God's unrelenting judgment?

There is another way to read this prayer, and I am grateful to Rabbi Ed Feinstein for sharing his thinking about this. The decree is not anyone's individual fate—not yours, not mine. It is the human condition itself. It is the fragility, the vulnerability of being human—the blunt truth that we do not control the fundamental fate of our own existence.

We cannot alter the fundamental facts of human existence, but we can make the world a bit more gentle. Acts of righteousness and acts of goodness might ripple across to world to heal an aching soul far beyond our horizon. A Hasidic teaching says that when we are challenged by difficulty and the loss of hope, try to perform one selfless act of goodness. At that moment, we might feel God's presence in our fingers. In our act of love, we might feel God's power to heal. This is *tzedakah.*

Human life is fragile, vulnerable and finite. We possess gifts that enable us to transcend the limitations of the human condition. We are free to shape our character. We are able to share our common suffering and find moments of celebration and song. We are equipped to heal and to help one another and to bring a small measure of peace to the world. These actions can help affirm the meaningfulness of our existence and our belief that God is present among us.

There was a time—not so very long ago—when people would stop before they did something that was illegal or immoral or deceitful, no matter how tempting it might be, because they had a nagging fear that, if they did, it would end up on their Permanent Record. And then, at some point many people realized that there was no Permanent Record! They realized that the claim that there was one was just a story that the teacher had used in order to keep them from misbehaving.

Now people go on television and reveal things about themselves that we would have kept secret for fear that people would not like us if they find out about them. Now people write books in which they reveal things about themselves and about their families that we would never have admitted in public. Now things that we would have never revealed even to our closest friends are talked about in magazines and on talk shows without any embarrassment. Now things that we did not do for fear that they might go on our Permanent Record are not only done; they are talked about and even boasted about as if they were not a *shandeh*.

Let me give you just one example of what I mean. A couple of weeks ago, I was listening to a television program and heard a certain celebrity being interviewed. And I heard him say casually, in an off-hand manner as if what he was saying was funny, that he and his brother both were born out of adulterous relationships that his mother had with two different men. And then he dismissed the whole matter by saying, "I suppose my mother must have been going through a difficult time when she did these things."

When I heard him say that, I sat up in shock, and I said to myself, "Is this man going through a difficult time too? And even if he is, does that justify shaming his mother and shaming his brother and shaming himself on national television?" Is there no such thing as privacy left in this world? Or does this man think that his words have no consequences?

If that is what he thinks, let me tell you that he is wrong. And the proof that he is wrong—the proof that deeds and words have consequences—is that ever since I heard that broadcast in which he mocked his mother and shamed his brother and embarrassed himself, the first thing that comes into my mind whenever I hear his name mentioned is what he said that night on television. And so let me tell you what I wish that I could tell him: words and deeds have consequences. And they do go on your Permanent Record.

And even if you no longer believe that there is a Permanent Record that is kept in the school principal's office, know that there is a Permanent Record of what you say and what you do that is kept in your conscience and that is kept in the memories of those who hear you and that is in the records that are kept by God.

This is the sad spiritual state of the world in which we live today. Without thinking much about it, we have accepted the notion that there is no Permanent Record and that nobody is keeping track of what we do, and, therefore, we can say what we want, and we can do what we want with no fear that it will ever come back to embarrass us.

I imagine that if a teacher tried to threaten a child today by saying that if you don't behave, it is going to go on your Permanent Record, the kid would probably file a suit under the Freedom of Information Act and have a copy of his Permanent Record in his possession by the time recess arrived. Either that or else the kid would call up his Permanent Record on his computer and would purge any information that he did not want to have there with just a couple of keystrokes.

Many people no longer believe that there is such a thing as a Permanent Record—and without oversimplifying—that may be the real reason why they stay away from the synagogue on Yom Kippur.

For the central theme of this day is that there IS a Permanent Record and that all that we do is written down and read and judged. That is what the central prayer of these holy days, the *Unitane Tokef,* says. "We acknowledge the awesomeness of this day—because it is the day when the books are opened, and the records are read—and the signature of each and every person is found on his record, and the deeds that we have done are witnessed and judged." And many of us think that we are too smart and that we are too sophisticated to take such an idea seriously. We have outgrown the idea of a Permanent Record that the teacher tried to sell us when we were in elementary school, and so we are not going to buy it when the High Holy Days tries to sell it to us again now that we are grownups. And that is why many of us do not come to the synagogue on these holy days.

I want to answer this question: Is there a Permanent Record or not? And I want to make clear the differences between the Permanent Record that they told us about in school and the Permanent Record that we will face up to on these Holy Days. But there is one problem. The problem is that those who are not going to be here on Yom Kippur are probably not here in *shul* today either. And so I need your help if I am going to reach them. So let me give you the reasons why I believe that there is a Permanent Record, and why I think it is important to know that there is, and then let me ask you to please share what I am going to say to you today with anyone you know who is not planning to be here on Yom Kippur.

Will you do that for me, please? I mean it. Will you please do that for me? Because you probably know more people who are not planning to be in *shul* on Yom Kippur than I do, and I can't think of any way of reaching these people except through you. And so I hope that you will help me by telling these people what I am now about to tell you.

The first thing that I want to say is that the Permanent Record is a figure of speech. And if you do not know what a figure of speech is, then woe to you. Not only are you unable to understand the prayer book. You cannot understand a play or a song or a poem or a love letter either.

When the prayer book says, "I will bring you back from the four corners of the earth" it does not mean that the earth has four corners. It means, "I will bring you back from wherever you are."

To say that something is a figure of speech does not mean to say that it is not true. It means to say that it is true, but in a different way than "It is two miles from here to the grocery store" or "Water is composed of hydrogen and oxygen" are true.

There are two languages that human beings use: the language of prose and the language of poetry. Both are true, but they are true in different ways. The language of prose says that two and two are four. The language of poetry says that the heavens declare the glory of God. And both of these languages are equally true, and both of these languages are equally important to human discourse. And if you do not understand that, if you do not know what a figure of speech is, I feel sorry for you, I really do. It means that you are as rigid and as doctrinaire in what you don't believe as any fundamentalist is in what he does believe.

The *Unitane Tokef* prayer is written in the language of poetry. And what the *Unitane Tokef* says—in the language of poetry—is that our deeds have consequences. They have consequences for us, and they have consequences for those with whom we live and for those who will follow us.

If you don't believe that, ask the bruised and battered children who have grown up in the home of an abusive father or an alcoholic mother, and they will tell you. They will testify that not only have the deeds of these people ruined their own lives, but they have ruined the lives of those who live with them and those who will follow after them. Ask the children whose parents abandoned them or ask the children whose parents who have gone to prison for their crimes, and they will tell you that the deeds of these parents have had consequences, not only for their own lives but for the lives of their children as well. Ask the people sitting here on Yom Kippur who cannot say the *Yizkor* prayer because the words stick in their throats because they cannot think of their parents without remembering all the harm that they did to them, and they will tell you.

Or ask those people whose parents brought them up to appreciate music and art or ask those people whose parents taught them respect for their elders, or ask those children whose parents brought them up to value ethics, or ask those children whose parents taught them to treasure and appreciate the Jewish heritage, and they will tell you that their lives, to this day, have been molded by what their parents taught them.

Our deeds have consequences. That is what *Unitane Tokef* says to us on Yom Kippur, and we had better hear those words and take them to heart, for they are true—terribly true. They are true for our good deeds, and they are true for our bad deeds. They have consequences for our lives—and they have consequences for the lives of those with whom we live. And therefore, we had better stop—at least once a year if not more often—to realize this truth and to re-realize this truth to comprehend this truth and to absorb this truth for our sakes and for the sakes of those with whom we live.

Our deeds have consequences. We need to know this truth, and we need to understand this truth. And therefore, anyone who is not here on Yom Kippur, anyone who misses out on the annual confrontation with this truth, sins against himself and sins against those with whom he lives. Will you please tell this to those whom you know who may not be planning to be here with us on Yom Kippur?

Tell them—in my name and in the name of Jewish tradition and in the name of *Unitane Tokef*—that Yom Kippur is more than just the annual reunion of the Jewish people, although it is that, too. Tell them—in my name and in the name of Jewish tradition and in the name of *Unitane Tokef*—that Yom Kippur is more than the day for facing up to our mortality and for thinking about what we are doing with our few days upon this earth, although it is that, too. Tell them—in my name and in the name of Jewish tradition and in the name of *Unitane Tokef*—that Yom Kippur is the day when we realize and understand that deeds have consequences. Tell them that it is the day when BOTH—BEING HERE AND NOT BEING HERE—BOTH have consequences on the character and the meaning of our lives and in the lives of our families.

Will you please help me get that message to those who are not planning to be here on Yom Kippur? If you do, I will be very grateful.

And now let me tell you the two main differences between the Permanent Record that they told us about in elementary school and the Permanent Record that we face up to on Yom Kippur.

The first difference is that the principal kept your Permanent Record hidden away under lock and key. It was hidden in his office, and there was no way that you could steal a look at it. It was his property, not yours, and there was no way that you could get hold of it and find out what it said

But the Permanent Record that *Unitane Tokef* talks about is not like that. You can access it by being here on Yom Kippur, because, as you listen to its words, you will find that many of the things that you have done during this last year—both the good things and the bad things that you have done—will come welling up into your consciousness. God will show you what is written in your book, not just at the end of days but now on Yom Kippur if you are here and if you are open to reading the record of your deeds.

I don't know about you, but I must tell you that when I hear the words of *Unitane Tokef* every year on Yom Kippur, a host of memories come up into my mind . . . memories of the things that I did wrong this year and memories of the things that I did right this year...both come up into my mind and they make me think about what I am doing with my life and what I need to change.

That is the first difference between the Permanent Record that they told me about when I was in elementary school and the Permanent Record that we will face up to when we come to *shul* this week on Yom Kippur. That one was kept hidden away from us so that we could not read it. This one is right there in front of us for us to read and face up to.

And there is one more difference between the Permanent Record that they told us about in elementary school and the Permanent Record that we will face up to on Yom Kippur. And that is that the Permanent Record that we confront on Yom Kippur is not really permanent. It can be changed. I do not mean that we can make the deeds we have done disappear. No one can ever do that. I mean that WE can change, and if we do, our record will change as well. We cannot erase our past. It is written in indelible ink. But we can write a new chapter. And if we do, the story of our life will take on new meaning, and the mistakes and the sins that we have done will be seen in a new perspective.

And so, this is what I want you to hear today. And this is what I want you to tell those of your friends who are not planning to be here with us on Yom Kippur. Tell them that I know that it has been a long time since any of us believed in the Permanent Record that our teachers threatened us with when we were in elementary school. And tell them that I don't blame anyone who smiles at that *bubbe maiseh* or teacher *maiseh* or whatever it was that they told us back then. But tell them that *Unitane* Tokef is not *bubbe maiseh* and that it is not a teacher *maiseh*. Tell them that *Unitane Tokef* is a declaration that our lives matter and that our deeds matter. And tell them that it is a lesson that we and they need to know. And tell them that *Unitane Tokef* is an opportunity to look at the record of our lives and to see what it says while we still have time to change it—if we really want to.

Let me tell you a bit of literary history, and then I will let you go. You may not know this, but scholars say that there are some religions that have versions of *Unitane* Tokef that are much, much older than ours is. It is clear that our *Unitane Tokef* is based on theirs. Their versions speak of a day when even the angels tremble, and so does ours. Their versions speak of a day when the book will be opened and our deeds will be judged, and so does ours. Their versions speak of our signature being written on the record of our lives, and so does ours. Their versions speak of a great horn being sounded, and so does ours.

But there is one difference between those versions and our version. Do you know what it is? In those versions, the book of deeds is opened, and the still small voice is sounded, and the angels in heaven tremble, and each person is judged—just as in our *Unitane Tokef.* But in those versions, the judgment takes place after lives are over. In those religions, the book that contains the record of each person's deeds is only opened on the Great Judgment Day that will take place at the end of days—which means that when people see the record of their lives, it will be too late to change.

But that is not the way it is in our *Unitane Tokef!* That is not the way it is in Judaism! In Judaism, the book that contains the record of our lives is opened every year on Rosh Hashanah and on Yom Kippur so that we can read it, so that we can see what we are doing with our days and so that we can change.

We show up on Yom Kippur in order to access our record and in order to resolve to write a new chapter in the new year that now begins, a chapter that we hope will be better than last year's chapter was, a chapter that we hope will contain *teshuvah* on our part and pardon on the part of God. And that makes all the difference!

If our record is hidden away from us in the principal's office or if our record is not opened until after we die, then by the time we get to read it, it is too late to do anything about it. But if we can read our record every year, then we can change it, we can transform it, we can improve it, and we can do so NOW—NOW and not when it is too late.

The Permanent Record that they told us about in elementary school was meant to scare us. The *Unitane Tokef* that we will hear here on Yom Kippur is meant to awaken us. And that makes all the difference!

Therefore, I hope to see all of you in *shul* on Yom Kippur, and who knows? Perhaps you will be good enough to bring some of those whom you know do not usually come to *shul* on Yom Kippur but will come along with you this year. I hope to see all of you and even some of them here this week on Yom Kippur. I hope and I pray that when the book is opened and the days of our lives are examined on Yom Kippur, that we—and God—will find many good things written there. I hope and I pray that when we look back over this last year as we recite *Unitane Tokef*, we will find many good deeds—many deeds that we are proud of. I hope that we will find more good deeds than deeds that we are ashamed of written there. I hope and I pray that after we have looked back over what is written in last year's pages of our record, we will resolve to write a better chapter in the new year that now begins.

And I pray that this Yom Kippur will be a time when you and those whom you bring with you and I, as well, will learn the two central spiritual lessons of this day—the two lessons that we must learn if we are to live worthwhile lives—which are: that our deeds matter and that we have the power to change. And to this, let us all say: Amen.

# Beginnings

## Rosh Hashanah Morning—2015

*L'shanah Tovah*—Happy New Year. What I really mean is happy first of four. Ancient Judaism established four separate new years to provide boundaries and markers for various activities. (Mishnah *Rosh Hashanah* 1:1)

The first is today, the first of Tishrei, the few year for seasons. Rosh Hashanah literally means "the head of the year." This day is the new year for celebrating creation.

The second is the fifteenth of Shevat (*Tu B'Shevat*), the new year for trees. This date was selected because most of the winter rains are over, the sap has begun to rise, and the fruit has started to ripen.

Then comes the first of Nisan, which corresponds to the season of Passover, the redemption from Egypt and the birth of the Israelite nation.

Finally, just a month ago, the first of Elul, is the new year for the tithing of cattle.

When something is repeated—recurs—that is a clue about what is important. New years are about beginnings, and the first word in the Torah is *beresheit*, beginning. The first word is not "God" or "world" but "beginning." If there is no beginning, then we are trapped in a circle in which the times of our lives are erased, and time is collapsed. If there is no beginning, then imagine a life without birthdays, anniversaries and unique moments to celebrate.

A beginning means that we can have a fresh start, another chance. For this whole Jewish enterprise in which we are engaged is one great unfinished story, a story in which each of us, in every generation, has a chapter to write. For our personal lives, the opportunity to begin—to move forward, to try something new—can be wonderful. But beginnings also are fraught with risk and uncertainty. Like little kids, many of us might prefer to hide our heads under the covers, at least on some days, and not come out until we are good and ready. But the truth is that we can't. Even if it were an option, hiding wouldn't help. This is the moment—one of many moments that add up.

But we moderns didn't invent the concept of the moment. The ancient Greeks had it, and our Jewish ancestors did as well. The Greeks had at least two different notions of time: *chronos*, the vast, inhuman, infinite stretch of time and *kairos*, the moment.

I want to apply to the concept of time two Hebrew words from the language of prayer. The first is *keva*, a fixed point which returns again and again—like the beginning of every day, the first of each month and the first of the year. The second term is *kavannah*, which in prayer is used to describe intentionality and spontaneity. In the context of time, it can refer to what is ever-changing and to that which changes depending upon the time and circumstances.

Life is beginnings, *keva*, fixed at one point and then we measure from there. Life is constant change, *kavannah*. Life and time never stand still. Ironically, this is what makes life both a great adventure and such a great challenge. We are always in the process of becoming. We may be in the process of becoming better or worse—but we are always becoming.

Biology also teaches us about continuously becoming because all the cells in the human body change every seven years.

And so I offer to you and to myself as well three suggestions of how to capture new beginnings and bring about the changes in ourselves that we would like to achieve. They are chain-smoking, micro adventures and MVP.

The first one is "chain-smoking." Strange to use that term! Creative output such as making something new is hard work. It feels like it's bound to Newton's First Law of Motion. The tendency for a body in motion is to stay in motion, and the tendency for a body at rest is to stay still. In other words, it is a lot less work to stay put when you're not moving than it is to gather momentum. Author and artist Austin Klein has a solution to the issue of maintaining creative momentum. He calls it chain-smoking. (*Show Your Work* 2014) If you have seen real chain-smokers—who light up their next cigarette before they have finished the one they are smoking—you know what this means. Working on multiple projects—or goals—concurrently uses momentum you've gathered in one part of your life and pushes it onto the next. And anyone of us who is seeking to begin anew can use whatever techniques are available to sustain momentum.

The second comes from the work of Alastair Humphreys, *National Geographic*'s Adventurer of the Year. While he has had some huge adventures under his belt, like rowing across the Atlantic Ocean, his passion now is all about going small. Humphreys is on a mission to encourage everyday people like you and me to experience adventure through small expeditions he calls microadventures (www.alaistairhumphreys. com). For Humphreys, adventure represents a simple mechanism to trade the rushed and mundane world for something fun and unpredictable. It's the perfect way to push ourselves outside of our own box.

Adventures can be messy and starting something new can be as well. But for all their risks and difficulties, adventures offer up some amazing benefits. They spark new synapses in the brain. Like a complex highway system, it is hard to have new experiences and novel ideas if we're constantly driving up and down the same roads. We need to break out of our rut. In the brain, this is referred to as neuroplasticity, the ability of our brain circuitry to change.

Adventures are fascinating, but they can be hard to rationalize in a busy life. This is where the concept of microadventures comes to the rescue. Adventures don't have to be week-long; they can be at hours when we are not otherwise committed to work or school. As with most new habits, the key is to start small.

The third suggestion is all about MVP. Not the "Most Valuable Player" award that Stephen Curry won last basketball season and maybe Buster Posey will win again at the end of the current baseball season. This MVP is Minimum Viable Product. This term comes out of the tech world and applies to an approach in which a new product is developed with just enough features to satisfy early adopters. The final, complete set of features is only refined after considering feedback from the product's initial users.

This way of thinking leads us to ask what in our lives have we made needlessly complex? Like the expression that the "perfect should not be the enemy of the good," we need to take first steps, get started, embrace beginnings in order to move forward and change ourselves to be who we want to be.

Don't think that we can do it all at once, because we can't. And if we try to do that, we will fail and be disappointed. Instead, we can try to change one step at a time, one day at a time. We can't move overnight from being shy to being confident, from being frugal to being generous. It doesn't work that way. It is not easy to change the habits of a lifetime, and it can't be done all at once.

Each step takes courage: first day of school, new job, new neighborhood, new friend, a pledge to do new things this year. Maybe that is why we come to synagogue on these days of Rosh Hashanah and Yom Kippur. We may not be able to explain even to ourselves why we come. One reason may be that we come because, when we stand on the threshold of a new year, we feel anticipation. There is a desire for *kavannah*, something spontaneous, something new. Who knows what the new year will bring? Will we be at peace or will we have to wander? Will we be well or will we be ill? And above all, will we live or will we die?

What are the High Holy Days? Some parents send their children to what are called "finishing schools" so that they will learn how to be refined and well mannered. We come to these days because they are "starting schools," an opportunity to begin a new page in our lives, how to look inside and decide what needs changing and how to go into the new year with courage in our hearts.

> The devil who once called a meeting of his staff and said to them, "We're doing very badly this year. The number of sins that people commit is way down. What are we going to do about it?" He gave them twenty-four hours to come up with an answer. When they reconvened, the first demon said, "My technique is that I try to tell people that there is no God, and they don't need to keep the Torah or do the commandments. But it doesn't work. People aren't stupid. They look around, and they see how magnificent the world is—and so they realize that there must be a God. And so I fail." The second demon said, "My strategy is I tell people that there is a God, but that God didn't give the Torah. And they don't have to connect with Jewish tradition and the Jewish people. But it doesn't work. People are not stupid. They look into the Torah, and they see how wise it is, and they realize that God must have given it. And so I fail." The third demon said, "My strategy always works. I tell people that there is a God, and I tell people that God gave the Torah. But I say to them, 'What's the rush? Stay in bed—you can always do the commandments tomorrow.' And that always works!"

I conclude with words from the songwriter John Boutte who wrote these lyrics for his song "The Eternal Now" (*Good Neighbor,* 2008). "We are living in the eternal now. The past is gone; the future is tomorrow . . . . Maybe the moment is talking to you now."

This is the moment—the time of *kavannah*. May we each find courage to hear what this moment is saying to us—and begin.

# Relationships

## Yom Kippur Evening—2015

Each one of us is an expert in something, like a gem with great potential. Though not yet fully polished, we have the capacity to be someone special and unique—to be *kadosh*, holy. We all are simply diamonds in the rough. We polish our rough humanity by treating others with justice and compassion. When we meet one another, we strive to see the gem and not be side-tracked by the flaws.

Our synagogue is based upon relationships. The Latin word for "religion" is *religare*, and you can find the same root in the word "ligament." It means "to bind, to connect." Religion aims to connect us to other people so that together we can successfully connect with ancestors, with family and friends and perhaps even with God. That's what group prayer is all about.

This service, what we are doing right now, will be a failure if we feel no different from the experience of being one of several hundred people showing up to see the same movie or concert. There has to be some sense that the prayers, the liturgy, the chanting—that they lift each of us out of our isolation and transform us into a congregation, a community for today, for tomorrow and for longer.

Relationships are at the heart of Judaism. That's why a child's becoming *Bar* or *Bat Mitzvah* is more than just an expensive birthday party. It signifies welcoming the youngster into the community of people who share their humanity with each other. That's why when we visit a house of mourning, we create a connection that builds relationships. That's why we witness a couple under the *chuppah* for a wedding and why we have three witnesses at the *mikveh*. We connect to build special and unique relationships. We are witnesses to moments of holiness.

Rabbi Mordecai Kaplan many years ago distinguished between dependent and independent nouns as a way of understanding relationships. He suggested that "God" is a dependent noun. Kaplan explained that just as a man can't be a husband without being somebody's husband

and a woman can't be a wife without being somebody's wife, so God can't truly be God unless God is somebody's God.

God is about inspiring human beings to behave in a human way. In the first chapter of the Torah, the account of the creation of the world, God creates human beings, unique creatures blessed with the capacity to have a relationship with God. Without human beings acting compassionately and morally, God is only God in potential. It's up to us to make God real in the world.

In the Genesis story of the Garden of Eden, Adam and Eve hear God coming for them after eating the forbidden fruit, and they believe God is coming to punish them. They try to hide. God calls out to them, "Ayecha"—"Where are you? Where are you hiding? What makes you think you can hide from Me?"

Perhaps God is saying to us, "Where are you?" because God needs us. Without us, God can be the Creator of the world, but God can't be God without being somebody's God. And there are no other candidates other than Adam and Eve and their descendants.

If that is correct, the Torah's message would be: God created human beings with the unique ability to know the difference between good and bad, because only creatures with that ability can have a real relationship with God and with each other. God must have known that this unique creature would get a lot of things wrong because the challenge of living morally is so complicated. But it would defeat God's purpose if we should feel disqualified from a relationship with God because we get some things wrong.

Imagine that God comes looking for us, calling out "Ayecha"— "Where are you?" And God might be saying to us, "Don't hide from Me because you've done things you think I won't like. It's not news to Me," God says to us and especially on Yom Kippur, "that you make mistakes, that you fall short of moral perfection." That's why we have Yom Kippur every year. We don't come here to grovel, to make excuses, to apologize. We come here to renew our relationship with one another or with our tradition or with a God who needs people like us who make mistakes and wish we were better.

Indeed, it was Martin Buber who explained that when we seek to find God, don't look only to the beautiful mountains or spectacular sunsets or the gorgeous colors, designs and musical notes in the sanctuary. Look for God between people—because God is in relationships. That is where I believe we can find holiness and meaning in our lives.

This could lead us to thinking that there is a right way and a wrong way to do Yom Kippur. We may think that the right way to do Yom Kippur is when we confess our sins and beg to be forgiven. But I believe that could be wrong. The right way is to use this day to rediscover what it means to be a human being, to access our humanity by using this day to connect with other people, to move the needle back from Me to Us.

On this day—if we do it right—we reach out to those around us. And we reach inward to connect with a God who is not out there or up there but right here, inside each of us. In the process, we are reminded who we are and who we might become.

May it be so.

# Trying to Do the Right Thing

## Yom Kippur Evening—2018

I heard about a diner in a small town far from here that I'd like to visit someday. The story goes that they have good food, strong coffee and an old-fashioned, somewhat charming greasy spoon atmosphere. They have t-shirts with the business name on front and an unusual slogan on the back. It reads "Not trying to please everyone, just a solid 75%."

Who is it we are trying to please? Is it our friends, our family or ourselves? We cannot make everyone happy. So what if we use this measure to consider our actions—aim for a solid 75%. Does that sound good?

Here we are together on the Day of Atonement where there are no experts and no masters. No one of us is better than any other. Each one of us is exposed in our basic humanness as mortal. The rituals and worship on Yom Kippur are arranged to be a near-death experience. And, as death approaches, we have the opportunity to turn our thoughts to confessing our sins and seeking forgiveness. We can try to reach for goodness in life and to seek to put our thoughts and prayers into action.

Martin Buber was a twentieth century teacher and philosopher. He was raised in a Hasidic community in a small town in Poland but went to Berlin for his academic studies. He struggled with what it meant to live an authentic Jewish life in a world that was increasingly hostile to Jews. He authored many books, including *I and Thou*, and much of his work focused on human relationships. He argued that our behavior and our deeds are the most important determinant in the quality of our life. Authentic Judaism, in his view, has little to do with superficial spirituality and narcissism. Instead, Buber challenges us to understand that genuine religiosity exists as part of a social framework and what truly matters is not intellectualizing but actions." (*The Knowledge of Man: Selected Essays*, 1952)

Another twentieth century Jew was Victor Frankl, an eminent Viennese psychiatrist who practiced in the 1930s. Even though he had a visa for America, he decided to stay in Europe to be with his aging parents. He and his parents were captured by the Nazis and sent to Auschwitz—where he miraculously survived. He wrote a book about his experiences called *Man's Search for Meaning* (1946), which is an attempt to understand why some of his fellow prisoners not only survived the horrifying conditions but managed to grow in the process.

Frankl asks questions that are vital for each of us to face, even here in the lovely Santa Ynez Valley. The questions revolve around the concept of control. We know, because we say this to ourselves often: In our lives, there are many things we cannot control, and we know that. So what are the things we can control? Are we just passing through this life like a leaf blowing in the wind or a fallen leaf flowing down a river? Or can we control our flight . . . our direction . . . our trajectory?

I believe that the answer is YES . . . and NO. No, we may not be able to control our life . . . however, yes, we can take charge of how we respond to our life.

Frankl said that in Auschwitz and in every other camp, the Nazis controlled every moment and every action for the Jews. The one thing the Nazis could not control was how each person reacted. No matter what, the response was entirely up to the individual.

And that is a powerful insight. If people in a time like that had control, then we, in our time, can take charge even in small ways of how we respond—verbally, emotionally and physically. Tonight and tomorrow remind us of our mortality and give us the opportunity to take control.

We can learn much from a Buddhist teaching. If you're out watering your flower garden by hand, you naturally concentrate the flow of water to benefit your beautiful flowers. If there's an area of weeds, you don't waste water there. As best you can, you avoid watering the weeds.

It's the same with your consciousness. You can learn to selectively water the positive seeds and flowers in you by attending to them. There are enough weeds. You don't have to encourage them. Sometimes we unwittingly water the weeds within us. If you see this clearly, you won't want to continue exposing yourself to this kind of experience. There are many lovely things in the world. Why focus so much on the potentially destructive ones?

Let me conclude with a story attributed to King Solomon that addresses this challenge of what we can and cannot control.

> The king had many servants, but one, Benayah ben Yehoyada, was his favorite. Solomon made his preference quite obvious to all the others, and because of this, the other servants teased Benayah about his seeming arrogance. Solomon decided Benayah needed a lesson in humility.

The king summoned Benayah and two other servants and gave them an impossible mission to fulfill—a mission impossible. He thought all of them would fail and then Benayah would no longer be teased for being Solomon's favorite. King Solomon began, "I have heard rumors of a fabulous ring. It has a unique power. When a sad man gazes upon it, he becomes happy. But when a happy man gazes upon it, he becomes sad. Find this ring and bring it to me. You have three days to complete this task."

Benayah set out in search of the ring. He traveled from town to town, inquiring about this ring. However, no one had ever heard of such a ring. His time was almost over, and he was about to give up when he spotted a trinket shop whose proprietor was sitting out front drinking coffee. Benayah approached the man and told him about his search.

"A ring that cheers the sad and saddens the cheerful?" asked the junk dealer. "Come inside." They entered the shop. Benayah waited as the junk dealer brought out a boxful of baubles. The junk dealer took out a plain silver ring. He engraved some words on it and gave it to Benayah. Benayah read the inscription, smiled, nodded and headed back to the palace.

Solomon summoned all his servants to assemble for the reports of the three "mission impossible" servants. The first came up empty handed. The second brought a ring made out of gems. When Solomon summoned Benayah, he expected an unsuccessful—and humbled—Benayah. So, when Benayah strode in and handed the king a ring, the king was taken aback.

King Solomon inspected it, read the inscription—and let out a melancholy sigh. He slipped the ring from the trinket shop on his finger. "It was I who needed a lesson in humility," he said. "This ring has reminded me wealth and power are fleeting things."

The inscription on the ring read *"Gam zeh ya'avor"*—"This too shall pass." At that moment, King Solomon realized all his wisdom, fabulous wealth and tremendous power were but fleeting things, for one day he would be nothing but dust. And so the words of the humble merchant taught the king and increased his wisdom that nothing is permanent.

That thought—*gam zeh ya'avor*—interrupts us in the midst of the life we are living to tell us nothing lasts forever, neither joy nor sorrow. In difficult situations these words provide a glimmer of comfort. In joyous situations these words provide perspective.

Numerous times on Yom Kippur we recite, *"al chet shechatanu l'fanecha"* which often is translated as "for these sins, our God." The Hebrew word *"chet"* is from a root meaning "to miss the mark," as in archery or stone throwing. As with a stone thrower or archer, our intent is to aim true and do the right thing. Wrongdoing does not cause a permanent stain. With practice and attention, we can improve our aim and do better in the future.

As 5779 begins, let us remember these points:

First, if a Holocaust survivor can learn that though he is not be able to control his life, he can control how he responds to life. We, too, can control how we respond to life.

Second, remember Solomon's ring: *gam zeh ya'avor*—this too shall pass. The ring should remind the sad among us of the transience of their suffering, and it should remind the happy among us of the transience of their happiness. Try to stay balanced.

And finally, as this new year 5779 begins, remember that living is not about trying to please everyone—but trying our best to do the right thing. And if it is 75% of the time, that's awfully good.

May this be a sweet and peaceful new year. May God's blessings rest upon good people the world over.

# Commentaries

# A Tribute to Rabbi Lawrence Raphael

## Norman J. Cohen,
## Rabbi, PhD*

After twenty years in his uncle Laban's house in Haran, in Northern Mesopotamia, Jacob was on his way home. He fled Canaan as a young adult, caught up solely in himself; he was returning with two wives, thirteen children and an array of flocks. He left fearing Esau, after stealing his birthright and blessing; he was returning home to encounter his brother once again.

When Esau and Jacob finally approached each other, Jacob said: "If you would do me this favor, accept this gift from me....for to see your face is like seeing the face of God." (Gen. 33:10) How utterly powerful! Truly seeing Esau's face . . . recognizing his essence, the core of his being...is tantamount to Jacob acknowledging the Divine in him and in the world.

When we are able to see the faces of other human beings...not just those closest to us, but all those we encounter on the way, then we truly acknowledge God's presence. That perhaps was the "gift" Jacob gave to his brother . . . the gift he bequeathed to us.

To me, this quality surely characterized Rabbi Larry Raphael z"l in every interaction that I and others had with him. Our relationship spanned nearly forty-five years. I began teaching at the New York School of Hebrew Union College–Jewish Institute of Religion (HUC–JIR) a year after Larry was ordained and had already begun working at the College-Institute. Just as the first moment of meeting between

*Dr. Norman J. Cohen is Professor Emeritus of Midrash at HUC–JIR/New York. He served as Provost of HUC–JIR from 1996-2009, Interim President of HUC–JIR from December 1999—June 2000 and as Dean of the New York Campus from 1988-1996. He was ordained by HUC–JIR in 1971 and received his PhD from HUC–JIR in the field of Midrash in 1977. He lectures widely on the Modern Interpretation of the Bible and has published many books in his areas of expertise.

Jacob and Esau upon Jacob's return to Canaan spoke volumes about who Jacob had become, from the very beginning I knew that Larry was a special human being. Larry was a consummate mensch who cared deeply about people, and it was not surprising at all that our relationship quickly became more than colleagues...we soon became friends. And especially in the years we both served in the Administration of the New York School, I was able to witness firsthand not only the depth of his dedication to Jewish life and values, but how much he loved and was truly interested in others.

It didn't matter who they were or the status they possessed. He was the same genuinely concerned human being, be they family, friends, colleagues in every venue in which he worked, congregants, students, guests in the HUC–JIR Soup Kitchen or the people he encountered in the communal activities in which he regularly participated. He touched so many people and affected their lives in significant ways because he was a compassionate human being who cared about the well-being and growth of others. He was driven by essential values, none more important to him than the dignity and worth of every person. This was the gift that Larry gave to all the people in the myriad of institutions to which he dedicated himself.

The Reform movement was the primary beneficiary of Larry's many gifts. For some thirty years, the students and faculty of the Hebrew Union College–Jewish Institute of Religion benefitted from Larry in his roles as Assistant and Associate Dean, Dean of Administration and member of the Faculty. We learned from his teaching and insights, were buttressed by his support and counsel, were moved by his humility and caring and were challenged by his integrity. He always was willing to stand up for what was right. The greatest impact he had as an administrator came in his devotion to professional and adult education. His work as Chair of the Professional Education Department radically altered the training our Rabbinic and Cantorial students received, and his spearheading of a vibrant Continuing Education program for our alumni enabled them to continue to grow after completing their formal training. Beyond his administrative and teaching roles, Larry devoted himself to a multitude of *mitzvah* projects, none perhaps more important than the HUC Soup Kitchen. He was a leading force in the creation of the Kitchen in the mid-1980s and in sustaining it. After some thirty-five years, it continues to exemplify the central role Social Justice plays in the life of the College-Institute and of the Reform Movement, and Larry embodied that commitment by himself working in the Soup Kitchen every Monday evening. He also was a role model for our community in leading a High Holiday Congregation for College Students and Unaffiliated Adults for decades.

A core commitment of Larry's was his passion for learning, with the goal of teaching others, which he conveyed to all of our HUC–JIR students. This passion led to his service as Director of Adult Jewish Growth of the Union of American Hebrew Congregations, where he was instrumental in creating material for adult and congregational study, shaped and led numerous spirituality retreats across the country for the Reform Movement, created a synagogue para-rabbinic program and provided leadership training for Temple presidents.

And his teaching over the years . . . no matter the focus . . . whether it was rabbinical, cantorial, or Jewish Education students, congregants, campers at Camp Eisner or participants in Jewish communal study, touched all who were blessed to sit with him.

In his service as a congregational rabbi, chiefly as Senior Rabbi of Congregation Sherith Israel in San Francisco for some thirteen years, his passion and ability to teach and touch others, no matter their circumstance or background, his desire to help shape institutions which would respond to the needs of other human beings and his overriding concern that we shape lives of value . . . all were evident during his rabbinic service.

Yet, his essential commitment to others frequently took him beyond the pale of Reform Judaism, impelling him to serve communal institutions, including ones outside of the Jewish community. Nevertheless, embodying the core values of Judaism, he was involved with organizations such as the San Francisco Interfaith Council, the Jewish Fund for Justice, the Park Slope Food Coop, the North American Conference on Ethiopian Jewry and Mazon: A Jewish Response to Hunger.

And through it all...touching the lives of a myriad of individuals through his intelligence, insights and teaching ability . . . his utter humility was ever apparent. He invited people into his life, he was always present for all of us, and we could feel his embrace and his willingness to share himself.

His contributions to Jewish organizational life—intellectually, educationally and personally—are well-documented. His leadership and vision in many ways helped shape the contours of the many institutions in which he served, their programs, the bases upon which they measure success and the nature of their influence. Yet, it was the very personal relationships he established in his many roles that is the measure of his profound influence. All of us who were lucky enough to work with Rabbi Larry Raphael z"l can attest to the fact that what we gained from

our relationship with him went far beyond the specificity of the professional role that he played. And the testament to that is the fact that we
all considered Larry to be a lifelong friend.

Though he was taken from us all too soon, his memory will surely
remain a blessing through the gifts he gave us which are now a part of
us.

# Rabbi Larry Raphael— My Teacher, Mentor, Friend

## Rabbi Jessica Zimmerman Graf*

It is with great pride that I became the tenth senior rabbi of historic Congregation Sherith Israel in San Francisco on July 1, 2016. Founded as a synagogue with social justice at its core, Sherith Israel has been a significant institution in the city of San Francisco since 1851. It was established by Jewish leaders of the city immediately following the Gold Rush of 1849 to serve the growing Jewish population that had migrated west. San Francisco has always been a frontier town, a place of innovation and pioneering spirit. Still today, we are a congregation—and a city—that leads the way in creativity while remaining firmly rooted in our history. I follow in the footsteps of forward-thinking rabbis who inspired our community to employ Jewish values and texts to engage with the issues of our day. The rabbis who served this community before me continue to be an integral part of our identity. I am greatly influenced by the vision of my immediate predecessor, Rabbi Larry Raphael.

Rabbi Raphael believed in building relationships that would create a network of friendships within our community. He got to know people well and helped them to connect to one another. By allowing people to feel "seen," Rabbi Raphael helped people to make a home at Sherith Israel. He is remembered for his incredible ability to retain

*Rabbi Jessica Zimmerman Graf is a graduate of Columbia University and was ordained by Hebrew Union College in 2003. She has worked in congregations from New York City to Juneau and is active in several major Jewish organizations. During her tenure as Director of Congregational Engagement for Synagogue 3000 from 2006-2014, Rabbi Graf was on the cutting edge of synagogue renewal and transformation. At Sherith Israel, Rabbi Graf served for two years as Director of Magalim (circles of Jewish community). She focused on designing programs to create new dimensions of Jewish practice involving Jews from their 20s through their 40s in learning, prayer and shared experience before becoming Senior Rabbi of Congregation Sherith Israel in San Francisco in 2016.

detailed information about the lives and families of people he met. He was a master at greeting people and putting them at ease.

Rabbi Raphael worked hard to welcome everyone to Sherith Israel. His vision of social justice and inclusivity continue to inform our ethos. Rabbi Larry often spent time in our kitchen, helping to make meals to serve to people in shelters. He saw our responsibility as wide-reaching and inspired people to think far beyond the doors of the synagogue. Our Hamotzi/Chicken Soupers program, which feeds over 200 people a week, continues to serve our larger community, helping to fulfill Rabbi Larry's vision of *tikkun olam*—repairing our world.

In addition, Rabbi Larry was extremely committed to interfaith work. He followed the instruction of our Torah to welcome the stranger into our midst. He always invited people to make their home in our beautiful sanctuary, whether it was their first visit or they had been around for decades. Rabbi Raphael proudly served on the board of the San Francisco Interfaith Council, working with leaders from all faith communities around the city. He was devoted to building relationships with clergy from other faiths and to creating lasting relationships between Sherith Israel and other communities. After Rabbi Larry died, I was invited onto the board of the San Francisco Interfaith Council. I very proudly accepted, ensuring that Sherith Israel would continue to be a leader in interfaith coalition building in our city. I agreed to serve in memory of Rabbi Raphael.

I had the privilege to meet Rabbi Raphael nearly twenty-five years ago when I was a student in his class at the Hebrew Union College–Jewish Institute of Religion in New York. I never imagined then that I would follow in his footsteps as leader of this synagogue. Rabbi Raphael was a legend in the rabbinic community—a colleague and friend to so many during decades of service to the Jewish people. He knew almost all Reform rabbis, having served in several capacities at the College-Institute and directly helping to train a generation of Jewish clergy. Many of the programs or ideas that I have for Sherith Israel come directly from values that Rabbi Larry held deeply or from conversations we had in our time together. I think of him often. Rabbi Raphael's wisdom, humor and even-keeled demeanor influence my own leadership.

Rabbi Larry Raphael's legacy at Sherith Israel is vast. He inspired congregants to become lay leaders; he inspired curious folks to become life-long learners; he inspired rabbinic students to devote their lives to serving the Jewish people. I am grateful for having known Larry as a teacher, mentor and friend. And I am honored to have had him as my rabbi emeritus. In that role, he demonstrated humility and vulnerability—powerful lessons. His legacy will long be remembered at Congregation Sherith Israel. His teachings will continue to influence generations of people who cherish Judaism, as he did.

# Rabbi Larry Raphael, A Model of *Menschlekeit*

## Rabbi Hara E. Person[*]

It's hard to remember when I actually met Larry, because I feel like I always knew him. It's possible that I met him in high school, when I was involved in a program for teens that met at Hebrew Union College (HUC). Or perhaps I met him when I was in college, as a prospective HUC student. But what I do remember clearly is that it was very comforting to know that Rabbi Larry Raphael was a Dean at HUC. I knew that when the time came for me to think about applying to HUC, I would have someone there who would be rooting for me.

When I finally began to think seriously about going to rabbinic school, I made an appointment to meet with Larry. He was warm and encouraging and made me feel that going to HUC could work for me, despite that fact that I wasn't a typical student. We shared certain things, like living in Brownstone Brooklyn, and sending kids to St. Ann's, and a mutual love of mystery novels. I felt like he got me and accepted me for who I was.

I don't know if I could have gotten in to HUC or for that matter made it through without Larry's support and his belief in me. He was my main cheerleader at the school, willing to bend rules so that it could work. I couldn't pick up and go to Israel for the year—his approach was, no problem, we'll make this work. He made all of this possible

*Rabbi Hara Person is the Chief Executive of the Central Conference of American Rabbis (CCAR), the Reform Rabbinic leadership organization. The CCAR enriches and strengthens the Jewish community by fostering excellence in the Reform Rabbis who lead it, in whatever setting they serve. Previously, Rabbi Person was the CCAR's Chief Strategy Officer. In that capacity, she oversaw the Communications Department and served as Publisher of CCAR Press. Before coming to the CCAR, Rabbi Person was the Editor-in-Chief of URJ Books and Music. Since 1998, Rabbi Person has been the High Holy Day Rabbi of Congregation B'nai Olam, Fire Island Pines, NY.

for me—of course I had to do the hard work of studying and passing the exemption test, but he made it clear that if I could do my part, he would do his. And he did. And then when I asked if could go less than completely full-time because of my family and work responsibilities, he again managed to figure out a way to make it work.

When I first applied to HUC, I did not share that I was pregnant with my first child. Larry coached me through the application process, and his investment in my success meant the world to me. When I got accepted, I had to then tell Larry that not only was I going to try to place out of the year in Israel, but also that I was pregnant and was also going to defer a year. I was worried that he would be disappointed, but instead he was delighted to hear my news. Throughout that year before I enrolled, he would get in touch periodically and ask how I was doing. I remember that when my daughter was born, he sent me a gift with a lovely note. That kind of caring and generosity was such a hallmark of Larry's presence.

Larry was someone who cared deeply about people and their lives. He understood that lives were complicated, and raising children was complicated, and that managing it all took a lot of work. He understood that the commitment to becoming a rabbi could take a toll on the people around us, and he was supportive about how and when to make compromises that could help keep the whole together. Rather than making me feel bad for not fitting neatly into the program, he made it all feel possible. That was no small gift.

I was recently going through files from my time at HUC and found notes from the professional development class that Larry used to teach the second year students. In that class we learned the practical skills that most of us still use today—how to do a baby naming, how to do a funeral, how to talk to a bereaved family or a couple preparing for their wedding. But the class wasn't just Larry's personal views on these issues—he generously brought in many other rabbis to speak to us so that we would get a well-rounded view and a multiplicity of approaches. And Larry also understood that talking about life cycle events wasn't just a clinical kind of how-to conversation, but rather, one that brought up all kinds of emotional baggage for us. In a non-judgmental and compassionate way, Larry was able to get us talking honestly to each other about our fears and our concerns, our hopes and our anxieties related to these major life moments. In his uniquely caring way, he helped us grow into the rabbis we would become.

When Larry left HUC to work at the Union for Reform Judaism (URJ), I missed him and felt his absence deeply. I missed the way that he had had my back and his caring presence on the fourth floor of HUC. Without him, the school felt a little colder and less caring. Little did I know then that I would go to work at URJ as well, and that I would get to work with Larry as a colleague. That was a wonderful time, to be able to continue to be enriched by Larry and to know again that I had a caring friend in the workplace. During those years, Larry ran many programs of adult learning around the country among other things. He was able to connect people to ideas and great teachers and enable them to find inspiration and community as Reform Jews. What a gift that was. In keeping with my experience of him as a Dean at HUC, he was a gentle, encouraging presence with adult learners, not judging them for what they did or didn't know but inviting them in to a meaningful experience through which they could grow.

We had fun together during those years. We loved talking about mystery novels and sharing recommendations of books. When Larry was working on his books with Jewish Lights Publishing—*Mystery Midrash* (1999) and *Criminal Kabbalah* (2001)—it was great fun to speak about the process of writing and putting those books together. At one point I tried my hand at writing a mystery, and Larry read early drafts. He tried to help me find a professional editor who might be interested in my book—that didn't come to fruition but it was another example of his caring and how far he would go to help someone. Another topic of our ongoing conversations was about the care and upkeep of Brooklyn brownstones. Larry was always up for a story about what wasn't going well and often had suggestions about who I could call to help.

One lesson that I particularly learned from Larry, and still think about to this day, was how he approached leaving URJ. It was a difficult and sad time, and I'm sure that I knew only the smallest details of what Larry was going through. But what I remember being so impressed by was that Larry gathered himself up and, with great intentionality and careful planning, got himself ready for a new challenge. I remember him telling me that he was taking some classes so that he could brush up on and learn new skills in order to be a congregational rabbi. He recognized that, given his career up to that point in institutions, there were tools he didn't have and skills he had learned as a student but hadn't used in many years. I was so moved by his ability to take a good look at himself and to be able to honestly evaluate his own strengths and weaknesses and then to do something about it. Of course, I don't know what he said in private, but publicly he faced the situation with grace, courage, and humility. At a moment where others might have insisted that an injustice had been done and that he deserved better, he picked himself up and got to work, shaping himself into a different kind of rabbi and preparing himself for a new kind of rabbinate. In that way, he served as an incredibly important model for me, not feeling sorry for himself and not letting his ego get in the way. And he went on to lead his congregation admirably, serving with strength until retirement.

That was one of the things about Larry that I most came to love and cherish, that he never let his ego get the better of him. He didn't have to be the star of every situation. Like when he brought in guest rabbis to speak to us as second year students, he didn't need to have all the answers. He had a deep appreciation of everyone's unique gifts and that made him well equipped to be realistic about his own. In an environment of huge personalities, he made room for other people and their successes. He was incredibly loyal to people, and to the institutions he served. He cared about and championed his students. And he took great pride in us. Having been a student of Larry's was always to be a student of Larry's. And that was a great feeling, to know he was in our corner and that he was proud of us.

One of the last times I was in touch with Larry, I wrote to thank him for his contribution to a book we had just put out. I had emailed Larry a few months earlier to ask if he wanted to contribute a chapter on ethical wills, something I knew he had written about previously and a topic close to his heart. I was delighted to be able to publish the chapter ("Ethical Wills," Rabbi Larry Raphael, PhD, IN *Navigating the Journey: The Essential Guide to the Jewish Life Cycle*, Rabbi Peter S. Knobel, PhD, editor, Central Conference of American Rabbis, 2018) and grateful that he had been willing to write for us. It was a treat to be in communication about a project and to have that kind of comfortable back and forth as the book was being readied for publication that I hadn't had with him in a while. And the conversation wasn't just about the book—almost twenty-five years after I'd been his student, he still remembered all the stories about my children and my house. He wanted to know how they were, shared with pride about his own children and of course asked about the ongoing adventures of brownstone ownership.

I think now about his interest in ethical wills, and it seems so fitting. This man, this teacher and this leader, who was such a model of *menschlekeit* and caring, left all of us who were lucky enough to be his students a living model of an ethical will. The way that he lived his life and cared for those around him was itself an ethical will—a model to live by. I was so deeply sad to hear that Larry had died and that I hadn't been able to say a proper good-bye or thank you. I am comforted by knowing that I have carried his rabbinic model with me and that he knew how appreciative I was for having been his student. In a world of outsize egos, Larry was a caring presence, a big-hearted man of humility and grace. And for that, I am incredibly grateful.

# Lawrence W. Raphael: A Good Friend and a Guiding Influence

## Gary Phillip Zola, Rabbi, PhD*

Among the writings of the ancient rabbis, the private prayers of several great sages have been preserved. One scholar, Rabbi Eliezar, an Amora who lived during the fifth century C.E., is said to have recited a touching personal prayer three times a day:

> May it be your will, O God, that our lives be filled with love and fellowship, peace and friendship . . . [and] may you sustain us in Your world with a good friend and a guiding influence.

Over the course of my professional career, Larry Raphael became the instantiation of this lovely benediction. Our bond began in the context of a professional encounter, but Larry Raphael quickly became a friend and a rabbinic role model. His ideals and personal values endure to this day as a guiding influence in my life.

Our first contact, however, took place long before we began working together. In the fall of 1975, I spoke with Larry by telephone in order to schedule a visit to the New York campus of Hebrew Union College–Jewish Institute of Religion (HUC–JIR). Planning this visit to New York was

*Professor Gary Phillip Zola, Rabbi, PhD, is the Executive Director of The Jacob Rader Marcus Center of the American Jewish Archives (AJA) and Edward M. Ackerman Family Distinguished Professor of the American Jewish Experience & Reform Jewish History at Hebrew Union College–Jewish Institute of Religion (HUC–JIR) in Cincinnati. Professor Zola edits The Marcus Center's biannual publication, *The American Jewish Archives Journal*—one of only two academic periodicals focusing on the total historical experience of American Jewry. He received both his rabbinical ordination and his Ph.D. in American Jewish History from HUC–JIR. Professor Zola is a historian of American Jewry who specializes in the development of American Reform Judaism.

an unexpected turn of events. In the spring of 1974, I gained admission to HUC–JIR in Cincinnati, where I assumed I would soon matriculate. Those plans changed unexpectedly when, while working at Olin-Sang-Ruby Union Institute in Oconomowoc, Wisconsin, during the summer of that year, I met a beautiful young woman from Manhasset Hills, New York, named Stefi Rothberg. I fell madly in love with Stefi and, rather than begin rabbinical studies the following academic year, I decided to request a deferment from HUC–JIR so I could remain in Chicago (my hometown) and dedicate all my time to winning Stefi's heart. By the spring of 1975, I had (thankfully) achieved my goal and now as a newly engaged couple, Stefi and I were considering where I should study—New York, which would place us near Stefi's family, or Cincinnati, in the familiar Midwest? To make this decision, it seemed sensible for me to visit the New York school, and I quickly learned that Assistant Dean Larry Raphael would help me to schedule my visit to the campus.

On the day I visited the campus, then still located on 68th Street next to the Stephen S. Wise Free Synagogue, Rabbi Raphael was away, and a student intern was to be my host. I recall sitting in Larry's office admiring his handsome rabbinical diploma hanging on the wall. What a surprise to discover that the Assistant Dean had just been ordained one year earlier, in 1974! I assumed that if Larry Raphael had become an Assistant Dean at HUC–JIR only one year after completing his rabbinical education, he must surely be one of the school's most gifted alumni.

Six years later, I was able to confirm that assumption. After completing HUC–JIR's rabbinical curriculum in 1982, I was invited to serve as the school's National Director of Admissions. This meant I would be working in close collaboration with Larry Raphael who, during the interim, had become the Associate Dean of HUC–JIR's New York school. During our first phone conversation, we assured one another that we looked forward to working together. Little did either one of us know that this conversation would mark the beginning of a close friendship that would endure for thirty-seven years.

Larry's rabbinate was unique. From 1973 to 1996, he served as Assistant and Associate Dean as well as Dean of Administration at HUC–JIR, New York. Over the course of those twenty-three years, Larry played a vital role in the admission, education and professional training of over a thousand Reform rabbis, cantors and educators. It did not take me long to learn about the ideals and values that were pivotally important to my colleague.

Family was unquestionably the brightest star in Larry's constellation of values. In the rabbinical world, where one encounters many colleagues who through dedication or personal ambition prioritize their professional obligations, Larry's love for his family stood out. He spoke regularly about Terrie, her work and her interests. He enjoyed telling me about his three children—Matthew, Andrew and Rachel—and I recall hearing about their childhood interests and activities. Over the years, I developed a personal bond with the members the family that brought Larry such fulfillment.

Beyond love of family, Larry was also skillful in building friendships. In his role at HUC–JIR, he was always a friend and an advocate for the students. Many of the pioneering women who studied for the rabbinate in New York testify to the invaluable role Larry played in helping the school adjust to the needs of a co-educational student body. Responding again to the interests and concerns of his students, Larry played a central role in founding the school's Soup Kitchen, which has fed over 150,000 guests since its inception over thirty years ago.

Larry and I worked on our doctorates during these years, and we commiserated about the difficulties we faced as part-time graduate students with growing families and full-time professional duties. Larry was two or three years ahead of me on this arduous path. His counsel and support eased the way. We celebrated when he completed his PhD in higher education and leadership at New York University (1990). His doctoral dissertation, "Leadership and Excellence in Theological Seminaries," equipped Larry to play a critically important role in guiding HUC–JIR through the massive technology revolution that swept over the world in the 1980s. From the earliest days of personal computing to the advent of the Internet, Larry intuitively understood that this newly emerging technology would transform the entire educational enterprise. He embraced technology with the conviction that it should enhance community—a concept that was so central to his thinking—as well as offer students, faculty, and alumni exciting new learning opportunities.

While I was National Director of Admissions, Larry and I worked in tandem to nurture prospective students and, ultimately, to guide applicants through the school's demanding admissions process. We sat together in countless meetings wherein the current generation of Reform rabbis were invited to begin what would be their lifelong association with HUC–JIR. It was in these meetings that Larry's wisdom, sensitivity and openness benefitted many applicants. He urged us to embrace non-traditional candidates—those for whom the rabbinate was a second career choice or those whose leadership ideas challenged conventional thinking. Larry understood that the Jewish community—especially the Reform Jewish community—would benefit from innovative and creative rabbis and cantors who aspired to be pathfinders.

Our professional/personal bond continued to flourish when, in 1996, Larry became the first director of the Union of American Hebrew Congregation's (now the Union for Reform Judaism) Department of Adult Jewish Growth. Larry directed an array of national study programs, weeklong learning seminars and adult learning initiatives. With Larry's encouragement, the American Jewish Archives and the Department of Adult Jewish Growth created and co-sponsored a biennial study program "Travels in American Jewish History." This innovative educational program attracted many dozens of adult learners to these five-day programs, where they gained knowledge about the heritage of historic Jewish communities in cities such as Charleston, Philadelphia and Savannah. These programs (which incidentally continue to attract attendees to this day) enabled the both of us to expand our professional repertoire. We worked as team-teachers and, in doing so, our friendship continued to blossom.

In 2003, Larry became the ninth senior rabbi of Sherith Israel in San Francisco, where he shepherded this venerable congregation during a time of generational and demographic change. His devotion to community moved the congregation to welcome interfaith families and Jews by choice. Larry also inspired his congregation to accomplish a nearly impossible feat; the community raised the unprecedented amount of funds needed to bring its beautiful and historic synagogue building into compliance with San Francisco's seismic retrofit mandate. Future generations of American Jewry owe Larry a debt of gratitude for the role he played in modernizing this majestic house of prayer, allowing it to continue to serve the needs of his spiritual community.

Larry's efforts to preserve Sherith Israel's historic building may have contributed to his growing interest in the American Jewish experience. During his years in the pulpit, Larry began to offer adult education programs on the history of Jewish life in America. Once again, our partnership evolved toward a new phase. Two or three times a year, Larry and I would speak over the telephone or exchange emails to brainstorm about historical subjects for these programs. I would suggest topics and accompanying primary source documents from the American Jewish Archives. Subsequently, Larry would give me a report on how the subject matter had been received by his class. This dialogic partnership on the teaching of American Jewish history continued for many years, even after Larry became Rabbi Emeritus of the congregation in 2016.

Sometime during the summer of 2018, I received a voice message from Larry on my cellphone. In his typically warmhearted fashion, he wished me well and said he was looking forward to speaking to me. I assumed he was planning his fall teaching schedule and was calling to remind me it was time for the two of us to chat about a course or seminar he might teach. He concluded his message, however, with some words that caught my attention. "Let me hear from you, Gary" he intoned. "You know time is short, and I have become increasingly cognizant of how important it is to keep in touch with good friends."

I had no idea that the wisdom of Larry's final voice message would reveal itself so forcefully only months later. We never had a final chat, and this missed opportunity plagues me to this day. Was he teasing me playfully when he warned me time was short, or was he subtly telegraphing a dawning awareness of his own health concerns? It is impossible to know, but Larry's untimely and (to many) unanticipated death occurred the following March.

In 1996, HUC–JIR held a farewell luncheon for Larry when he left the school to join the staff of the Union. I flew to New York to participate in the event and, on the spur of the moment, was asked to say a few words to the large audience that had gathered to wish Larry farewell. Having no time to prepare my words in advance, I turned to a reliable failsafe: Gematria.

In feting Larry on that occasion, I noted that the Hebrew word for friend—*yedid*—is made up of the repetition of the Hebrew word for hand, *yad*. This makes sense because two clasped hands constitute an age-old sign of friendship. Two human beings who greet one another by placing hand-in-hand (or, in Hebrew, *yad b'yad*) are symbolically saying: "you are my friend—*yedid*."

Yet the numerical value of the word *yedid* is 28—a number that is shared with the word *koach*, which means strength. From this we can understand that a true friend serves simultaneously as a source of strength *and* support. Larry Raphael, I concluded, was a guiding influence, a rabbinic model and a true friend for me and for all those who had gathered that day to salute his contributions to HUC–JIR.

Thankfully, I had the opportunity to express those sentiments to Larry on that occasion, long before he went from time to eternity. Rabbi Larry Raphael sustained so many of us in this world by being a genuine friend *and* a guiding influence.

It is our hope that future generations who read Larry's teachings in this volume will fully appreciate why this special rabbi's persona touched so many lives.

# Appendices

# Building Bridges—
# My Role as a Rabbi

## Appendix I

My passion as a rabbi is helping a community to fulfill the covenant between the Jewish people and God. I have dedicated my years in the rabbinate to teaching and counseling young people and adults because I believe that the inner search for meaning must be matched with an outer quest to connect with the larger Jewish world. Congregations are places to enrich spiritual and communal life through worship, study and social action.

> Rav Hanina says: "I have learned much from my teachers, and from my colleagues more than from my teachers, but from my students more than from them all."
>
> (Talmud, Taanit 7a)

When I began my rabbinate, I engaged with a community of students as my congregation. I taught, counseled and learned from the future rabbis at the Hebrew Union College–Jewish Institute of Religion. I gained a deep understanding of the power of study to transform lives and the value of connecting individuals in a community. Over the years, I have been honored to serve congregations large and small, work with dozens of lay leaders in the Reform movement and teach hundreds of adult learners around the country along with interfaith communities seeking *tikkun olam*, repairing the world. All have been my teachers in a journey of learning.

> If each and every person was enabled to taste the manna according to his particular capacity, how much more and more was each and every person enabled according to his particular capacity to hear the Divine Word.
>
> (Pesikta De Rav Kahana 12.25)

People travel along diverse paths to find life-sustaining prayer and enter into lifelong learning. The rabbi has a sacred duty and awesome responsibility to help people of all ages find enrichment and encouragement for their religious journeys. Routes to understanding and faith may be marked by life-cycle events of joy or sorrow, relationships with teachers or mentors, the light of understanding through study or a celebration that becomes tradition.

Prayer and learning build bridges that connect past and future, practice and meaning, individual souls and the community of *Am Yisrael.* It is work that takes place through the formal study of texts, in dialogue and silence, by accepting obligations and creating rituals, by nurturing questions and finding answers as a community.

> The world stands on three things, Torah, worship and good deeds.
>
> (Pirke Avot 1:2)

The congregation that learns and prays together is a vehicle for *tikkun olam,* repairing the world. In these challenging times, the synagogue is a community in which the power of Torah is present and where study, prayer and good deeds are the highest priority.

> When two sit and study, the *Shechinah* dwells in their midst.
>
> (Pirke Avot 3:2)

Torah encompasses all the texts of our people stretching from biblical times to our own day. My role as rabbi is to open the gates of our tradition. It is a holy process, whether it takes place within a structured service, in a heartfelt question, in a weekend retreat or during a *mitzvah* project. All these opportunities to learn are also moments of connection to God, to our people, to our history and to our experience as Jews.

*Rabbi Larry Raphael, 2003*

# Rabbi Larry Raphael

## Professional Biography
## Appendix 2

A native Californian, Rabbi Larry Raphael grew up in Los Angeles. He earned a Bachelor of Arts in Psychology from the University of California at Santa Cruz in 1967, founded and then became the first president of the UC Santa Cruz Alumni Association. Rabbi Raphael was ordained at Hebrew Union College–Jewish Institute of Religion (HUC–JIR) in 1974, earned a PhD in Leadership and Higher Education from New York University in 1990 with a doctoral dissertation on "Leadership and Excellence in Theological Seminaries." He was awarded a Doctor of Divinity by HUC–JIR in 1999.

Rabbi Raphael served the New York Campus of HUC–JIR as an administrator and faculty member for many years. He filled a vital role in the admission, education and professional training of more than a thousand Reform rabbis, cantors and educators. From 1973—1978, he was Assistant Dean and then became Associate Dean until 1986. For the next decade, he was the Dean of Administration. Through these years, his responsibilities included counseling rabbinic, cantorial and education students; raising funds for scholarships and social action projects; organizing national colloquia and regional alumni courses; liaising with architects and contractors for new building design and construction; chairing the Department of Professional Education; serving as the National Director of Continuing Education for the Joint Commission on Continuing Rabbinic Education of the Central Conference of American Rabbis and the Rabbinic Alumni Association. He spearheaded *mitzvah* initiatives, including a weekly soup kitchen at the College which has fed over 150,000 guests since its inception. In addition, he was a faculty member of the school's Department of Professional Development from 1977 through 2003. He created and taught a highly influential year-long course to prepare rabbinic students for pulpit responsibilities. He taught other rabbinic education courses, including: "Professional Orientation to the Rabbinate," "Transformational Leadership" and "Leadership in Formal and Informal Education Settings."

During the five decades between 1973—2002, Rabbi Raphael led an annual High Holy Days congregation in New York City for college students and unaffiliated young adults with as many as a thousand worshippers. The participatory services, sponsored by the Metropolitan Conference of the National Federation of Temple Brotherhoods and HUC–JIR, created a unique community for people building their adult lives in the midst of a busy city. He officiated at weddings, funerals and baby-naming ceremonies for these annual congregants, provided pastoral counseling, taught and supported the lay leaders of the Metropolitan Conference.

In 1996, Rabbi Raphael joined the Union of American Hebrew Congregations (now known as the Union for Reform Judaism) as the first Director of the Department of Adult Jewish Growth. He developed adult education materials for congregational and individual Jewish study. These included weekly on-line and print *Torah Hayim: A Reform Torah Commentary*, handbooks on adult education for congregations, holiday study guides and *Go and Study: Text Materials for Lay-Led Discussions*. As well, he created and led study and spirituality retreats serving 700 adults annually, led the Synagogue Associates (Para-Rabbinic) Program and co-directed a leadership training program for Temple presidents.

Adult education courses that Rabbi Raphael taught in formal and informal settings included "Psalms and Contemporary Literature," "*Kohelet* (Ecclesiastes) Past and Present," "Before Saying Kaddish: Readings and Reflections When Praising God," "Our Faith and the Bible," "Creating Your Own Ethical Will," "Spirituality and Adult Faith Development," "Styles of Jewish Leadership," " Poetry and Meditation for Worship," "Jewish Themes in the Poetry of Yehudah Amichai" and "Jewish Identity and Detective Fiction."

In addition to being admired as a wise and engaging teacher, he published articles on such diverse topics as Bob Dylan and rabbinic messianism, the future of the Reform rabbinate, ethical wills and personal spirituality. Rabbi Raphael edited *Mystery Midrash* (Jewish Lights Publishing, 1999) and *Criminal Kabbalah* (Jewish Lights Publishing, 2001), two volumes of Jewish mystery fiction that reflected his fondness for a good mystery, Jewish and otherwise. A seductive way to think about Jewish identity, he shared these stories with congregants to open dialog, discuss values and make life choices.

Rabbi Raphael became the ninth Senior Rabbi of Congregation Sherith Israel in San Francisco on July 1, 2003, and led it through an era of dynamic changes until 2016. His legacy included spearheading the complex architectural and fund-raising challenges of bringing the domed synagogue, dedicated in 1905, into compliance with the city's seismic retrofit mandate after the Loma Prieta earthquake. Rabbi Raphael built a strong sense of community among congregants in a city with high rates of intermarriage and low rates of affiliation. This included creating a welcoming spiritual home for interfaith couples and a dynamic member-based mentoring program for people exploring becoming Jews by choice. He introduced a variety of adult learning opportunities in addition to individual counseling, weekly Torah study and a Talmud class. He organized special Shabbat afternoon programs on topics such as restorative justice and innovations in relationship-centered medical care. He team-taught a course on exploring Jewish beliefs and practices as an introduction to Judaism and evening classes such as "Jewish, Lincoln and the Civil War," "Reading (and Understanding) Emmanuel Levinas" and "Godspeak: Making Space for God in Judaism."

During an active retirement, Rabbi Raphael became an officer of the San Francisco Interfaith Council Board, was a hospice volunteer at the Jewish Home in San Francisco and taught at several venues in the Bay Area, including The Fromm Institute at the University of San Francisco. He travelled monthly to lead services and teach at the North Tahoe Hebrew Congregation and served as the rabbi for the Santa Ynez Valley Jewish Community.

*For a Good Year* is a selection of High Holy Day sermons on themes of social justice, faith and community that Rabbi Raphael shared with his congregations in New York and California over many decades.

CPSIA information can be obtained
at www.ICGtesting.com
Printed in the USA
LVHW021030100921
697438LV00011B/539